The Arc of Human Experiencing

A Journey of Being and Becoming

Nicholas Hatcher, DNP

The Arc of Human Experiencing: A Journey of Being and Becoming

© 2025 by Nicholas Hatcher

Catharsis Publications

Printed in La Vergne, TN, United States of America.

Cover Design by Katarina @nskvsky

Connect:

 https://www.DrNicholasHatcher.com/
 @drnicholashatcher
 @DrNicholasHatcher
@DrNicholasHatcher0

For my son, Damian Hatcher

May you always remember that who you are is not something you must earn, achieve, or fix.

You are already whole. Already worthy. Already home.

The journey is for you, and because of you.

For my wife, Sarah Hatcher

Your unwavering presence, deep wisdom, and quiet strength have been the ground beneath every word of this book.

Thank you for seeing me, holding me, and walking beside me.

This would not exist without you.

Author's Note

"You are not in the universe, you are the universe expressing itself as human for a little while."

— Eckhart Tolle

This book is not a manual, a method, or a map in the traditional sense. It is an invitation—a rhythm, a remembering, a return.

The ideas shared here arise from years of clinical practice, inquiry, teaching, and personal transformation. But more than that, they emerge from listening to the body, to suffering, to silence, to the subtle intelligence that lives beneath words. What follows is a layered exploration of what it means to be human: to become fragmented, to adapt, to long, and to find our way back.

The Arc of Human Experiencing is meant to be read slowly, with the same kind of presence it hopes to evoke. My hope is that something in these pages touches a truth you already carry, a coherence that has always been waiting to be lived.

— Nicholas Hatcher, DNP

Contents

Part IV. Returning Tides: Descent Into Presence

Part V. The Ocean Beyond: Resting in the Rhythm of Wholeness

Introduction

A New Way of Seeing Human Experience

"The real voyage of discovery consists not in seeking new landscapes, but in having new eyes."

— Marcel Proust

Human experiencing is like the life of the ocean—vast, rhythmic, and layered in depth. At its stillest depth lies the Unitive, the boundless field from which all experience arises, undivided and whole. As energy stirs from these depths, it crests into the Sensorial, where presence takes form and the felt texture of being meets the world. From there, waves of meaning gather into the Symbolic, shaping language, image, and narrative; codes through which experience is given coherence. With time and repetition, the tide etches grooves into the shore, forming the Patterned, where roles, defenses, and identities solidify into structure.

Yet in the motion of these layers, something can be lost. When the inner sun is obscured, an eclipse occurs, not by erasure, but by shadow. What cannot be fully met is not gone, but cast into the unconscious, echoing through behaviors, symptoms, and cycles that seek return. Still, the ocean remembers. Coherogenesis is the ocean's memory in motion, the process by which the field of the Self organizes toward wholeness, drawing even the fractured and forgotten back into the tide. Each wave, each return, is not a repeat, but a rhythm— an invitation to remember what we are beneath the surface.

An Invitation to Experience Differently

This book is an invitation. Not to adopt a new belief system or therapeutic technique, but to shift the way we *see* and *experience* ourselves. It offers a map, not of symptoms or diagnoses, but of wholeness: a movement through layers of selfhood, fragmentation, and return. It is about coherence. Not as something imposed from outside, but as something already present, waiting to emerge.

You may be a clinician seeking more integrative ways to understand trauma, transformation, and healing. Or you may be a seeker, someone who senses that your suffering is pointing to something deeper, something whole. Wherever you are, this model welcomes you as you are.

Why This Book, Why Now

Modern psychiatry and psychology have offered important insights, but often at the cost of fragmentation. The self has been divided into parts, behaviors, neurotransmitters, and labels. Suffering is pathologized, and the human story is reduced to symptom checklists.

This book takes another approach. It sees symptoms not as errors, but as signals. It sees fragmentation not as failure, but as part of a larger movement toward integration. It draws from trauma theory, developmental psychology, neurobiology, psychotherapy, complexity science, and contemplative traditions but it is not confined by any one system. It is a weaving, an interrelated field of understanding.

What is Coherogenesis?

At the center of this book is a term you may not have encountered before: *coherogenesis*. Simply put, it is the process by which wholeness emerges from complexity. It is the movement from fragmentation toward integration, from chaos to pattern, from multiplicity toward a felt sense of wholeness. It is how life organizes itself.

This process is not linear. It is recursive, emergent, and dynamic. The self is not a fixed object to be discovered but an ongoing unfolding, a dance between being and becoming.

A Map Made of Waves, Not Lines

Rather than seeing development as a staircase or a ladder, this model envisions waves moving through the ocean of being. Each wave (sensorial, symbolic, patterned) arises from a deeper ground: the unitive field of presence, the formlessness that precedes form. The journey is not from brokenness to repair, but from unconscious organization to conscious coherence.

This book follows the arc of that wave. It begins with the unitive ground of being and traces the emergence of differentiated selfhood. We explore how each layer gives rise to the next, how sensation becomes story, and how story becomes

3

structure. Then, as the wave begins to turn, we descend into the shadowed waters of fragmentation. Here we meet the eclipse, the veiling of the light of wholeness, and its echoes, which ripple through the psyche, body, and soul. These echoes are not errors, but signals: symptoms, patterns, and inner conflicts that speak in the language of return.

This exploration unfolds through a holistic lens, recognizing that human experiencing cannot be reduced to mind or brain alone. We examine the psychological imprints, the physiological reverberations, and the spiritual disconnections that arise when parts of the self go underground. By honoring each of these dimensions, we glimpse how the system, devoted to coherence, organizes around what has not yet been fully integrated.

And then, the wave begins its return. Not backwards, but inward. The second half of the book traces the pathways of reorganization and reunion. Here, the wave folds back into the sea. The journey ends where it began: not in the dissolution of identity, but in the rediscovery of the unitive ground as the source and sustainer of all becoming.

Who This Book Is For

This book is written for:

- **Psychiatric and mental health professionals** seeking frameworks that honor both science and soul.

- **Therapists and healers** who long to work from wholeness, not just pathology.

- **Clients and seekers** who intuit that their experiences, however painful, carry meaning and potential.

- **Anyone** who has ever sensed that they are more than their story, diagnosis, or role.

No prior clinical training is necessary to engage with this material. While it draws from technical domains, it is ultimately grounded in direct human experience.

A Note on Metaphor and Language

Throughout this book, metaphor plays a central role. Rather than presenting the psyche as a machine or a pathology to be fixed, we speak in terms of ocean, mirror, light, eclipse, and play. These are not poetic decorations; they are invitations to think and feel differently.

Because much of what we explore exists below or beyond language, metaphor allows us to approximate what cannot be directly named. We invite you to engage with these metaphors not just with your mind, but with your whole being.

A Field of Possibility

What follows is not a manual or a set of rules. It is a field, a living field, of possibility. It speaks to the unfolding of energy, pattern, perception, and presence. You will meet layers of the self, moments of eclipse, and paths of return. And through it all, you are invited to recognize that what you seek is already here: the one who is aware, the one who holds it all, the field in which all of this appears.

Welcome to the journey of *The Arc of Human Experiencing: A Journey of Being and Becoming.*

Part I. Sounding the Depths: Preparing the Vessel

Before the journey of becoming can unfold, we must listen deeply to the waters we inhabit. This section lays the foundation for understanding the fragmented landscape of modern psychiatry and introduces *coherogenesis* as a living process of reorganization toward wholeness. We explore the Self as a unified field, the origins of suffering through separation, and the map that guides us—not by fixed direction, but by resonance. Like mariners preparing for voyage, we attune to the inner tides and begin to sense the deep rhythms beneath the surface.

CHAPTER ONE

The Problem of Fragmentation in Modern Psychiatry

"The range of what we think and do is limited by what we fail to notice. And because we fail to notice that we fail to notice, there is little we can do to change—until we notice how failing to notice shapes our thoughts and deeds."

— R.D. Laing

Modern psychiatry, for all its advances, often resembles a cracked mirror with each shard offering a glimpse of the person before it, but none capturing their wholeness. Diagnostic manuals, treatment protocols, and even the language we use to speak about the mind have become fragments, pieces, categories, and clusters. As if the richness of human experience could be neatly partitioned into discrete sections and still retain its vitality.

Part I. Sounding the Depths

This chapter is not an indictment of psychiatry, but an inquiry into its current limitations; a compassionate examination of how a field once grounded in the study of the soul (*psyche*) has drifted toward compartmentalization. And in doing so, it has often lost sight of the person behind the pattern, the story behind the symptom, the self within the system.

Something essential has gone missing. Not from malice or neglect, but from a growing dependence on tools that cut things apart rather than bring them together. We are left with ever-expanding checklists, rigid treatment algorithms, and a mounting sense that something doesn't quite add up.

In this chapter, we'll explore what has been fractured and why. We'll examine how historical shifts, diagnostic structures, and treatment models have divided what was once understood as whole. We'll consider the ways in which this fragmentation not only limits healing but may actively obscure it. And finally, we'll begin to glimpse another possibility: a path toward coherence. A way of seeing that invites not just categorization, but integration. Not just management, but meaning. Because beneath the fragments, the whole is still there waiting.

The Historical Turn Toward Fragmentation

To understand the fragmentation of modern psychiatry, we must look to its lineage. Psychiatry did not begin as a biological science. Its roots reach back into philosophy, religion, and early medicine—traditions that treated the soul, the spirit, and the psyche as inseparable from the body, the world, and the divine. For centuries, suffering was interpreted as meaningful, even sacred. Madness, in many indigenous and mystical traditions, was not merely illness, it was initiation.

10

But with the Enlightenment came a shift. The rise of rationalism, scientific materialism, and empirical medicine brought immense progress and with it, a narrowing of vision. The body became a machine. The mind, a function of the brain. And suffering? A symptom to be managed.

Psychiatry's birth as a medical specialty in the 19th century was deeply shaped by these values. As it sought legitimacy alongside other sciences, it traded mystery for measurement, depth for diagnosis. The soul was exiled, and the symptom took center stage.

The 20th century accelerated this trajectory. Freud's psychodynamic approach gave way to behaviorism, and later to cognitive models, each offering valuable tools, but also reinforcing a tendency to divide the mind into parts, mechanisms, or processes that could be controlled. By the time the Diagnostic and Statistical Manual of Mental Disorders (DSM) gained prominence, psychiatry had become firmly anchored in classification. The goal shifted: from understanding the *why* to documenting the *what*.

In many ways, this was a response to practical needs. Clinicians needed shared language. Researchers needed standardized terms. Insurance companies needed billable codes. But the consequences of this medicalization were profound. Psychiatry became a system of surfaces, observations and measurements, rather than a discipline of meaning.

And so, the fragmentation began. Human experience, once held as sacred and layered, became flattened into categories. Depression. Anxiety. Trauma. Psychosis. Terms that point to phenomena but do not explain them. Words that describe without truly seeing. The irony is striking: in our effort to treat suffering, we may have reduced it to something less than human.

The Diagnostic Maze: Naming Without Knowing

A diagnosis can be a relief. It can offer language for a person's inner world, a way to make sense of chaos, and even a path to treatment. But in modern psychiatry, the diagnostic process often stops at the naming, leaving the deeper knowing behind.

The DSM presents itself as a neutral tool: a collection of symptom clusters organized into categorical disorders. But what it gains in structure, it often loses in depth. These clusters describe surface features (e.g., moods, behaviors, thoughts) without attending to the person's story, development, relationships, or environment. They are snapshots, not narratives.

Take "major depressive disorder," for example. Two people may share the same diagnosis, yet one grieves the collapse of a marriage while the other is silently unraveling under the weight of unspoken childhood trauma. Both are labeled "depressed," but the path that brought them there, and the path out, may be entirely different. The name unifies them, but the knowing does not.

As more diagnoses have emerged, the maze has grown denser. We now speak of "comorbidities", multiple diagnoses coexisting in the same person, as if the psyche were a filing cabinet of disorders. The overlapping criteria between categories (e.g., anxiety and trauma, ADHD and bipolar disorder) create diagnostic ambiguity, and yet we continue to treat the labels as fixed realities. As if the psyche had clean edges.

But human experience does not fit neatly into checkboxes. The psyche is fluid, adaptive, and expressive. Diagnoses, by contrast, are static. They freeze movement. They convert a living process into a coded identity.

There is a risk here: that naming becomes a form of forgetting. That we forget to ask where the pattern came from, what it protects, what it longs for. That we forget the person in the pursuit of the label. Naming is not the problem. Naming without curiosity, without inquiry, without reverence for the wholeness behind the suffering, that is the problem.

Treatment Silos and the Fragmented Practitioner

Modern psychiatry does not just fragment the person receiving care, it fragments those who provide it. Clinicians, too, are caught in a system of silos. Each discipline trained to master its portion of the human experience, often without learning how to speak across the divide.

The psychiatrist prescribes. The therapist listens. The nutritionist advises. The bodyworker intervenes. The spiritual guide prays. Each may be skilled, sincere, and dedicated. Yet rarely are they taught to collaborate as if the person before them were one integrated system, a human being with mind, body, meaning, memory, biology, spirit, and story.

This fragmentation is not accidental. It's embedded in the very structure of professional training. Psychiatrists learn pharmacology and neuroscience, but often little about trauma, meaning, or embodiment. Psychologists master theory and behavior, but may know little of physiology or spiritual process. Somatic therapists understand felt sense, but are rarely consulted in clinical decision-making. Even within a single field, subspecialties rarely speak.

The result is a divided care plan for a divided person. An individual may be on multiple medications prescribed by someone who has never spoken to their therapist. They may be encouraged to meditate without understanding their trauma history, or to change their diet without support for underlying relational wounds. Each provider does their best, but without a shared map, the person's inner coherence is easily missed. This kind of care can feel like being passed from hand to hand without ever being held.

And the practitioners suffer, too. Burnout rises in part because clinicians are asked to treat slices of a whole they never get to witness. They are trained to manage symptoms, but not to make meaning. To follow protocols, but not to listen for the deep intelligence beneath the distress.

The system, in its current form, mirrors the problem it seeks to solve. It treats human fragmentation with clinical fragmentation. And so, the cycle continues. But what if our work as practitioners was not to fix, but to reconnect? Not to control, but to relate? What if each modality were a language, and the person before us a poem waiting to be read in full?

The Missing Developmental Lens

Perhaps the most profound omission in modern psychiatry is not the absence of compassion or knowledge, but the absence of time. Not time in the scheduling sense, but in the developmental sense. A way of seeing that recognizes the human psyche as something that *unfolds*, not merely something that malfunctions.

Within the DSM framework, symptoms are treated as if they appeared fully formed detached from history, context, or meaning. But patterns of thought, feeling, and behavior are not random occurrences. They emerge through a lifetime of adaptation, shaped by relationship, experience, and environment. They are attempts at coherence.

A child who learns to suppress anger to avoid punishment may grow into an adult with anxiety and chronic muscle tension. A teen who dissociates in the face of betrayal may become a grown-up with mysterious lapses in memory or a sense of unreality. These are not broken systems—they are creative ones, shaped by necessity. Psychiatry's failure to recognize this developmental coherence leads to mislabeling adaptation as pathology.

Trauma, in particular, reveals this gap. While there is growing awareness of its role in mental health, the frameworks used to address trauma are often fragmented themselves, separating the psychological from the physiological, the narrative from the nervous system, the present from the past.

What's missing is a developmental arc, a way of tracing how a person's inner world formed in response to what they lived through. Without it, clinicians are left to treat symptoms in isolation, rather than understanding them as echoes of a longer journey.

The developmental lens allows us to see structure where others see dysfunction. It lets us ask: *What happened to you?* instead of *What's wrong with you?* And more importantly:

Part I. Sounding the Depths

What did you learn to do to survive? and *Is it still serving you now?*

Without this lens, interventions risk being premature or misdirected. But when we honor development, something shifts. We begin to see not just patterns, but *paths*—pathways toward integration, coherence, and growth.

Development is not linear, nor is healing. But both require a context that allows the self to be seen in motion, not a static object of diagnosis, but a dynamic being, always in process.

The Problem of Subpersonalities and Multiplicity

If we listen closely, we'll notice that people rarely speak from a single voice. One moment they're confident, the next unsure. A part of them wants to leave the relationship, another part is terrified to be alone. One voice seeks growth, another clings to safety. These are not contradictions, they are expressions of an inner multiplicity. And yet, psychiatry often treats this multiplicity as pathology.

The prevailing model of the self in mainstream psychiatry is monolithic. The self is assumed to be singular, consistent, rational—until something goes wrong. When someone exhibits conflicting internal states, they are labeled with terms like "mood instability," "identity disturbance," or even "dissociation." But what if these states are not malfunctions, but subpersonalities, parts of the self that formed for good reasons?

Multiplicity is not a disorder. It's a feature of being human. We are not one thing. We are constellations of experience (e.g., inner children, caretakers, critics, protectors,

16

and exiles). Each formed in relationship to life events, often carrying forward the burdens and beliefs of past moments. In integrative therapies like Internal Family Systems (IFS), this is honored as natural and workable. In psychiatry, it is often pathologized, minimized, or ignored.

Subpersonalities are not the enemy. They are messengers. They represent unmet needs, frozen adaptations, and unprocessed experience. They emerge because the system was intelligent enough to create them.

But in a diagnostic framework that values consistency and symptom reduction, these inner figures are forced into the shadows. A person might be prescribed a mood stabilizer to flatten the inner conflict rather than being invited into a relationship with it. The fragmentation is seen as illness, rather than as the psyche's attempt to preserve coherence under strain.

This misrecognition compounds suffering. Not only is the person in pain, but now parts of them are rendered invisible, or worse, treated as pathological.

True healing does not come from suppressing these voices. It comes from making space for them. From listening, relating, and reintegrating. Multiplicity, held within the presence of an observing self, is not fragmentation. It is the beginning of wholeness.

We do not need to eliminate parts of ourselves to be well. We need to *include* them gently, relationally, with respect for the intelligence that formed them in the first place.

The Silence of Meaning and Spirit

Something essential has gone missing in modern psychiatry. Not simply a theory or a technique, but a quality of presence, a willingness to explore the deeper currents of human experience. In the drive toward objectivity and quantification, psychiatry has fallen silent on matters of meaning and spirit.

The absence is subtle but profound. An individual may sit in an office, describing despair, loss of purpose, or a longing they cannot name. Yet the clinical response may be limited to adjusting medications or updating diagnoses. The question of *why* this suffering exists, what it might be pointing toward, what truth or transformation it carries, is rarely asked.

This silence is not malicious. It is cultural. Psychiatry, shaped by the norms of scientific materialism, has inherited a discomfort with the intangible. Meaning cannot be measured. Spirit cannot be graphed. And so, these dimensions are often left out, not because they are irrelevant, but because they defy standardization.

But the human psyche is not a closed system. It hungers for coherence, for narrative, for transcendence. People seek not just relief from symptoms, but a deeper sense of self, connection, and purpose. They want to know that their pain means something, that it is not just a malfunction, but a message.

Spirituality, too, has become estranged from psychiatric care. Experiences that might once have been held as mystical or sacred are now viewed with suspicion, sometimes misdiagnosed as psychosis or mania. Yet throughout history and across cultures, altered states of consciousness have been honored as openings to the divine, the unconscious, or the symbolic. These inner movements are not inherently pathological. They are invitations to heal, to integrate, to grow.

The work of meaning-making does not belong only to religion or philosophy. It belongs in the therapy room. It belongs in the diagnostic process. It belongs anywhere a person is suffering and searching for wholeness.

When meaning and spirit are exiled from the clinical encounter, a kind of second wound is created, not just the pain of the original experience, but the pain of having it flattened into something that no longer resembles the truth of it.

Healing is not just about resolution. It is about recognition. It is about remembering who we are beneath the symptom. Why we're here, and what it all means.

Consequences of Fragmentation

Fragmentation leaves a mark, not just on individuals, but on the entire field of mental health. When systems of care mirror the divisions they aim to heal, both patients and practitioners suffer. The cost is not only clinical, it is human.

For the individual, fragmentation often creates confusion and despair. Being passed from one provider to another, receiving disconnected treatments, or being labeled with multiple overlapping diagnoses can feel like being dismantled rather than understood. Each symptom is targeted in isolation, while the person's deeper coherence, what holds their experience together, is left untouched.

An individual may be medicated for depression while carrying unacknowledged grief. They may be taught cognitive strategies for anxiety while their body remains in a perpetual state of hyperarousal. They may explore childhood trauma in therapy while being prescribed medications that suppress inner child work. The pieces do not align. The whole is never addressed.

This kind of care often reinforces the very disconnection it seeks to resolve. The individual internalizes the fragmentation. They begin to believe they truly are broken into parts: a diagnosis here, a behavior there, a history scattered across providers and paperwork. Healing becomes harder, not because they are resistant, but because the system is incoherent.

And the practitioners? They are not spared. Clinicians, too, are trained in pieces. They are taught to treat disorders, not persons—to follow protocols, not patterns. Many feel the quiet ache of disconnection in their work, the sense that something vital is missing. Burnout becomes common, not simply from workload, but from soul-weariness. From being asked to touch suffering without the tools or the time to honor its depth.

When fragmentation becomes normalized, psychiatry risks becoming mechanistic. Symptoms become checkboxes. Interventions become formulas. And the sacred dimension of healing (the relational, the mysterious, the meaning-making) is lost.

But fragmentation is not the final word. It is the symptom of a deeper forgetting. The forgetting of wholeness. Of coherence. Of the truth that each person is not a collection of problems, but a living system seeking to heal, to grow, to become.

When we treat the parts without seeing the whole, we risk reinforcing the very suffering we aim to relieve. But when we begin to see through the fragmentation, to sense the intactness behind the adaptation, something remarkable becomes possible. We remember. And in that remembering, healing begins.

Toward a Re-Visioning: Coherogenesis Over Categorization

If fragmentation has been psychiatry's default mode, then coherence must become its new aspiration. Not the false coherence of rigid categories, but a living, dynamic coherence, one that honors complexity, development, and meaning.

We don't need to abandon everything psychiatry has built. The problem is not the presence of categories, but their overuse. It's not the existence of medications, but their isolation from context. It's not the desire to reduce suffering, but the tendency to reduce people in the process.

The re-visioning begins when we shift our orientation: from managing disorders to understanding patterns; from eliminating symptoms to supporting transformation; from naming to *knowing*.

This vision does not reject the multiplicity of the psyche. It *includes* it within a broader framework of integration. Subpersonalities, symptoms, and defenses are no longer problems to fix, but expressions to decode. They become intelligible when seen through the lens of development, adaptation, and the body's deep intelligence.

To do this, we must move beyond silos. A truly integrative psychiatry will not choose between biology and psychology, or between neuroscience and spirituality. It will learn to hold all of these (brain, body, behavior, meaning, and relationship) as expressions of a single, interrelated system.

In this vision, coherence replaces categorization as the guiding principle. Diagnosis becomes one tool among many, not the foundation. Treatment becomes individualized, responsive, developmental. And the clinician's role transforms: from fixer to facilitator, from expert to co-investigator, from technician to companion on a path of healing.

We begin to ask different questions:

- *What is this symptom trying to say?*

- *What part of the person is expressing itself here?*

- *How did this system come to organize itself in this way?*

- *What new coherence is trying to emerge?*

The result is not a loss of rigor, but a shift in orientation, from fragmentation toward wholeness. From suppression toward listening. From control toward collaboration.

Coherence is not perfection. It does not mean being free of suffering. It means being connected internally, relationally, and developmentally. It means that each part belongs, each experience fits, and each expression points toward something meaningful.

This is not just a new method. It is a new stance. A remembering of the deeper purpose of psychiatry, not to manage people, but to witness them. Not to divide them, but to walk with them as they find their way back to themselves.

Closing Reflection: Seeing Through the Cracks

If modern psychiatry is a fractured mirror, then the task before us is not merely to glue the pieces back together, but to see *through* them. To recognize that even in the shattered state, light still moves between the cracks. That the wholeness we long for has never truly disappeared, it has only been obscured.

Fragmentation is not a failure. It is a stage. A necessary moment in the process of differentiating, protecting, and surviving. But when we stay there, when our models, diagnoses, and treatments remain fragmented, we risk confusing the strategy with the self.

This book is, in many ways, an invitation to return. To remember the coherence that underlies all expression. To see symptoms not as errors, but as signals. To recognize that multiplicity is not the opposite of unity, it is its unfolding.

The field of psychiatry stands at a threshold. It has the tools. It has the science. But it needs the *soul*, the capacity to listen beneath the surface, to honor the full spectrum of human experiencing, to witness the system that lives and breathes behind every diagnosis.

We cannot integrate what we refuse to see. But if we are willing to look again with presence we may begin to see not just the brokenness, but the beauty that lives within it. The intelligence behind the defenses. The longing behind the symptom. The person behind the pattern. And perhaps then, the cracks in the mirror will reveal not distortion, but depth.

As Leonard Cohen wrote, *"There is a crack in everything. That's how the light gets in."* Let us begin there.

Key Takeaways: The Problem of Fragmentation

Part I. Sounding the Depths

- **Fragmentation as a core issue**: Modern psychiatry often divides rather than integrates; treating symptoms, not systems; parts, not people.

- **Historical shift**: Psychiatry's evolution from meaning-based traditions to mechanistic, symptom-focused models has led to a loss of depth and coherence.

- **Diagnostic limitations**: The DSM offers structure but flattens complexity, prioritizing naming over understanding and fostering poly-diagnosis and confusion.

- **Siloed treatments**: Clinical care is divided across disciplines (medication, therapy, nutrition, etc.) with little integration, mirroring the fragmentation it seeks to heal.

- **Lack of developmental context**: Without a framework for how patterns emerge over time, adaptive responses are misinterpreted as static pathology.

- **Misunderstanding multiplicity**: Subpersonalities and internal parts are pathologized instead of understood as normal, functional responses to experience.

- **Exile of meaning and spirit**: Psychiatry has marginalized the existential and spiritual dimensions of suffering, neglecting the person's search for coherence and transformation.

- **Consequences**: Individuals feel unseen, over-labeled, and disconnected; clinicians feel constrained, burned out, and unable to practice holistic care.

- **Re-visioning the field**: A shift toward coherence invites developmental understanding, integrative practice, and curiosity about meaning, not just symptom control.

- **Hope through the cracks**: Fragmentation is not failure; it is an opening. Healing begins when we see beyond the pieces and rediscover the whole.

If fragmentation reflects psychiatry's current dilemma, then coherence must become its path forward not as an abstract ideal, but as a living process. Beneath the divided diagnoses and disjointed treatments lies a deeper truth: human beings are not assembled from parts, but arise from a single, unfolding field of experience. Healing does not come from managing fragments, but from restoring relationships within the self, between selves, and with the world. The next chapter turns toward that possibility. It introduces *coherogenesis*: the dynamic process by which life reorganizes toward wholeness, not by erasing difference, but by weaving it into meaning.

CHAPTER TWO

Coherogenesis: A Return to Living Wholeness

"Wholeness is not achieved by cutting off a portion of one's being, but by integration of the contraries."

— Carl Jung

Modern psychiatry, with all its advances in pharmacology, diagnostics, and neurobiology, has paradoxically become a discipline marked by fragmentation. We see it not only in the growing number of diagnostic categories and subtypes, but in the disjointed way we often conceptualize the human experience. We divide the mind from the body, biology from narrative, symptoms from meaning.

This fragmentation extends beyond clinical categories. It is woven into the very fabric of how the field approaches suffering. A mood disorder is treated separately from a trauma history; a panic episode is addressed without curiosity about its symbolic or relational origins. Psychotherapy and psychopharmacology are often siloed, as though they treat different people rather than different expressions of the same whole. In attempting to make the complex manageable, psychiatry has risked losing sight of the living person altogether.

At its core, this fragmentation reflects a particular worldview. One that privileges parts over patterns, problems over processes, and mechanical intervention over mutual unfolding. It mirrors the paradigm of totality, where the self is treated as a sum of its components, and healing is thought to occur by adjusting or correcting discrete variables. Within this framework, relationship becomes background, the body becomes a machine, and suffering becomes a defect.

But what if this view, while sometimes useful, is ultimately insufficient? What if the crisis in psychiatry is not simply a matter of misdiagnosis or inadequate treatment, but a reflection of a deeper confusion about what it means to be human? The challenge may not be in refining our categories, but in reimagining our foundations.

To address fragmentation, we need more than new tools. We need a new organizing principle. One that affirms complexity without resorting to chaos, honors multiplicity without dissolving unity, and guides healing not through forceful correction, but through natural reorganization. What we are seeking is not merely an answer to pathology, but a way of restoring coherence to the human experience. This is the invitation of coherogenesis.

Introducing Coherogenesis

If fragmentation is the problem, then coherogenesis offers a path toward integration not as a technique or treatment protocol, but as a principle of healing and human development. The term coherogenesis blends two root concepts: coherence, meaning integration, harmony, and resonance; and genesis, meaning origin or becoming. It refers to the dynamic, living process by which the human system reorganizes itself toward greater wholeness across sensation, thought, relationship, physiology, and meaning.

Unlike reductionist models that aim to fix or suppress symptoms, coherogenesis invites us to understand healing as something emergent. It is not imposed from the outside. It arises naturally, like a flock of birds shifting direction in mid-air or like sediment settling in water when the turbulence clears. It occurs when the conditions are right, when the system feels safe enough, supported enough, or simply ready enough to reorganize.

This reorganization is not linear or logical. It often begins with a subtle shift in body awareness, a moment of emotional resonance, or the loosening of a long-held identity. A gesture, a dream, a relational rupture. Any of these can become the catalyst. Coherogenesis is not limited to the consulting room. It can unfold in conversation, in grief, in silence. It is not something we control. It is something we allow.

What makes coherogenesis so distinct is that it does not aim to create coherence from scratch. Rather, it assumes that coherence is already inherent in the system, obscured by fragmentation, defense, or dissociation. The work, then, is not to invent wholeness, but to remove what interferes with it. In this way, coherogenesis is fundamentally different from strategies that seek to enforce order. It is a process of remembering, not constructing.

In the clinical encounter, coherogenesis shifts the therapist's role from that of a fixer to a facilitator, from engineer to companion. The question is not, How do I fix this part? but rather, What would allow this system to begin reorganizing itself from within? This perspective reframes the symptom not as a problem to be eliminated, but as a messenger from a deeper process seeking integration.

Coherogenesis is the movement of the self toward resonance with itself. It is the unfolding of inner life into more harmonious relationship with the body, the world, and meaning. It is the quiet force behind all genuine healing, the rhythm of coherence returning to its source.

As this deeper coherence unfolds, it also reveals something equally profound: the emergence of truth. Just as coherogenesis is an ongoing, dynamic process, so too is truth an ever-deepening discovery, a pattern that arises from the lived experience and becomes clearer as coherence increases. Truth, in this context, is not a fixed concept, but rather the authentic emergence of what is most real in the present moment. It is a pattern that flows organically from the integration of all that was once fragmented, a revelation that deepens as we grow in coherence.

Truth: The Undistorted Emergence of Authentic Pattern

In this context, truth is not a static, predefined entity, but rather a dynamic unfolding. It is an ongoing emergence of what is most real in the present moment, deepening as coherence increases. It is the undistorted pattern that arises from the field of lived experience, shaped by the interconnectedness of mind, body, and spirit. As we engage with life, we are continuously moving toward an ever-deepening understanding of truth, one that becomes more refined as coherence increases.

To conceptualize truth within the scope of this model, we must recognize that it is a process, not a fixed destination. It is not something we impose on the world but something that reveals itself organically through the interactions of experience, presence, and awareness. This pattern is not only an intellectual recognition but an embodied knowing: a realization that emerges through the unity of our senses, symbols, behaviors, and relationships.

As coherence deepens within us, the pattern of truth becomes more distinct. It is as though the layers of the self—sensorial, symbolic, patterned—gradually align, allowing us to perceive with greater clarity. The truth is always present, yet it is often obscured by fragmentation, by the layers of unintegrated experience that prevent us from seeing what is most real. As these layers are reintegrated, truth reveals itself, not as a singular, unchanging fact, but as a process of continual alignment with the deeper ground of being.

Thus, truth is not an absolute, unchanging statement of facts but a living, evolving expression of coherence. It is the flow of life itself, unfolding through each moment, deeper and more authentically with each return to presence. It is a dance between the known and the unknown, where each step taken reveals more of the underlying unity of existence.

This understanding of truth invites us to embrace the ongoing process of discovering and aligning with what is most real in our lives. As we increase in coherence, we come to see the truth that was always there, hidden in plain sight beneath the surface of experience. In this way, truth becomes not just a concept but a lived reality, something that emerges organically as we grow in presence, awareness, and integration.

Rethinking Wholeness

To fully understand coherogenesis, we must first re-examine what we mean by wholeness. In much of modern psychiatry and medicine, wholeness is often conflated with symptom-free functioning, a kind of mechanical totality in which all systems appear to be working properly. But this view carries an implicit assumption: that the human being is a collection of parts, and that health is achieved when those parts are correctly assembled or adjusted.

This perspective aligns with what nursing theorist Rosemarie Parse describes as the paradigm of totality: a view in which body, mind, and spirit are considered separate entities, functioning in a cause-and-effect relationship with the environment. Within this framework, human experiences are broken down into observable phenomena, and intervention becomes a matter of managing discrete components.

Yet there is another paradigm, one far more aligned with the process of coherogenesis. Parse calls this the paradigm of simultaneity, where the human being is understood not as the sum of separate parts, but as a whole pattern, irreducible and continuously evolving. From this perspective, a person is always in fluid, simultaneous interaction with their environment, their meaning-making, and their inner experience. Cause and effect dissolve into a more dynamic and nonlinear field of becoming.

From the view of this model, totality is not wrong it is simply incomplete. In fact, it is best understood as an emergent property of simultaneity. Imagine a vast ocean: the body of water as a whole represents simultaneity—fluid, undivided, immeasurable. From this ocean, waves arise. These waves can be seen, measured, and tracked; they appear distinct. But they are not separate from the ocean. They are expressions of it.

Simultaneity is the ocean; totality is the wave. The wave never leaves the ocean, though it may seem, in its arc and crash, to exist on its own.

This metaphor reveals the danger of clinging too tightly to the paradigm of totality: we mistake the wave for the whole, and in doing so, we lose sight of the ocean. We diagnose the wave's shape, try to manage its height, or even suppress its movement without asking what deeper currents or environmental forces gave rise to it. In this way, wholeness becomes an abstraction divorced from lived experience.

Coherogenesis invites us back to the oceanic view. It reminds us that what appears as fragmentation on the surface is often the result of deeper processes seeking realignment. It teaches us that wholeness is not a fixed state, but a living pattern of movement, a relational rhythm between surface and depth, part and whole, form and field.

Wholeness as a Dynamic, Living Process

If we free ourselves from the idea of wholeness as a static state (something to be achieved, restored, or maintained) we can begin to see it as something far more organic: a dynamic process of becoming. In this light, wholeness is not perfection. It is not the elimination of difficulty or the erasure of wounds. It is the capacity of the system to integrate all parts of experience, including what was once split off, rejected, unmetabolized, or unformulated.

From this perspective, a person is not whole *because nothing has gone wrong*, but because their system is able to bring what has gone wrong into relationship with the larger field of self. This is where coherogenesis becomes vital. It is the process by which the fragments are not discarded but woven back into the fabric of being.

Wholeness is not found in a return to innocence, nor in the suppression of complexity, but in the ability to hold contradiction, ambiguity, and difference within an integrative field. The self does not become coherent by eliminating multiplicity, it becomes coherent by allowing multiplicity to resonate with unity.

This view is crucial in clinical work. A symptom does not signal failure. It signals a system struggling to cohere. A traumatic memory, a disowned part, a recurring pattern—all are not intrusions into the self, but invitations to reorganize around deeper truth. When we relate to these not as malfunctions but as messages, we participate in the process of coherogenesis. In this way, wholeness becomes a verb, not a noun. Not something we have, but something we do. It is a rhythm, a movement, a returning.

And this returning is never complete. Life continues to stir the waters. New experiences bring new challenges and awaken dormant parts. Each moment of disorientation carries within it the potential for deeper coherence if it is met with presence, safety, and space.

This is why wholeness, in the context of coherogenesis, must remain open-ended. It is not a final state, but a capacity, a fluid responsiveness to life that reflects the movement of the Self through time. Just as the ocean continually reshapes its shores, so does the self reorganize in response to what arises.

To be whole is not to be unbroken, but to be capable of reweaving oneself, again and again, from the fabric of experience.

Wholeness is the simultaneity of being made visible through the totality of becoming. Coherogenesis is the rhythm by which this movement unfolds, where multiplicity harmonizes with unity, and form continually realigns with the formless field from which it emerges.

Clinical and Existential Implications

When we shift our understanding of healing from fixing parts to facilitating coherence, the entire orientation of clinical work changes. In a fragmented model, the therapist is trained to identify problems and apply solutions—to diagnose, correct, and control. But from the perspective of coherogenesis, the clinician becomes something different: a companion to the reorganization of the self, a facilitator of the system's innate movement toward integration.

This does not mean abandoning skill or structure. It means recognizing that the most powerful therapeutic interventions are often those that create conditions for the system to reorganize itself: safety, attunement, reflection, and presence. When the system no longer needs to defend against fragmentation or threat, it naturally begins to re-pattern.

This re-patterning often begins subtly: an insight that shifts perspective, a somatic release, the emergence of a long-buried image or emotion. These moments may seem small, but they mark a profound shift in orientation; from protection to participation, from surviving to integrating. What once stood outside the field of awareness begins to move toward it, seeking inclusion.

Symptoms, in this light, are not disruptions to be silenced, but signals from the system. They reveal where coherence is incomplete, where energy has become stuck, where expression has been inhibited or misdirected. A panic attack, for example, may be a wave rising from a deeper ocean of grief, of separation, of misattunement. Instead of suppressing the wave, coherogenesis invites us to track it back to its source. Every symptom is a messenger of unfinished coherence.

This framework is not only clinically transformative, it is existentially liberating. It reframes suffering not as failure, but as part of a greater process of becoming. Life itself becomes the curriculum of coherence: every rupture an opportunity to deepen integration, every conflict a mirror revealing an unseen pattern, every loss a reorientation toward what matters.

In this way, coherogenesis gives meaning to disorder. Not by romanticizing it, but by recognizing that all experience, even suffering, is part of a living system seeking to return to itself. Healing, then, is not an act of will, but of listening. The system is already speaking. The role of the clinician, and of the self, is to learn how to hear.

This view is both humbling and hopeful. It reminds us that healing does not require perfection. It requires presence. And when presence is sustained within the therapeutic space, within the body, within the field of experience coherence begins to unfold, not through force, but through resonance.

The Movement Toward Unity

As coherogenesis unfolds, something deeper begins to reveal itself. Something not imposed, but remembered. Beneath the changing layers of sensation, emotion, and story, beneath the symptoms and the subpersonalities and the adaptive patterns, there is a quiet constancy. A field of presence. A ground of being.

This deeper ground is not a part of the self, it is the source from which all parts arise. In moments of coherence, we don't just feel regulated, we feel whole. Not because we've resolved every issue, but because we've realigned with something that was never broken. This is not coherence as structure, but coherence as being.

Here, the movement of coherogenesis reveals its full significance. It is not merely a process of repair, it is a return. A return to the unity that underlies multiplicity. A return to the deeper intelligence that lives within every system, every symptom, every fragment. As the system reorganizes, what emerges is not a new identity, but a more authentic alignment with the Self—not as persona, but as presence.

The ultimate movement of coherogenesis is a movement toward the unitary.

This is not the erasure of difference, but the re-contextualization of it. Subpersonalities are still present.

36

Emotions still rise and fall. Patterns still echo. But they are no longer scattered or at war. They are in relationship with the whole. The wave recognizes itself as the ocean. According to Thich Nhat Hanh, this is enlightenment.

In this light, the journey of healing becomes something much more than symptom relief. It becomes a spiritual and existential unfolding, a gradual reorientation from fragmentation to presence, from defended form to dynamic openness. The human being is not reconstructed, but re-membered, each part returned to the body of the whole.

This prepares the way for a deeper exploration. If coherence emerges from within the system, what is the nature of the Self that gives rise to it? What is the organizing principle behind coherogenesis itself? What is this field in which coherence, compassion, curiosity, and flow spontaneously arise? To answer these questions, we must now turn inward (beyond pattern, beyond symbol, beyond sensation) to the unitary Self as the ground of coherogenesis.

Key Takeaways: Coherogenesis

- Modern psychiatry often reflects a fragmented view of the person, grounded in the paradigm of totality: isolating mind, body, and behavior.

- Coherogenesis offers a new organizing principle: the emergent reorganization of the system toward greater wholeness through presence and internal resonance.

- It is not a technique but a natural process that unfolds when conditions are safe enough for the system to realign.

- Drawing from Parse's paradigms, totality is reframed as an expression of simultaneity, form arising from field.

- Wholeness is not a static ideal, but a living, dynamic capacity to include and integrate all aspects of being.

- Clinically, this means recognizing symptoms and patterns as invitations to reorganization, not malfunctions to suppress.

- Healing becomes a movement not toward perfection, but toward authentic alignment with the Self.

- This sets the stage to explore the unitary Self, the source from which coherence, presence, and integration arise.

To fully understand the nature of coherogenesis, we must now turn our attention to the source from which coherence arises. If wholeness is not constructed but remembered, then what is it that holds the memory? What is the ground that gives rise to presence, to the healing intelligence of the system, to the rhythm of returning? In the next chapter, we will explore the unitary Self not as a structure within the psyche, but as the undivided field from which all experience, expression, and integration flow.

CHAPTER THREE

The Self as Field: Foundations of Coherogenesis

"What you are looking for is what is looking."

— St. Francis of Assisi

In the previous chapter, we explored the concept of coherogenesis, the living process through which a human system reorganizes itself toward wholeness. Coherogenesis is not merely a response to fragmentation; it is the deeper rhythm of life itself, an unfolding that was always underway, even when obscured by protection, dissociation, or developmental rupture.

At the heart of this process lies a deeper presence, the Self, not as identity or structure, but as a unitary field of awareness. This Self is not a product of psychological construction. It is not formed by experience, though it expresses itself through experience. It is the ground of being—

spacious, luminous, and indivisible. In moments of quiet clarity, it is intuited not as something we have, but as what we fundamentally are.

From this ground, the movement of coherogenesis arises. It is the way in which wholeness gives rise to form without dividing itself, how the ocean expresses itself through waves. This process is not separate from life but inherent within it. When allowed to flow unobstructed, it brings about healing, integration, and transformation. Not by force, but by resonance.

This chapter articulates the core propositions that link the Self and coherogenesis. These propositions offer a new way of seeing the nature of the Self, not as a fixed or fragmented entity, but as a dynamic field whose coherence reveals itself through differentiated experience. They invite us to look beneath the layers of symptom, role, and identity and recognize that all human experience, in its multiplicity, emerges from a single source.

Coherogenesis is not a clinical intervention or a cognitive technique. It is a principle of life, operating subtly beneath the surface of every therapeutic encounter, every developmental leap, every moment of genuine presence. It is the Self's natural unfolding toward integrative harmony.

This chapter begins with the Self as undivided field. From there, we follow the ripples outward to presence, to qualities of being, to the differentiated layers of experience, and to the ways the system remembers its wholeness. These propositions will form the philosophical foundation upon which the journey of transformation rests, a journey that will be mapped in the following chapter, *A Map of the Journey*, and entered experientially in *The unitive*.

The Self is the Unitary Field and Coherogenesis is its Dynamic Expression

The first and most essential proposition is this:

The Self is not a structure, identity, or collection of parts. It is the unitary field from which all experience arises.

This Self cannot be located within any particular layer of experience—sensorial, symbolic, or patterned. It is not the sum of subpersonalities, memories, or traits. Rather, it is the ground of being that precedes all differentiation. It is not made, it is *given*. Not found in form, but in the formless spaciousness from which all forms emerge.

From this field arises a movement, a rhythm, an unfolding. This movement is coherogenesis: the process by which the undivided field gives rise to coherent form. Coherogenesis is not imposed from outside. It is the Self's dynamic expression, the way in which wholeness becomes particular without ever ceasing to be whole.

The Self is the ocean; coherogenesis is the rhythmic unfolding of its tides.

This metaphor is foundational. Just as every wave on the sea is an expression of the ocean's movement, distinct yet never separate, every experience, every pattern, every expression of the human being arises from this indivisible ground. The system is not *becoming* whole through external correction, it is revealing its wholeness as it reorganizes around the field.

Part I. Sounding the Depths

In developmental terms, the Self does not form through the accumulation of experience, it is present from the beginning, though it may be obscured by the protective strategies that form in response to overwhelming circumstances. In healing, we are not *building* the Self; we are uncovering it. Coherogenesis is not additive, it is clarifying. It is the inner rhythm by which experience reattunes to its source.

And so, this first proposition reorients our view: instead of seeking a self to assemble from fragments, we begin with the recognition that the Self is already present—undivided, whole, and alive. What follows in the therapeutic or spiritual journey is not the construction of a new identity, but the discovery of the field beneath all identities. From this perspective, coherence is not something we create, it is something we return to.

Coherogenesis Unfolds Through Presence, the Felt Signature of the Self

If the Self is the indivisible field, then presence is how that field is felt. It is the signature of the Self within lived experience: the direct, unmediated quality of being in contact with what is. Unlike attention, which can be directed or fragmented, presence is whole. It is not a function of focus, but of being-with, a soft, unguarded awareness that touches life without interference.

Presence is not something we manufacture. It is what arises when the system relaxes into coherence. It emerges when protective mechanisms soften, when striving ceases, when identity loosens its grip. In this way, presence is not only the felt sense of the Self, but also the organizing force through which the process of coherogenesis unfolds.

Presence is the radiance of the Self meeting experience without interference.

In moments of true presence, something begins to shift. The frozen parts of the psyche begin to thaw. Dissociated experiences drift toward the light. Protective structures, long held in tension, begin to soften. This is coherogenesis initiating itself. Not because we force it, but because the Self has touched itself through the field of now.

When presence meets fragmentation, reorganization begins. Not through interpretation, control, or resistance, but through resonance. Like a tuning fork placed near a dissonant string, presence vibrates in such a way that forgotten or exiled parts begin to remember their belonging. This is not a metaphor, it is a felt experience. A subpersonality that once operated in isolation softens in the light of awareness. A pain that was once overwhelming begins to integrate. A sensation that was once avoided becomes a doorway.

Presence is the organizing force that allows multiplicity to remember its source.

This proposition reframes healing not as problem-solving, but as re-contact. Presence is not a technique. It is not reserved for the awakened or enlightened. It is the innate capacity of the Self to know itself through experience. The more we trust this presence, not as a tool, but as a mode of being, the more the field of coherence begins to shine through the complexity of form.

Thus, presence is not a passive state. It is generative. It initiates, amplifies, and stabilizes the movement of coherogenesis. It is the living bridge between the unitary field and the multiplicity of lived experience.

The Morphologies of Presence and Catalysts of Coherogenesis

Presence is not uniform, it takes on different qualities as it moves through the layers of experience. These qualities are not manufactured states or cultivated traits; they are morphologies of presence, spontaneous expressions of the Self as it touches different dimensions of human life. When the field of the Self expresses itself through differentiated layers, it reveals itself in distinct, coherent forms.

Compassion, curiosity, and flow are not tools applied from the outside, they are expressions of coherence arising from within.

Each quality corresponds to a particular layer of the human experience:

- **Compassion** emerges in the **sensorial** realm as presence touches sensation, pain, or the embodied residue of trauma.

- **Flow** reveals itself in the **symbolic** realm as presence moves through meaning, metaphor, language, and narrative.

- **Curiosity** arises in the **patterned** realm as presence engages with habit, behavior, structure, and identity.

These are not simply emotional states. They are intelligent expressions of the field, ways in which the Self meets the world and supports its return to coherence. When defensive structures loosen and presence begins to flow, these qualities naturally arise. They are indicators that the system is reorganizing around the field of being.

These qualities emerge spontaneously when protective patterning softens and the Self shines through.

- **Compassion** opens space around pain without collapsing into it. It allows the body to feel without fear, making room for sensation to become contact.

- **Flow** loosens rigid narratives and opens the symbolic mind to spontaneity and resonance. Meaning is not fixed, but alive, constantly reorganizing around coherence.

- **Curiosity** softens control and perfectionism, inviting exploration, flexibility, and humility. It signals the system's willingness to reorient without shame.

These qualities do not need to be cultivated, only allowed. They are catalysts of coherogenesis, not because they impose change, but because they are signatures that coherence is already in motion. They are the fragrance of a system beginning to remember itself.

In clinical and contemplative work, the emergence of these qualities often marks a turning point not because insight has been achieved, but because the field of Self is beginning to unfold. When an individual shifts from self-judgment to curiosity, or from numbness to compassion, or when their narrative becomes fluid rather than fixed, we are not just witnessing progress, we are witnessing coherogenesis expressing itself through presence.

Coherogenesis Occurs When the Self is Unobstructed

In many therapeutic paradigms, healing is framed as something the individual must *do*. It is seen as a task to be achieved through insight, effort, or strategy. But from the view of coherogenesis, healing is not a product of doing. It is what naturally occurs when the field of the Self is unobstructed. It is a shift from "doing" to "being".

Coherogenesis is not something the Self does, it is what happens when the Self is unobstructed.

This view turns the process inside out. Rather than building coherence through intervention, we are invited to clear the debris that obscures what is already whole. Fragmentation arises when the differentiated layers (sensorial, symbolic, and patterned) become disconnected from the unitary field. When this disconnection softens, even momentarily, the system begins to reorganize on its own.

This reorganization is not effortful. It is not directed by an ego. It does not require control. It is more like water flowing downhill once the stones have been removed—spontaneous, responsive, intelligent. The therapist does not orchestrate coherogenesis; the individual does not force it. Both participate in allowing it.

It is not effortful or willful... it is spontaneous, like water flowing downhill when the debris is cleared.

The system wants to heal. It is not neutral. It is not passive. It is biased toward coherence, just as a plant leans toward light or a heartbeat seeks rhythm. This is not teleology in the sense of an external goal, but an intrinsic movement toward integrative harmony. Left undisturbed, and supported

46

with enough safety, the Self unfolds. Not into something new, but into what it always was.

This proposition invites a radical trust. It suggests that our work, whether as therapists, guides, or individuals, is not to fix, but to make space. To listen. To soften. To be with the system long enough and gently enough for the process to begin remembering itself. What emerges in this space is not something added, it is something revealed.

The Self is Immanent in All Parts and Coherogenesis Realizes This

From the perspective of coherogenesis, there are no parts of the psyche that are *outside* the Self. There is no subpersonality, no defense, no reaction, no symptom that does not, in some way, contain the field. The Self is not elsewhere, it is everywhere within the system, even in the places that seem furthest from wholeness.

The Self is immanent in all parts; coherogenesis is the realization of this immanence.

What we often label as pathology, dysfunction, or distortion can be re-seen as the Self in obscured form, like light bent through fog. A reactive pattern, a compulsive loop, a dissociated fragment: each of these holds a trace of the field, a forgotten coherence beneath the surface. Coherogenesis is the process by which that forgotten wholeness is remembered. It is not imposed, but uncovered.

This is why integration does not require eliminating parts, silencing symptoms, or erasing complexity. It involves welcoming the full multiplicity of experience into relationship with the Self. Each part becomes an entry point, not to a

47

problem to be solved, but to a deeper belonging. What appears as disconnection is often simply a disrupted resonance waiting to be restored.

Every subpersonality, symptom, or reaction contains the field in obscured form.

When presence touches a previously exiled part, when curiosity meets a rigid identity, or compassion holds a painful memory; coherogenesis becomes active. Not because the part is fixed, but because it is recognized. It is no longer other. It is no longer isolated. It is seen as of the same field, and in that recognition, it begins to soften, reorganize, and realign.

Coherogenesis occurs as the Self is remembered in each of its expressions, bringing a sense of unity to the diversity of form.

This proposition reframes integration as a process of revelation, not reconstruction. The goal is not to manage parts, but to *recognize the Self in all of them.* From this view, unity is not the opposite of multiplicity, it is what holds multiplicity together. Integration is the dance of the many returning to the one.

Integration is the recognition that every wave belongs to the same sea.

Differentiated Layers as Modes of Self-Expression

In the coherogenic model, the differentiated layers of human experience (the sensorial, symbolic, and patterned) are not seen as separate from the Self, but as modes of its expression. Each layer is a distinct way in which the unitary field moves into form. They are not additions to the Self; they are the Self expressing itself in differentiated frequencies.

The sensorium is the Self felt; the symbolic is the Self in meaning; the patterned is the Self in form and function.

This proposition reinforces the view that human complexity is not a deviation from essence, but a deepening of it. The emergence of layers through development is not fragmentation, but articulation. It is how the Self becomes knowable in time, how presence finds shape in the world.

Problems arise not because there are layers, but because the layers lose attunement to the field. When they forget their source, they become rigid, reactive, or dissociated. But even in this dissonance, the origin remains unchanged. Coherence is not something we must insert into the system, it is something we realign with.

When these layers realign with the Self coherence is not created, it is revealed.

This understanding reframes both development and healing. The task is not to transcend the layers or bypass their complexity, but to allow them to reorganize around the field of presence. The Self does not need to "return" to itself, it never left. What changes is the degree of alignment between the differentiated and the undifferentiated, between form and field.

Coherogenesis is not the construction of coherence, but the unveiling of it.

Each layer has its own morphology, tempo, and vocabulary. Yet all arise from the same ground and return to it through presence. When the sensorium is held in compassion, the symbolic is allowed to flow, and the patterned softened through curiosity, we begin to see the inherent continuity among them. The human being is not built from parts, but revealed in layers, each one a different voice of the Self.

Coherogenesis is a Mutual Process

Although the Self is unitary and immanent, its unfolding does not occur in isolation. Human experience is inherently relational. We are born into relationship, shaped by resonance, and transformed through contact. Thus, coherogenesis is not solely an interior process. It is mutual, emerging within the relational field.

The individual does not heal alone; the system reorganizes through resonance with other systems.

In infancy, the field of Self is first mirrored through the presence of another, through gaze, touch, voice, and rhythm. The child's experience of being *felt* initiates the early movements of coherogenesis. Presence meets presence, and coherence begins to take shape. This foundational truth continues throughout life: the Self is awakened in relationship.

Coherogenesis unfolds within the relational field through therapist-client resonance, attuned caregiving, nature, culture, and shared presence.

In psychotherapy, this mutuality is not secondary; it is primary. The therapist's coherent presence does not fix the individual. Rather, it creates a field in which the individual's own coherence can emerge. The therapeutic space becomes a resonant vessel, where defenses soften, subpersonalities come into contact, and fragmented layers begin to realign with the Self.

But this mutual process is not limited to formal healing relationships. Coherogenesis also arises in friendship, nature, art, music, movement, stillness, and collective ritual. Any field that reflects the presence of the Self invites coherence to unfold. We are never reorganizing *against* the world, we are reorganizing with it.

This proposition affirms that the movement toward coherence is not self-contained. It is ecological. The individual system is always in relationship with the nervous systems of others, with the environment, with culture, and with time. Healing is not an escape from these influences, but a reorientation within them.

The Self reorganizes with the world, not apart from it.

Mutuality means that we do not bear the work of coherence alone. We participate in a larger field that is also becoming. The Self's unfolding is part of a larger dance, a choreography of reorganization that includes every other living system. In this way, coherence is not just personal, it is transpersonal, and ultimately, universal.

Wholeness Was Never Lost, Only Obscured

As we step back from these propositions, a single truth becomes clear: the Self was never absent. It has always been here—spacious, immanent, whole. The fragmentation we experience, the symptoms we carry, the roles we assume, and the defenses we construct do not arise from the absence of the Self, but from the obscuring of its presence.

Coherogenesis is not a function of an ego, nor a product of psychological technique. It is the intrinsic movement of the unitary Self toward differentiated expression and integrative harmony.

This movement is not forced. It is not something we must achieve. When the layers of the human system soften, when protection yields to presence, when multiplicity is held rather than judged, the Self does not do coherence, it radiates it. The ocean does not need to remember how to move. The wave need only remember it is not separate.

These propositions are not just ideas to be believed, they are experiential invitations. They ask us to look again at what we thought was broken, and to see instead the process of reorganization already underway. They ask us to listen for the subtle pulse of coherence behind the noise of the psyche. They call us to trust the process, not as a strategy, but as the very nature of the field itself.

What we call healing, integration, or growth is not the imposition of something new, it is the unveiling of what was always true.

"The wave is the dance of the ocean. You are not separate from what you seek. You are its movement." — Adapted from Rumi

With this foundation in place, we now turn to the next chapter: *A Map of the Journey*. There, the differentiated layers will be named and explored as living expressions of the field described here. The journey forward is not a path away from the Self, but a deepening into its many forms. The field remains the same. What changes is our capacity to feel it, to trust it, and to move with its rhythm.

Key Takeaways: The Self as Field

- The Self is a unitary field, not a structure or identity. It is the indivisible ground from which all experience arises.

- Coherogenesis is the dynamic expression of the Self, the spontaneous movement of the field into differentiated coherence.

- Presence is the felt signature of the Self and the initiating force of coherogenesis.

- Compassion, curiosity, and flow are morphologies of presence; expressions of coherence emerging through different experiential layers.

- Healing unfolds when the Self is unobstructed; coherogenesis is not effortful, but natural and self-organizing.

- Every part of the system holds the Self in obscured form; integration is the realization that no part is separate from the whole.

- The differentiated layers (sensorial, symbolic, patterned) are not outside the Self but modes of its expression.

- Coherogenesis is mutual, arising within and through relationship, resonance, and the broader field of interconnectedness.

- Wholeness is not achieved; it is revealed as the obscurations fall away and the Self begins to radiate freely.

Part I. Sounding the Depths

With these propositions as our foundation, we can now begin to trace how the Self unfolds into differentiated form. In the next chapter, *A Map of the Journey*, we will explore how human experience coheres into layers (sensorial, symbolic, and patterned) each reflecting a unique aspect of the Self's expression. This map is not a rigid sequence or hierarchy, but a living landscape through which the journey of becoming unfolds. As we move into this territory, we carry with us the understanding that every layer is not separate from the field, but born of it. And that the return to wholeness is not a path forward, but a deeper return to what has always been.

CHAPTER FOUR

A Map of the Journey: Being and Becoming

"We shall not cease from exploration, and the end of all our exploring will be to arrive where we started and know the place for the first time."

— T.S. Eliot

Having glimpsed the Self as a field, unitive, indivisible, and ever-present, we now shift our focus from essence to expression. This chapter offers a map of movement, not to explain away the journey, but to orient us within it.

Healing is not a ladder we climb, nor a straight line from brokenness to repair. It is a return to something fundamental that was never truly lost. The Self, like the ocean, is already whole. But its wholeness unfolds through waves of sensation, symbol, and structure—layers shaped by development, relationship, and time.

Part I. Sounding the Depths

The purpose of this map is not to impose direction or fix the path. Rather, it helps us recognize a deeper rhythm, one in which the Self expresses, differentiates, becomes entangled, and remembers. This rhythm is what we call coherogenesis: the dynamic movement by which the field of being organizes, fragments, and reorganizes toward wholeness.

What follows is not a formula, but an invitation. We will explore the layered terrain of the journey ahead: how we descend into embodiment, story, and structure—and how, through awareness, we return again and again to the presence from which all experience arises.

Coherogenesis: The Organizing Principle

At the heart of this journey is the movement of coherogenesis, the natural rhythm by which the Self, as a unified field, expresses into form and reorients toward wholeness. This is not a linear process or a fixed protocol. It is a living intelligence, unfolding uniquely in each moment.

Coherogenesis does not shape the Self, it reveals it. In any experience, we may find ourselves drawn outward into roles and narratives, or inward toward stillness and integration. These movements are not mistakes or detours. They are the currents of becoming, shaped by need, memory, context, and presence. Wholeness can be achieved in either direction when there is a harmonizing of human experiencing, yet it is augmented when both being and becoming are intimately aligned.

The map that follows traces this unfolding not as a strict route, but as a rhythm of descent and return. We do not follow it to reach a final destination. We follow it to become more intimate with the ways the Self expresses through form, forgets itself in fragmentation, and remembers itself in coherence.

Developmental Arc: The Descent and the Return

The journey of human experiencing unfolds in two interwoven movements: the descent into form and the return to presence. Like waves pulled by the gravity of the moon, these movements are not separate phases but interwoven currents— one gives shape, the other gives depth.

The *descent* is the movement of differentiation. From the unitive ground of pure being, experience begins to take shape first through sensation, then symbol, and finally structure. Emotions gain texture, identities form, relationships mold the self, and survival strategies organize behavior. We come to know ourselves in form, in language, in roles. This is not a fall, it is a flowering. The formless becomes expressive.

Yet, in this flowering, we often lose touch with the deeper field from which all form arises. We become identified with the wave and forget the ocean. The self constricts around strategies of survival and coherence gives way to compensation.

The *return* is not a reversal of this process, but a remembering. It begins when presence meets what has been forgotten. It is when the patterned, symbolic, and sensorial layers are approached with curiosity rather than control. In this meeting, the system begins to soften. Awareness returns to the places that have been exiled. What was fragmented begins to move again in rhythm with the whole.

This process is rarely linear. It moves in spirals and cycles. We revisit the same themes with new awareness, touch familiar wounds from new depths. Each loop brings us closer to coherence not through perfection, but through inclusion.

These tidal movements, descent and return, are not stages to complete, but ongoing rhythms to feel. In any given moment, we may find ourselves deep in the patterns of survival or resting in the stillness beneath them. To live within this rhythm is to honor both being and becoming. To recognize that our patterns and parts are not obstacles to overcome, but waves to be understood. And that beneath them all, the ocean waits, not as an escape, but as the very source from which the next movement will rise. The task is not to transcend one and dwell in the other, but to allow both movements to inform our becoming. What follows is a view of the layered field through which these rhythms unfold.

The Layered Field of Being

Human experience is not flat or linear. It arises through interwoven layers, each with its own texture, language, and logic. These layers are not stages to be climbed or separate compartments to be analyzed. They are living expressions of the same field, shaped by development, adaptation, and the imprint of lived experience.

To orient ourselves within the journey of coherogenesis, it is helpful to recognize four primary layers through which the Self expresses:

The Patterned Layer is the surface expression of identity: habits, roles, defenses, and relational strategies shaped by history. It organizes around survival and predictability. Though often rigid, it holds valuable clues about unmet needs and protective adaptations.

The Symbolic Layer lies beneath, shaping meaning through image, narrative, metaphor, and language. Here, the psyche weaves coherence through story. When disconnected from direct experience, it can become abstract or performative. When integrated, it becomes a bridge between insight and embodiment.

The Sensorial Layer holds the raw, unmediated pulse of life—sensation, movement, rhythm, and affect. It is pre-verbal and deeply embodied. Trauma, attachment, and vitality all express through this layer. It is often where the deepest reorganizations take root.

The Unitive Layer is not a developmental phase but the ever-present ground of being. It is the field from which all layers arise and to which they return. It cannot be constructed or achieved, only remembered. When touched, it brings stillness, spaciousness, and the sense of coherence beneath complexity.

These layers are not separate realms. They flow into and through one another. A memory may emerge as a symbol, become felt in the body, express as a pattern, and dissolve in presence. Healing arises not by bypassing any layer, but by restoring fluidity among them so that sensation can inform story, pattern can soften into awareness, and all can be held within the wider field of Self.

Multiplicity as Expression

The Self does not express as a single voice or fixed identity. It expresses as multiplicity: distinct parts, patterns, and perspectives shaped by context, memory, and need.

Part I. Sounding the Depths

This is not fragmentation in the pathological sense. It is texture. Just as the ocean gives rise to countless waves, the field of being gives rise to a wide range of internal expressions: protector parts, inner critics, exiled children, longing selves, rebellious impulses. Each is a current within the same field. They are not a departure from Self, but an imprint of experience seeking coherence.

The challenge is not that these parts exist. It is that awareness becomes fused with them. We don't just feel anger, we become the one who must defend. We don't just carry sadness, we collapse into the one who was never seen. In this identification, the wider field is forgotten. The part takes over, and the Self seems lost.

Healing begins not by eliminating these parts, but by entering into relationship with them. When awareness decouples from identification, a new space opens. We begin to be *with* the part, rather than *as* it. Presence becomes the shoreline where even the most fragmented wave can rise, crest, and return.

Multiplicity is not a threat to coherence, it is its music. When each voice is heard within the field of presence, something deeper harmonizes. The system reorganizes, not by controlling its parts, but by including them. The ocean does not reject its waves. It expresses through them.

Qualities that Guide the Journey

As the system begins to reorganize, moving from fragmentation to fluidity, certain qualities naturally arise. These are not strategies or virtues to cultivate, but signs that the field is remembering its coherence.

60

Presence is the spacious awareness in which all experience unfolds. It meets sensation, emotion, memory, and thought without needing to fix or control. In presence, parts are no longer exiled, they are welcomed and seen.

Compassion emerges when presence touches suffering. It doesn't analyze or explain, it includes. It is the capacity to hold space for what emerges, offering a container. In compassion, protectors soften, grief is allowed, and the longing beneath defenses can be felt and held.

Flow is the system's return to responsiveness. It is presence in motion. When no longer constrained by fear or fragmentation, experience begins to move organically. Emotions shift, insights emerge, and the body speaks in rhythm with the moment.

Curiosity invites us toward what has not yet been met. It is the eyes and ears of presence. It softens judgment and creates space for what lies beneath patterned reactivity. This is not intellectual inquiry, but a relational openness to the unknown.

These qualities are not separate from the Self, they are its expression. The qualities of compassion, flow, and curiosity are all morphologies of presence. They arise not through striving, but through safety, attunement, and the gentle loosening of contraction. When they surface, they signal that the waters are clearing and coherence is returning.

In practice, they are the subtle markers of healing: the felt sense that something is reorganizing, that the wave is returning, that the system is moving in rhythm with its source.

When these qualities begin to surface, the map is not just being followed, it is being lived.

The Role of the Therapist or Witness

In the unfolding of coherogenesis, the therapist or witness is not a guide with a map, but a presence that makes the journey feel possible. They embody the qualities that guide the journey, bringing them into the mutual process between the therapist and individual.

Healing does not come from being led, it comes from being seen. When another holds presence, compassion, flow, and curiosity, the system feels safe enough to soften its grip on old strategies. The field begins to reorganize, not through direction, but through resonance.

The role of the therapist is not to interpret or fix. It is to listen, across all layers of experience. To attune not just to what is said, but to how breath shifts, how tension lives in the body, how silence speaks. This is not technique, it is relational coherence.

When the therapist is anchored in their own presence, they become a steady shoreline, a place where even the most overwhelmed inner waves can rise, crest, and return. Their attunement creates space for parts to emerge, for sensations to be felt, for meaning to unfold without pressure.

In this way, the therapist becomes a resonance chamber not ahead on the path, but beside it. Not the source of healing, but a mirror in which the system begins to recognize its own wholeness.

Toward Freedom: Living the Map as a Dance

This map is not a prescription. It is a rhythm, an invitation to participate in the unfolding of experience, rather than to control it.

Healing is not a task to complete, nor is freedom the absence of complexity. Freedom arises when we can stay in relationship with the full texture of our experience, without collapsing into it or needing it to be different.

To live the map is to move with the tides of becoming and return. To feel the layers as they express (patterned, symbolic, sensorial) and to meet them with presence rather than resistance. It is to let each part, each wave, each moment become an opening into coherence.

Orientation, in this sense, is not about knowing where you are on the path. It's about remembering how to listen. To the part that needs protection. To the image that carries meaning. To the sensation beneath the story. To the presence beneath it all.

We will enter each of these layers in turn not to analyze them, but to attune to them. To meet them with the qualities that guide all transformation: presence, compassion, flow, and curiosity. The journey is not about arriving somewhere new. It is about remembering the ground that holds it all. The field of Self. The rhythm of coherence. The dance of being.

Key Takeaways: A Map of the Journey

- Healing follows a rhythm, not a straight line, coherogenesis maps the natural movement from fragmentation to coherence.

- Coherogenesis is the dynamic expression of the Self as field, unfolding through sensation, symbol, pattern, and presence.

- The journey includes two interwoven movements: the descent into differentiation and the return to presence, like tides within the ocean of being.

- Experience organizes through four interconnected layers: *Patterned*: habits, defenses, and identity roles; *Symbolic*: language, narrative, and meaning; *Sensorial*: raw, embodied experience; *Unitive*: pure awareness, the ground of being

- Multiplicity is not disorder but expression, healing arises when parts are witnessed in the field of awareness, not identified with.

- Presence, compassion, flow, and curiosity emerge as natural signatures of reorganization and coherence.

- The therapist or witness creates space, not solutions, supporting the system's innate movement toward integration through attunement and resonance.

- Living the map is not about achieving completion, but participating in the unfolding, letting each wave rise and return in rhythm with the oceanic Self.

As we've seen, the journey of coherogenesis is not a departure from the Self, but a movement through its layered unfolding. At the heart of every wave, whether patterned, symbolic, or sensorial, there is a deeper stillness. A presence that was never lost, never fragmented, never formed. This presence is not something we acquire. It is something we remember.

In the chapters that follow, we will enter each of these layers in turn, descending into the raw immediacy of sensation, the architecture of meaning, and the patterned rhythms of survival and adaptation. But before we begin that descent, we turn inward, to the source.

The unitive is not the beginning of the map, nor its end. It is the ocean beneath all waves. It is the ground of the Self, ever-present, ever-expressing. In returning to it, we do not arrive somewhere new. We remember the source from which we have always been moving.

Part II. Rising Currents: Formation of Self

Here, we trace the emergence of selfhood through the layered movement of becoming. From the silent fullness of the Unitive, waves rise into the Sensorial, where the body feels and presence takes on form; into the Symbolic, where meaning is constructed through language and image; and into the Patterned, where experience congeals into structure, identity, and adaptive roles. This upward arc mirrors the wave's ascent, life unfolding through differentiation, complexity, and the effort to make sense of being.

CHAPTER FIVE

The Unitive: Being Before Becoming

"You never enjoy the world aright, till the sea itself floweth in your veins, till you are clothed with the heavens, and crowned with the stars: and perceive yourself to be the sole heir of the whole world."

— Thomas Trapherne

To begin this journey, we return to the source—the unitive ocean from which all form emerges. Before identity, before boundary, there is only the sea of being. This is the realm of the unitive self: a state of pure being rather than becoming. Drawing from complexity science, physics, and holistic nursing, we explore this foundational layer not as a concept to grasp, but as a movement to sense and remember. As we unfold these ideas, we will draw upon the metaphor of the ocean as a vast, dynamic, and boundaryless field, to illuminate the nature of human development as a continuous flow of pattern and presence.

Human Beings as a Unitary Field

Like the ocean, human beings are not made up of isolated parts, but are expressions of a dynamic, indivisible wholeness—a unitary field of energy in constant flux. Martha Rogers (1970) articulated this beautifully when she wrote that human beings "are not disembodied entities, nor are they mechanical aggregates... they are a unified whole possessing their own integrity and manifesting characteristics that are more than and different from the sum of their parts." In this view, the body is not a container for the self, but a visible pattern within an invisible field—an expression of the Self, not its origin. It is a temporary crystallization, an expression of underlying energy configurations within the larger, unified field of being. The concept of field allows us to see individuals not as isolated within their environments, but as inseparable from them: co-emergent, mutually patterned, and indivisible.

A Field of Energy

The term energy in this context refers to the inherent movement, flow, and dynamism within the field. It is not metaphorical, but ontological, pointing to the ever-shifting, vibrating nature of reality itself. This understanding finds support in quantum field theory, which posits that every point in space and time is permeated by fields that generate the phenomena we perceive. We do not have energy fields; we are energy fields. As described in the previous chapter, we are not observers of the field, we are its living expression. Human beings, in this sense, are not biological, psychological, or social entities in a compartmentalized sense, nor are we simply the sum of biopsychosocial parts. Rather, we are patterned expressions of a unified energy field that cannot be reduced to any single domain.

Moreover, the human and environmental fields are not separate domains interacting across boundaries. They are in a state of continuous mutual process, open systems that co-create and influence one another in every moment. There is no true "inside" or "outside" in this view, only the ongoing emergence of pattern, resonance, and meaning within the indivisible whole. Just as waves are not separate from the ocean, our identities, behaviors, and experiences arise within and as the living currents of the field.

In Mutual Process

Within the unitary field, mutual process refers to the dynamic, co-creative movement that arises between beings or systems, though even "between" begins to lose meaning in this context. Mutual process is not a transactional interaction between distinct entities, but a seamless unfolding within a single, undivided field. From this perspective, the notion of interaction, as if between a subject and an object, implies a false separation. It presumes borders where none inherently exist.

Rather than envisioning two beings exchanging energy across a gap, we begin to see that they are expressions of the same field in motion. Mutual process is the field moving with and through itself, appearing as two but arising from one. This is not metaphorical; it is a direct description of reality as an indivisible whole manifesting in patterned relationships. What we call "relationship" or "connection" is, in truth, a continuous flow of resonance and rhythm within the field's own fabric, like eddies within a single ocean current, distinct in shape yet made of the same water.

In this light, mutual process is not interaction between two things, but the field flowing through itself, appearing as two, but arising from one. It is a dance of interbeing, where the sense of separation dissolves into the recognition that all differentiation is relative, not absolute. The appearance of twoness conceals a deeper oneness, a unity that is not behind or beneath, but fully present within every movement of connection.

A Universe of Open Systems

Unlike closed systems, which imply containment and isolation, *open systems* are inherently interdependent, continually exchanging and transforming energy within a broader, interconnected context. Each open system is nested within larger fields while simultaneously encompassing smaller systems, creating a holographic structure of interrelated wholeness. In this framework, fields are never static or confined; they flow fluidly between, through, and beyond all systems—blurring the lines between parts and wholes, self and environment.

In an open system, boundaries are not rigid or absolute. Instead, they are *permeable, fluid, and dynamic*—more like zones of transition than fixed borders. There is no absolute inside or outside, no ultimate subject or object. What appears to be separation is more accurately understood as differentiation within unity. Experience, then, is not fragmented or compartmentalized, but *immersive, continuous, and relational*. Reality reveals itself not as discrete units, but as a seamless unfolding of interbeing.

This perspective shifts our understanding of causality. In open systems, there is no linear cause and effect in the traditional sense, no isolated agent producing a discrete outcome. Instead, all phenomena *co-arise* through reciprocal shaping. Systems influence and are influenced simultaneously, in a choreography of mutual becoming. Every event, pattern, or experience is the emergent expression of countless interwoven processes occurring within the field.

In such a universe of open systems, energy fields are not static containers, but *living, breathing* expressions of possibility. They continually reorganize, adapt, and evolve through the dynamic flow of mutual process. The infinite nature of these fields reflects the *boundless potential* of life itself—to transform, to self-organize, and to reveal new patterns of coherence as it responds to the pulse of the whole.

The Expression of Unity: Presence

Presence is a natural expression of unity, an immediate and embodied resonance with the now. It is not something we acquire or perform; rather, it is the innate beingness of the field itself made palpable. In this view, we do not *have* presence, we *are* presence. This presence is the living current of the unitary field, expressed through rhythm, resonance, and moment-to-moment responsiveness. It arises not from effort, but from coherence with the undivided whole. Before the body-mind learns to split the world into subject and object, self and other, presence is the seamless immersion in being. It is the felt texture of unity, before cognition lays down names and narratives.

The etymology of *presence*, from the Latin *praeesse*, meaning "to be before one," points directly to its predifferentiated essence. In this context, *being before one* is both literal and symbolic: it means being fully here, but also existing before the emergence of "one"—before the internal concept of a separate self takes shape. This notion aligns with Zen teachings, such as Alan Watts' phrase, "walking the razor's edge of the present moment," which captures the delicate immediacy of presence. When the present moment is traced down to its smallest increment, beyond the mind's grasp, it reveals itself as inevitable, ungraspable, and untouched by the will. Nothing can alter it, and nothing lies outside of it.

This realization has profound implications. It invites radical acceptance, not as passive resignation, but as a dynamic attunement to the unfolding now. And yet, even as the present moment is unchangeable, it also brims with potential. Each moment becomes a threshold, an opening through which new patterning may arise. Our ability to respond emerges from this unbound immediacy, echoing the unbounded nature of the field itself.

It is here, within this open presence, that the foundational ground of being, I am, is recognized. Not as a concept, role, or identity, but as a direct, felt knowing. I am is not yet this or that; it is the unconditioned pulse of existence itself. A silent, ontological truth that stands prior to content, prior to form. Before "one," and certainly before "many," there is simply the undeniable reality: I exist. This affirmation does not require language or belief, it arises as a resonance, as the field recognizing itself.

In early development, the ground of being is veiled by relational demands. As development unfolds, differentiation gives rise to form, identity, and self-other boundaries. But beneath all of this, presence remains the trace of the unitary field - a doorway back into wholeness. Through attuned presence the system remembers. Thus, presence reopens the field, and in that openness, the simple truth of I am shines through. Not as ego, but as being itself.

Open to Infinite Potential

A field, in its essence, is open. Unbounded by fixed form and alive with *infinite possibilities*. It is not constrained by structure or identity, but exists as *pure potential*, unitive and ever-responsive. In the context of open systems, energy fields are never static or limited. Because they exist in continuous flux, they are inherently dynamic *capable of expanding, evolving, and reorganizing* without end. This movement is not linear or predetermined, but emergent, arising through the *relational shaping* of mutual process.

Importantly, this openness does not imply chaos. The field maintains *coherence*, not through rigid structures or fixed patterns, but through *resonance, rhythm, and attunement*. Like a primordial ocean, it pulses with life—currents flowing beneath the surface, not yet shaped into distinguishable waves or familiar forms. This oceanic potential is responsive, intelligent, and deeply sensitive to relational influence.

It is within this *infinite matrix of becoming* that early relational impressions begin to take form. Through repeated patterns of resonance, whether harmonious or dissonant, the field gradually develops constraints that give rise to recognizable patterns. Over time, these enduring impressions shape the contours of what we come to know as the *self*. From this perspective, the self is not an empty vessel or passive slate, but a rich, living field of potential, with patterns that are gradually sculpted by the ongoing interplay of inner and outer influences.

Rather than being a fixed identity, the self is an *emergent form* within the field, a patterned coherence that reflects the field's history of relational experience. It remains open to further shaping and transformation, always more than any one pattern, and always connected to the boundless field from which it arises.

The Visible Language of Fields: Pattern

Pattern is the distinguishing characteristic of an energy field perceived in form, *a singular wave within the greater ocean of being*. It is not a fixed or static structure, but a *dynamic expression*, a living signature of the field's uniqueness. Like a fingerprint woven from experience, pattern reflects the ongoing relational dance between a human and their environment. As Todaro-Franceschi (2008) emphasizes, patterns are not discrete, measurable objects. Rather, they are *emergent properties*—fluid, shifting manifestations of the mutual process between the self and the world.

In this view, *pattern is the visible language of the invisible*. It reveals itself in how we move, feel, respond, and relate. Each person's life becomes a *story told through pattern*—infinitely complex, in constant motion, and never reducible to single events. Behaviors, physiological states, emotional landscapes, and even symptoms are not isolated phenomena; they are expressions of deeper, more fundamental field configurations. What we perceive as parts or problems are actually patterned echoes of the whole, *expressions of an underlying unity*.

76

Because pattern is nonlinear and abstract, it resists being pinned down or explained through purely analytical terms. It unfolds in rhythm and resonance, reflecting not a fixed product but a *living process*. In this way, pattern offers a way of perceiving the continuity of being—not as a collection of discrete moments or traits, but as an *ongoing, unfolding form of life itself*. It speaks to the primacy of process over product, of becoming over being finished. And it reminds us that within each expression (each breath, gesture, or symptom) lies the full field, revealing itself in real time.

The identity of an individual is never fixed; it is always becoming, much like a weather pattern. Though we may speak of a storm or a sunny day as if they are discrete events, they are in truth dynamic expressions of larger atmospheric systems in constant flux. A breeze gathers into a gust, clouds converge, and a storm forms. Not because it was destined to, but because conditions aligned in a particular way for a particular moment. Likewise, who we are emerges from the convergence of patterns (relational, physiological, psychological) continually shifting, reshaping, and re-patterning in response to the field around us. Identity, then, is not a static structure but a living process, always in motion, always on the edge of becoming something new. The diversity of patterning across individuals reflects not pathology but creative variation in how fields express themselves through form and experience. Pattern is the emerging wave from the underlying current, still full of potential but you can begin to detect it. Within it are all of the possible outcomes of the emerging particle.

Part II. Rising Currents

From Formless to Form

Patterns begin to take form through the natural process of self-organization, a spontaneous unfolding that arises not from external control or linear causality, but through the dynamic, reciprocal interplay of mutual process. At the delicate boundary where order meets chaos, subtle rhythms and resonances emerge between the individual and their environment. These micro-alignments (fluid, intuitive, and often below conscious awareness) begin to cohere into recognizable patterns. They are not imposed from the outside, but rather *crystallize from within* the field itself, reflecting the unique flow of energy specific to that being.

This *edge of chaos*, a fertile terrain where structure and unpredictability mingle, is the ground from which novelty, creativity, and adaptive coherence arise. Here, cohering patterns emerge: configurations that are stable enough to support continuity yet fluid enough to remain responsive to change. These patterns do not constrain; they *organize*. They hold together identity as a rhythmic, living process rather than as a static structure.

It is within this dynamic field, where openness meets resonance, that identity begins to take shape. Not as a fixed form or role, but as a patterned expression of the field's deeper intelligence. What we begin to perceive are the first condensations of individuality: the particulate drops forming from the wave. The wave has not vanished; it is simply *expressing itself in new form*. This is the moment where being becomes *becoming*, where the boundless ocean of potential begins to articulate itself through shape, rhythm, and response.

Identity, then, is not a conclusion but a process, an ongoing co-creation between the field and its unfolding possibilities.

These early processes of emergence and organization can be deeply appreciated when viewed through the experience of an infant. In the earliest phases of life, the infant exists as a unitary field of being—open, unbounded, and immersed in a continuous flow of experience. There is no defined self, no "me" to locate or defend, no separation between body and world. Experience is not parsed into internal and external, subject and object; instead, it unfolds as a seamless, immersive field of sensation and presence.

At this stage, the infant is not a separate individual in relation to the caregiver, but part of a recursive mutual field, a dynamic interplay of rhythms, sensations, and attunements shared between bodies. This is what Winnicott pointed to in his famous assertion: *"There's no such thing as a baby."* His words emphasize that the infant cannot be understood in isolation, but only within the context of the relationship, especially the mother-infant dyad. The infant's early experience is formed within and through this relational matrix.

Inputs such as sound, touch, breath, facial expression, and movement do not simply affect the infant from the outside, they participate in the infant's becoming. They are not merely stimuli but are integrated into the emerging organization of the field, shaping the infant's patterning of safety or fear, connection or rupture, expansion or withdrawal. Yet, at this point, these experiences are not yet claimed as "mine" or interpreted through a personal identity. They are felt, registered, and patterned *pre-reflectively*, as part of the field's natural flow toward coherence.

In this fluid openness, the infant is exquisitely responsive to the subtle shifts in mutual process. It is through this resonance, rhythmic synchrony, shared affect, and attuned presence that the formless begins to coalesce into form. The mutual field begins to shape and be shaped, giving rise to early configurations of self and world. Mutual process, then, is not just a conceptual bridge between self and other, it is the cradle of becoming, where the infinite openness of the field begins its journey into distinct, embodied form.

Rhythmic Synchrony

Rhythmic synchrony is the earliest mode of connection through which the infant and caregiving environment come into subtle alignment. This alignment is not communicated through words or ideas, but through the body through shared rhythms that flow between the infant's internal physiological pulses (such as breath, heartbeat, muscle tone, and affective shifts) and the external rhythms of the caregiver's presence. The tone and cadence of the caregiver's voice, the warm rhythm of their touch, the soft timing of gaze, the rise and fall of their breath, and the gentle sway of movement, all provide a relational tempo that the infant entrains to, moment by moment.

This synchrony is not merely an exchange between two distinct beings. Rather, it reflects the deeper reality of a co-regulated field, in which the infant's nervous system is shaped and supported by the caregiver's more mature rhythms. These subtle exchanges serve as the primary regulators of the infant's sensory and affective systems, scaffolding the development of bodily coherence, emotional tone, and a sense of safety within the world. At this early stage, regulation does not occur *within* a separate self, but *through* the relational field. The experience is not yet divided by boundaries of "self" and "other," but remains continuous and unitive.

Rhythmic synchrony is the language of the pre-self, a primordial communication that precedes language, concept, and identity. It is a rhythm before form, a field before structure. This subtle dance lays down the first templates of continuity, offering the infant an embodied sense of being-with and belonging. Before the mind organizes experience into space and time, rhythmic synchrony provides a felt pattern of coherence, a kind of musical attunement that both contains and invites the unfolding of form.

In this way, rhythmic synchrony is not merely a developmental milestone, it is the music of mutual process, the foundation upon which all later relational, symbolic, and cognitive structures are built. It is through this embodied resonance that the infinite potential of the unitary field begins to shape into recognizable patterns of experience, forging the early architecture of self and other.

Resonance

While rhythmic synchrony shapes the temporal and sensory contours of early experience, resonance adds another dimension, the affective and tonal quality of the shared field. The infant exists in a state of mutual resonance with the environment, particularly with the caregiver. Unlike synchrony, which emphasizes timing, pacing, and physiological alignment, resonance speaks to the vibrational harmony of the relational field: how the emotional tone, energetic quality, and felt sense of the caregiver's presence ripple through the infant's being.

This is not a cognitive or interpretive process. The infant does not understand the caregiver's state; rather, they live it directly, as if their experience and the caregiver's are one and the same. The caregiver's tone of voice, muscle tension, breathing rhythm, emotional presence, and nervous system regulation all transmit signals that are not merely perceived. They are *absorbed*, *embodied*, and *inhabited* by the infant as part of the unitary field. There is no "me" and "you", only *this*, the shared texture of feeling.

Resonance creates coherence or fragmentation depending on the quality of the caregiver's attunement. A regulated, attuned caregiver fosters a sense of embodied coherence and safety, while dysregulated or inconsistent resonance can imprint fragmentation or alarm into the infant's system. At this early stage, it is not "I feel what you feel," but rather, "we are this feeling." The infant is not yet a separate self in relation to another, but a being-in-relation, a node within the greater relational field. This state of undivided experience forms the implicit memory of being-with—a deep, preverbal imprint that shapes the infant's sense of relational reality.

Over time, these early resonant experiences become the substrate upon which self-states, relational expectations, and emotional templates are formed. Resonance is the seedbed of future capacities such as empathy, mirroring, and symbolic meaning, but in this primordial stage, it is simply the tone of being, the raw material of human connection before identity has taken shape. It is the field's way of knowing itself through feeling.

Sensitivity to Conditions

In nonlinear systems, small inputs can have disproportionate impacts, a principle known as *sensitivity to initial conditions*, often illustrated by the butterfly effect. This is particularly true in early development, where the field of the self is still fluid, unformed, and highly responsive. In this phase, the unitive self is exquisitely sensitive to subtle relational cues. A moment of soothing presence, a fleeting rupture in connection, a tone of voice, or a touch. Each of these micro-events can shape the trajectory of development in profound ways.

The emerging self is not molded solely by dramatic or overt experiences, but through the accumulation of subtle, repeated patterns of attunement or misattunement. These moments ripple through the field, embedding themselves in the body, in implicit memory, and in the meaning-making structures that eventually coalesce into a sense of self. It is not the magnitude of any single input, but the *patterned quality of relational experience*, especially at formative moments, that contours the flow of becoming.

A Nesting of Systems

The unitive self exists within nested systems or fields, layers of experience that interact recursively, where patterns in one domain can shape and be shaped by others. Development unfolds fractally, meaning early relational or sensory patterns often re-emerge at more complex levels later in life. For example, the containment provided in infancy may echo in one's capacity for emotional regulation in adulthood. From this perspective, the self is not a fixed or singular entity but a dynamically mutual process—fluid, open, and inherently patterned.

Like a symphony, the self comprises multiple themes and tonalities, each arising from the same field of potential. Some patterns become more distinct over time, forming recognizable subpersonalities or "parts," each carrying unique emotional textures, histories, and adaptive roles. Yet beneath this multiplicity, there is a continuous thread, a core presence or "tone" of "I am" that gives coherence to the whole.

Just as each instrument in an orchestra contributes to the symphony without losing the unity of the piece, so too do the parts of the self arise from the same field, shaped by recursive interaction across time and experience. The symphony is never reducible to a single instrument, but its unity is unmistakable. In this way, the self is both one and many: a living expression of the field's rhythmic unfolding across nested levels of being.

The Body in the Unitary Field

From a physiological standpoint, before distinct body systems are anatomically differentiated, there exists a vibrational matrix. A dynamic field of resonance, rhythm, and relational attunement. This field is not inert or passive; it is alive and exquisitely responsive to the maternal environment, shaped by hormonal patterns, circadian rhythms, emotional tone, nutritional input, and the broader energetic field of the mother-child relationship. Even before neural or organ systems are fully developed, the body is already "learning" through resonance—absorbing the patterns of safety, stress, rhythm, and coherence within its environment.

Within this matrix, body system potentials are not simply genetically predetermined, they are co-shaped by mutual process. For instance, the hypothalamic-pituitary-adrenal (HPA) axis, responsible for stress regulation, begins to calibrate to the mother's neuroendocrine and emotional signals, laying down the template for how the body will perceive and respond to threat. Similarly, the gut-brain-immune network, now understood as a deeply interwoven system, develops in relation to microbial exposures, immune modulation, and affective resonance from the maternal field. The enteric nervous system, immune programming, and vagal tone are all being tuned in this early field.

Think of this phase as the primordial soil in which the seeds of the body systems are being planted, not in isolation, but within a living relational ecology. Every pulse of maternal presence, every fluctuation in tone, contact, or internal state becomes part of the energetic scaffolding from which the infant's physiology emerges. Body systems do not develop in a vacuum but arise through rhythmic participation in a shared field of becoming. In this light, physiology is not separate from psychology or spirituality, it is an expression of the same field, differentiated through pattern, tone, and rhythm. The body is the field in form.

Nurturing the Unitive: Supporting the Field Before Form

To nurture the unitive is not to shape it, but to protect the conditions in which it can remain open, coherent, and alive. This phase of development is not about instilling skills or achieving milestones. Rather, it is about safeguarding the field's natural intelligence, honoring its rhythms, its permeability, and its fluid responsiveness to the world.

In this early stage, care is not offered *to* a separate self, but *within* a shared relational field. The most powerful supports are subtle: presence, attunement, and resonance. These are not interventions, but *offerings*, ways of being that allow the unitive self to unfold without fragmentation.

- **Protect the rhythm, not the outcome.** Infants thrive not by being pushed toward structure, but by being held within rhythm. Gentle routines, patterned sensory inputs, and consistent relational availability help regulate the field without forcing form. Rocking, swaying, cooing, breathing in harmony. These rhythmic offerings echo the fluidity of the womb and reinforce continuity after birth.

- **Allow openness.** The unitive field is not empty, it is full of potential. Avoid premature categorization, overstimulation, or rigid expectations. Instead, create space where the infant can dwell in the mystery of being. Wonder, silence, and soft gaze all signal to the field: *you are safe to remain open.*

- **Become the ground.** When a caregiver attunes deeply without intrusion, they become a kind of holding environment not only physically, but emotionally and energetically. A grounded caregiver offers coherence through nervous system regulation, emotional tone, and non-reactivity. This allows the infant's own system to entrain to a stable, organizing presence.

- **Mirror, but do not distort.** The caregiver's face becomes the first mirror of the self not just in expression, but in emotional presence. When the caregiver reflects the infant's states with resonance and clarity, without overstating or under-attuning, the infant begins to sense itself as felt and known, before the idea of self arises.

- **Preserve the sense of unity.** This stage is marked by immersion, not separation. Practices that preserve this immersion (like skin-to-skin contact, eye contact without demand, and shared stillness) reaffirm the child's embeddedness in the field. Even brief moments of such presence offer a powerful imprint: *you are not alone; you are held within life.*

- **Repair ruptures gently.** Inevitably, misattunements occur. What matters is not their absence, but the rhythm of return. In the unitive, the caregiver's re-entry into attunement serves as the earliest lesson in trust and coherence. Through these reparative moments, the field learns that disruption is not the end of safety, it is part of the dance.

To nurture the unitive is to trust its intelligence. It is to support development not by imposing structure, but by staying close enough, soft enough, and coherent enough that form may arise gently, in rhythm with the field's own unfolding. In doing so, we protect the primordial memory of unity, the living pulse of *I am* that continues to echo within every wave of becoming.

Concluding Thoughts

Throughout this chapter, the ocean serves as a guiding metaphor for the unitive self and the unitary field of human experience. Like the vast, boundless sea, the self in its earliest state is fluid, immersive, and without fixed boundaries. An open system alive with rhythmic currents and infinite potential.

Part II. Rising Currents

Before the formation of identity or differentiation into self and other, there is only presence: a dynamic field of being, not yet shaped into distinct waves or forms. Just as patterns in the ocean arise from invisible undercurrents, our early experiences begin to cohere into stable, though still fluid, forms through mutual process, resonance, and rhythmic synchrony. The ocean captures both the mystery and the movement of becoming, how from a field of pure potential, the first gentle contours of self begin to emerge, not through separation, but through unfolding coherence.

"Out beyond ideas of wrongdoing and rightdoing, there is a field. I'll meet you there." - Rumi

In this unitive space, we glimpse the silent ground from which all form emerges, a unified, living field of resonance, rhythm, and relational flow. Before the self is shaped, before boundaries arise, there is only being: continuous, immersive, and deeply responsive. This field is not a blank canvas but a matrix of infinite potential, subtly sculpted by mutual process and the earliest patterns of connection. As presence becomes pattern, and resonance gives rise to form, we begin to see how complexity and coherence emerge from the dance of the field with itself. This chapter sets the stage for what follows—the slow crystallization of identity, the shaping influence of early relational rhythms, and the journey from being to becoming. In remembering the unitive, we do not regress, but recover the thread of wholeness woven through all experience. Wholeness is not something we become, it is what we return to when becoming falls away.

Key Takeaways: The Unitive

- Human beings are not separate parts, but unified fields of energy and consciousness, inseparable from their environment.

- The unitive self refers to the earliest phase of being, before identity, boundary, or differentiation; a state of pure presence.

- Mutual process, not external interaction, is the fundamental dynamic of life. It is a co-creative flow within one field, not between separate selves.

- Open systems characterize human experience: permeable, dynamic, and interconnected with no true inside/outside, self/other, or subject/object split.

- Presence is not something we generate but something we *are*; an expression of the unitary field experienced in the immediacy of now.

- "I am" precedes "I am this", identity arises from a deeper ontological ground of being, not as a construct, but as a felt truth.

- Pattern emerges through self-organization, shaped by mutual process, rhythm, and resonance at the edge of chaos.

- Infants exist in unitive mutual resonance with their environment, no "self" or "other," just shared states of being.

- Rhythmic synchrony and resonance between infant and caregiver lay the foundation for future emotional, relational, and symbolic development.

- Small relational inputs (attunements or misattunements) have significant impact, demonstrating the sensitivity of early development.

- Development is fractal and recursive, meaning early patterns echo throughout life in more complex forms.

- Physiological systems emerge from an energetic and relational matrix, meaning the body is shaped not just by biology, but by meaning and mutual experience.

- The ocean metaphor illustrates the unitive self as a vast, fluid, and formless presence, alive with potential and in constant motion.

As the unitary field continues to unfold, something subtle begins to shift. What was once completely fluid, immersive, and undivided begins to ripple with early patterns—faint, repeating impressions shaped by the rhythms of breath, touch, sound, and presence. These patterns do not arise from outside the field but emerge from within, born of mutual process, resonance, and the body's innate capacity to cohere. In this way, the infinite potential of the unitive begins to express itself through sensation, through texture, pressure, temperature, motion. The Self does not yet know itself, but it begins to feel.

From within the ocean of becoming, the earliest contours of form begin to rise. This is the sensorial self: a body before a name, a surface before an image, a pulse before a story. It is here that the first edges appear not as boundaries of separation, but as membranes of meaning. And with them, the field begins to fold into form.

CHAPTER SIX

The Sensorial: Where Presence Becomes Flesh

"The body is the shore on the ocean of being. It is the threshold between formless and form."

— Sufi Teaching

Having explored the unitive field, the rhythmic, resonant ground of being from which all experience arises, we now begin to trace the first contours of form. Where the unitary field remains fluid, immersive, and boundless, the sensorial phase marks the first differentiation, subtle edges within a field that remains whole.

This is not a rupture from unity, but a differentiation within it, a gradual organizing of the field through repeated rhythms, sensory impressions, and relational resonance. These first patterns are not yet mental or symbolic. They are felt. Lived through the body. Experienced at the skin, in the muscles, through tone, breath, and pressure.

In this chapter, we follow the movement from being to becoming not yet through thought or story, but through sensation. The infant, still fully embedded in the relational field, begins to register contrasts. Warmth and cold. Contact and space. Motion and stillness. These impressions become the raw material for the first sense of "I" and "not I" not as concepts, but as embodied patterns of experience.

The Self Felt Before Thought

It is here, in the sensorial, that the Self begins to express through form not as an idea, but as a body. Not as narrative, but as rhythm, tone, and touch. And from this, the earliest organization of identity and meaning begins to unfold.

From the unitive ground of being, pattern begins to take form. This movement toward form does not arise from outside the field, but emerges organically through self-organization, a process shaped by repeated engagement with the environment in what we've described as mutual process. Through rhythms of synchrony and the subtle affective attunement of resonance, the formless field begins to stabilize into recurring experiences. These repeated interactions lay down early patterns of coherence not fixed structures, but fluid, responsive configurations that gradually become recognizable.

Laying Down the Patterns of Coherence

Over time, these patterned interactions crystallize into predictable sensorimotor schemas, such as how it feels to be held or rocked, and give rise to the earliest affective templates, like safety, joy, or abandonment. At the same time, they shape implicit relational memory, forming a nonverbal imprint of what contact, closeness, and separation feel like in the body.

These emerging patterns create the first scaffolding of the self not through cognition or language, but through embodied repetition.

With each recurrence, the originally fluid and boundaryless field becomes increasingly contoured by experience. The infant begins to register the difference between self and other, inside and outside, presence and absence, now and then. These are not yet conceptual distinctions but felt differentiations, arising from the body's ongoing engagement with the world.

In this way, the Self is not imposed from above, nor constructed through accumulation. It is expressed through the field, as coherence taking shape through rhythm and relation. The earliest self-states take shape not as identities, but as patterns of becoming, drawn from the field's continuous relational flow.

Sensory Contours and Somatic Mapping

Through repeated sensory impressions (e.g., touch, temperature, pressure, sound, movement) the infant begins to encounter the first stirrings of form. These impressions are not isolated inputs but arise within the flow of rhythmic synchrony and relational resonance. Within this attuned field, sensations gain shape, repetition, and meaning. Skin-to-skin contact offers the warmth and firmness of another body; mouthing and sucking create contrasts between inner and outer sensation; rocking and being carried introduce vestibular rhythms; while voice and heartbeat provide auditory containment, defining the sensory space in which the infant is held.

As these experiences repeat, looping through relational feedback in a resonant environment, the infant begins to perceive differences and contrasts. Sensory contours emerge: breast versus no breast, warmth versus cold, motion versus stillness, internal versus external. These contrasts do not yet form cognitive categories, but instead give rise to felt differences, the earliest emergence of edges.

These edges are not sharp or fixed. They are porous, soft, and dynamic—living impressions formed on the surface of the body. They constitute a kind of somatic cartography: primitive surface mappings that register where one sensation ends and another begins. Not yet memories, not yet mental representations, but tactile and kinesthetic patterns etched into the psyche through the skin, breath, and body.

The Membrane of Self

At this stage, the psyche exists on the surface along the skin, the lips, the ears, the shifting textures of bodily contact. This is the membrane of experience, where the Self begins to take shape not as a solid interiority, but as a field of sensations held together by rhythm and touch. It is here that the earliest boundaries of selfhood form not to separate, but to give shape, coherence, and continuity to the evolving sense of being.

At this stage, the field begins to express increasing complexity. It remains unitary in essence, but is now becoming differentiated through mutual process—patterned, shaped, and contoured by ongoing relational exchange. The infant, still immersed in the shared field, begins to experience the formation of a proto-self not as a concept or image, but as a felt sense of coherence emerging through the containment of patterned sensory experience.

As sensory impressions repeat within a context of attunement, safety, and resonance, they begin to form stable but flexible containers for experience. This containment doesn't restrict; it organizes. It offers just enough structure for the infant to begin sensing themselves as something distinct, yet still deeply connected to the field around them.

From this, a bodily self begins to emerge, a self not yet organized by language, symbols, or reflection, but by sensorimotor coherence. It is a self made of surfaces and rhythms: the shape of being held, the cadence of breath, the tone of a voice. This expression of selfhood is not defined by narrative but by the integrity of felt continuity, a somatic rhythm that allows the infant to begin anchoring their existence in form.

At this level of development, there are no internalized objects, no symbolic representations, no structured self-concept. What exists is a pre-symbolic, embodied knowing, a self that is *lived* through touch, tone, and presence. This is the earliest articulation of identity: *not who I am*, but *that I am*—felt, sensed, and organized through the body's engagement with the world.

Containment as Field Function

Containment, at this stage of development, is a foundational phenomenon. It refers not only to being physically held, but to the infant's experience of being held emotionally, energetically, and rhythmically within a stable, attuned relational field. Containment is what allows overwhelming, unprocessed sensory input to be transformed into something tolerable, patterned, and meaningful. It is the relational envelope that makes coherence possible.

96

When we speak of containment, we are speaking of a field function, something co-created by caregiver and infant, moment by moment, through breath, gaze, tone, and touch. And this field performs several vital developmental functions:

First, containment regulates intensity. When the infant becomes overwhelmed by unfiltered sensation, whether from internal states or external stimuli, it is the caregiver's presence that helps hold that intensity. The infant cannot yet modulate their own arousal, and so the caregiver's regulated nervous system serves as a scaffolding for co-regulation.

Second, through repetition and predictability, containment supports the gradual organization and integration of experience. It helps the infant link one moment to the next, allowing a basic continuity of self and body to emerge. In this way, containment weaves the earliest threads of a coherent embodied self.

Third, containment supports differentiation. When the infant feels safely held, physically and emotionally, they can begin to notice where they end and others begin. Sensory boundaries become less threatening and more meaningful. This soft emergence of edges becomes the foundation for future distinctions of self and other, inside and outside, *without fear of collapse or fragmentation.*

Finally, and perhaps most importantly, containment allows for the formation of an inner container—a kind of *psychic skin*. Over time, the repeated experience of being held is internalized, giving rise to a capacity for self-holding. This becomes the basis for later emotional regulation, reflection, and the ability to stay present with internal experience without becoming overwhelmed.

Without sufficient containment, the infant may remain suspended in the pre-form field, flooded by sensation, unable to organize experience, and lacking the scaffolding needed to consolidate a stable sense of self. Boundaries may remain diffuse or fragmented, making it difficult to navigate the inner and outer worlds.

In this way, containment is far more than comfort, it is the *cradle of transformation*. It is what allows the infinite potential of the unitary field to begin self-organizing into form, identity, and relationship. It is the ground from which the earliest coherence of self is born.

When Containment Falters

Even with containment in place, there is often a profound fragility to the early sense of coherence. In these first stages of differentiation, the infant's emerging self can feel delicate—thin-skinned, porous, and vulnerable to rupture. When containment falters or is inconsistent, the infant may experience a sense of leakage, fragmentation, or even dissolution, as if the boundary between self and world is no longer holding. This is not yet a loss of self in the symbolic sense, but a collapse of felt continuity.

Drawing on the work of Frances Tustin and expanded by Thomas Ogden, we can understand certain early behaviors (such as rocking, flapping, or repetitive self-touch) as the formation of what are called autistic shapes. These are self-generated sensory experiences, used by the infant not to defend against psychological threat, but to maintain cohesion at a somatic level. In a world that feels too diffuse or too overwhelming, these repetitive sensations offer a point of anchor, a rudimentary rhythm that provides just enough containment to hold the self together.

These actions are not neurotic defenses or symbolic communications. They are pre-symbolic strategies of survival, primitive forms of psychic cohesion where the body takes on the role of organizer. In the absence of reliable containment from the caregiving field, the infant attempts to generate continuity from within, relying on sensation itself to preserve a sense of self.

Primitive Rhythms and Survival

This reveals just how tenuous the early experience of *being-with* can be. The infant is still in a phase of shared existence, not yet separate, but also not fully merged, and this in-between state is highly susceptible to disruption. In these earliest moments, the self is not formed through thought, but through tone, pressure, movement, and proximity. Safety is not yet a concept, it is a rhythm. Coherence is not yet a story, it is a sensory pattern.

When the field wavers, when the caregiver is misattuned, absent, or dysregulated, the infant's system registers the disruption not as a minor inconvenience, but as a threat to cohesion itself. Without a stable other to help regulate overwhelming sensations, the infant turns inward. Self-generated strategies emerge, not in words or images, but in touch, rhythm, and repetition. A rocking body, a clenched fist, a held breath—these are not random behaviors. They are the body's first efforts at organizing experience, anchoring itself through movement when the relational field cannot.

These primitive rhythms (sucking, swaying, arching, freezing) become the earliest scaffolds of self-regulation. In some infants, the absence of sufficient external soothing may lead to the development of subtle muscular contractions or breath-holding patterns. Others may find solace in repetitive motion, thumb-sucking, or the rhythmic tapping of a hand or foot. Even the fixation on certain textures or the insistence on specific routines can be understood as sensorial strategies for creating continuity in a world that feels too unpredictable.

Understanding these early self-generated patterns as *meaningful attempts at self-stabilization*, rather than pathology, allows us to bring compassion to even the most fragmented or confusing presentations later in life. The adult who flinches at touch, the child who rocks for hours, the teen who dissociates under stress all carry echoes of these early strategies. They are not signs of brokenness, but imprints of adaptation. They are, at their core, the body's memory of how to hold itself when no one else could.

In this light, the sensorial field is not merely a backdrop to development; it is the first canvas on which the story of survival is painted. To meet these patterns with presence is to begin the process of unwinding them, not through correction, but through resonance. Through attunement, safety, and embodied contact, the early rhythms of survival can become the new rhythms of coherence.

The Foundations of Presence

These early sensorial experiences serve as energetic templates for the development of both self-regulation and relational perception. Through consistent, responsive caregiving and the experience of being held (physically,

100

emotionally, and energetically) the infant begins to form a basic, embodied sense of "being". This foundational sense of presence is not based on reflection or recognition, but on the feeling of being coherently organized *within* and *with* another. It is this early sense of embodied being that later supports the emergence of more complex levels of development—those involving objects, language, symbolic thought, and narrative identity.

When this process is disrupted through trauma, neglect, or misattunement, the infant may struggle to develop adequate containment or coherence. Without a consistent field of resonance, the capacity to form stable boundaries, regulate internal states, and symbolically process experience may be compromised. These are not abstract psychological functions; they are *bodily capacities*, forged through relational experience. The capacity to symbolize, to link sensation with meaning, is rooted in the earliest ability to feel safely held.

Lifelong Echoes of the Sensorial

Importantly, these early sensorial layers remain active throughout life. They are not outgrown, but woven into the very structure of the self, quietly shaping perception, behavior, and the capacity for regulation. When the adult system encounters overwhelming stress, relational rupture, or existential threat, it may reach, not for logic or language, but for the earliest strategies of survival.

In these moments, the body remembers. An adult may suddenly find themselves dissociating during conflict, pulling inward to mute the overload. Others may rock gently, wrap arms around their torso, or begin humming, seeking rhythmic input to restore a sense of internal continuity. A person may stare out a window for minutes on end, or instinctively place a hand over their chest when faced with loss. These are not signs of dysfunction or immaturity. They are echoes of the original language of the self, where sensation, not story, was the means of coherence.

Such responses are not pathological regressions, but adaptive returns. The nervous system, in the absence of sufficient support or safety, instinctively reaches for what it once knew: self-generated movement, sensory withdrawal, or rhythmic input. These embodied gestures represent the body's effort to reestablish contact with itself—to find refuge in the familiarity of touch, tempo, and breath when the relational field is no longer reliable.

Even in moments of everyday overwhelm, these sensorial imprints may surface: the foot tapping during uncertainty, the hand fidgeting under pressure, the deep sigh released without thought. They are reminders that beneath our symbolic narratives and patterned roles, the sensorial layer remains alive—always scanning, always responding, always seeking coherence through rhythm.

Recognizing these gestures as meaningful, rather than dismissing them as maladaptive, opens the door to compassionate presence. It allows us, both as individuals and as clinicians, to work not just with thoughts or behaviors, but with the foundational rhythms of being. In the process of coherogenesis, these sensorial echoes are not erased, but integrated. They are brought into conscious relationship, not as relics of the past, but as portals through which the earliest layers of self can rejoin the whole.

Soma as the First Language

In this way, the sensorial self reflects a profound truth: that the body is the first symbolic system. But this symbolism is not linguistic or representational—it is *lived*. Before there are words, there is weight. Before there is narrative, there is nerve. Experience is encoded in movement, muscle tone, posture, breath, and rhythm. These are the pre-verbal languages of the self—the warmth of milk, the pulse of a heartbeat, the felt security of being held, the quiet tightening of the belly in the face of misattunement.

These sensations are not just experiences; they *are* meaning, made flesh. In the early phases of life, sensation is not a precursor to thought, it is thought, in its most elemental form. A curled fist, a turned head, a startled breath, these are expressions of the self, of need, of orientation to the world. The body does not wait for language to interpret life. It *responds*, and in doing so, it organizes experience into form.

The sensorial self is, in this way, a kind of *semiosis of the soma*—a bodily sign system through which experience is registered, interpreted, and expressed. It is a deeply intelligent, embodied system of coherence: an organizing matrix of patterned feeling, born from repeated interaction with the world. These patterns become the earliest framework for selfhood, woven through sensation rather than separated from it.

Before we speak, we move. Before we define, we sense. Before the world is known through language, it is felt through the skin. Even later in life, beneath the layers of thought and narrative, these primary sensorial meanings remain. A tight jaw may still carry the imprint of early protest.

103

A collapsed posture may still echo the experience of being unmet. These bodily patterns are not just reactions; they are stored symbols, somatic shorthand for the history of contact, rupture, and repair.

To honor the soma as the first language is to listen not only to what the body *does*, but to what it *says*, through weight, breath, stillness, and gesture. In the process of coherogenesis, re-contacting this original language offers a path to integration that does not bypass the body, but begins with it. It is here, in the quiet grammar of sensation, that the earliest truths of the self still speak.

The Soap Bubble Psyche

Metaphorically, the psyche at this sensorial stage is like a soap bubble—delicate, translucent, and barely holding together. The infant is not yet a fully formed "someone," but a being immersed in a field of sensations, trying to maintain coherence moment to moment. Each new sensory impression can ripple through the surface of the self; any disruption, too much stimulation, too little attunement, can feel like a rupture. Not a loss of identity in the narrative sense, but a collapse of *continuity*, as if the very envelope of being has burst.

This soap bubble represents the "skin" of the psyche, a primitive membrane forming through repeated sensory impressions and relational rhythms. It is thin, porous, and alive, holding the infant's emergent experience of self within a shimmering field of contact. The bubble is not separate from the environment but formed by it, its very existence shaped by pressure, balance, and surface tension. In the same way, the infant's early sense of self is shaped through resonant containment, held together not by internal structure, but by the relational field that surrounds and sustains it.

If we return to the earlier ocean metaphor, we might say that the soap bubble is like a small wave beginning to crest on the surface of the sea, not yet separated, but beginning to take shape. The ocean has not gone anywhere. It is still there, surrounding and sustaining the wave. But now, the wave begins to rise, distinct, yet inseparable. The soap bubble, like the wave, is a contour of the field, a first expression of form, fragile and temporary, but deeply meaningful.

At this stage, the self is felt before it is reflected. It is not yet symbolized or recognized, but sensed at the surface of the skin, in the rhythm of the breath, in the tone of a voice. The soap bubble metaphor invites us to feel the precarious beauty of early selfhood, the immense vulnerability and intelligence of a being trying to cohere within the flow of becoming. It reminds us that before we are names, stories, or roles, we are sensory rhythms held in relationship, and that even the most fragile forms are worthy of reverence.

Compassion as an Expression of Containment

Compassion, being with rather than doing to, plays a foundational role at this sensorial level of development. It mirrors and enhances the containment described earlier, serving as an *energetic quality* within the relational field that transforms sensation into coherence. At this stage, compassion is not an idea, not a moral stance or intention. It is a felt tone, an embodied presence, communicated through touch, breath, rhythm, and gaze.

The infant feels into the world not through thought, but through impression, through the texture of skin, the cadence of a voice, the warmth of proximity. These early experiences are preverbal and unitive, yet profoundly meaningful. In this context, compassion is the tone of being met, the subtle but powerful quality that tells the infant: *you are not alone in this experience.*

When distress arises, hunger, discomfort, and overstimulation are met with compassionate attunement rather than withdrawal, intrusion, or indifference; something profound happens. The overwhelming sensation begins to integrate. It becomes tolerable, then meaningful. It becomes part of a continuity rather than a rupture. In these moments, the caregiver offers not just regulation, but recognition. Not of the infant's thoughts or words, but of their raw, felt reality.

Over time, this consistent, compassionate response begins to lay down an internal tone: a subtle, bodily knowing that says, *my feelings are welcome here.* This is not yet the formation of narrative self-esteem or emotional literacy, but the pre-symbolic foundation of trust, a trust that sensation does not have to lead to fragmentation, that intensity can be held, and that the self can remain intact.

In this way, sensorial compassion becomes the first bridge between raw sensation and meaning. It is the soft, holding space in which the infinite becomes form. Without it, the infant risks encoding distress as danger. With it, the field begins to shape itself into a coherent container for experience. Compassion becomes the earliest architecture of integration, the invisible thread that binds sensation to self.

Containment, at its core, is the capacity to hold disorganizing or intense experience within a field that does not collapse under its weight. It is the spaciousness that allows distress to exist without it becoming the whole of experience. In this holding, compassion emerges as the binding and buffering agent; the quality that makes containment not just structural, but *relational*. It gives containment its tone, its warmth, its coherence.

When painful, overwhelming, or conflicting parts of the self arise, whether in infancy or adulthood, it is compassion that makes it possible to stay with what is difficult without disintegrating. It is the silent message that says: *This can be here, and I won't abandon you.* That message doesn't need to be verbalized. In early life, it is carried through presence, breath, rhythm, and attunement. Later, it may be carried through inner dialogue or therapeutic resonance. But in all forms, it is compassion that makes staying possible.

Compassion prevents containment from becoming suppression. Without compassion, the container may become rigid, an internal wall that holds things out rather than holding them through. But with compassion, containment becomes a receptive presence, one that can stretch, yield, absorb, and metabolize what is arising. It becomes a space not of avoidance, but of *inclusion*, a place where contradiction, ambivalence, grief, and fear can be held without collapse.

This internal spaciousness is not something that simply appears later in adulthood. It is seeded in the earliest relational field. When the infant is met consistently with compassion during moments of overwhelm, the body learns: *There is room for this.* And this knowing becomes the foundation for emotional resilience, self-trust, and the future capacity to remain whole in the presence of inner conflict.

In this way, compassion is not just a quality, it is a developmental necessity. It is what allows containment to breathe, to soften, and to integrate. It is what gives the field its elasticity, its forgiveness, and its wisdom.

As development progresses and the psyche becomes more complex, compassion remains the only inner quality capable of bridging the divides that emerge within the constructed self. Where once the infant relied on the caregiver's resonance to organize sensation, the adult must learn to offer that same presence inwardly, to the many *selves* that now inhabit the internal landscape.

These subpersonalities (the inner critic, the wounded child, the protector, the pleaser) each carry fragments of earlier experience. And while they may appear in conflict, each one has a reason for being. Each represents a pattern of adaptation, a part that emerged in response to sensation that needed containment, emotion that needed translation, or vulnerability that needed shielding. Compassion is the only force tender enough to say: *You all belong here.*

When compassion enters the field of the self, it softens polarization. The sharp lines between parts begin to blur not because they disappear, but because they are no longer at war. The internal critic doesn't have to be silenced; it can be understood. The wounded child doesn't have to be exiled; it can be held. Compassion creates the relational warmth necessary for inner systems to trust each other again, to risk coming into coherence.

In this way, compassion functions not just as a feeling, but as an internal field, an atmosphere of presence within which contradiction can be held, rather than resolved. Coherence doesn't mean uniformity or agreement; it means being able to stay whole in the presence of difference. Compassion makes this possible not by eliminating tension, but by making space for it.

Without compassion, we split. We suppress. We dissociate. We repeat. With compassion, we begin to integrate, to feel fully, and to transform. And all of this begins with that earliest tone of welcome, the preverbal sense that *what I feel is allowed to exist*.

Physiologic Correlations

From a physiological standpoint, the early sensorial field is not merely shaping perception, it is actively sculpting the organization of the body itself. Containment, regulation, and differentiation, those foundational psychospiritual processes, do not exist apart from the body. They are enacted *through* it. In this earliest phase, sensory impressions and relational rhythms begin to lay the blueprint for how body systems will function, adapt, and relate to the environment across the lifespan.

The nervous system, still plastic and forming, begins to calibrate to relational rhythms. Through cycles of co-regulation, being soothed, stimulated, settled, the infant's autonomic system starts to differentiate between states of arousal and rest. Sympathetic activation (mobilization) and parasympathetic settling (soothing, digestion, restoration) become increasingly responsive to cues of safety or danger embedded in the caregiving environment.

Meanwhile, the adrenal and immune systems are learning to read the field. In a consistent, attuned environment, the body begins to associate contact, rhythm, and voice with safety, enabling adaptive stress responses and immune calibration. In contrast, chronic misattunement can begin to encode dysregulated stress physiology, priming the system for hypervigilance, inflammation, or collapse. These aren't merely psychological states, they are biological adaptations to patterns of early relational experience.

The gut-brain axis, an intricate communication loop between the enteric nervous system, the vagus nerve, the microbiome, and central nervous system, also begins to organize around these early impressions. Feeding is not simply a transfer of nutrients; it is a ritual of regulation. Touch, eye contact, scent, and tone (all embedded in the feeding relationship) shape the infant's metabolic patterning, digestive tone, and sense of nourishment far beyond the biochemical.

Taken together, these systems begin to encode what we might call embodied memory, not just of events, but of how the world feels. These impressions are stored not as conscious recollections, but as implicit physiological patterns, reactions, responses, and thresholds. How the body metabolizes food, mounts an immune response, or handles stress is, in part, a somatic echo of early relational fields.

In this way, the body is not simply a container for experience, it is an expression of the field itself. Its systems are not separate from the psyche or spirit, but emerge in dynamic interrelationship with them. The rhythms of breath, the tone of digestion, the pattern of immune response. These are all biological reflections of early containment, co-regulation, and resonance. The body remembers. And it remembers in rhythm.

Nurturing the Sensorial

To nurture the sensorial is to return to the body not as object, but as living presence. The sensorial layer is not merely the registration of sensation; it is the way life flows through tissue, tone, movement, and pulse. This layer is easily bypassed, especially in systems organized around symbolic narrative or cognitive insight. Yet to truly inhabit the self, the sensorial must be reclaimed as ground.

Below are ways to support the reawakening and integration of the sensorial, both in therapeutic work and lived practice. Each is an invitation, not to force sensation into clarity, but to allow its natural rhythms to be welcomed with compassion and curiosity.

- **Slow the Pace to Meet the Present Moment**. Rather than seeking meaning, shift attention toward immediacy. Slowing down allows sensation to rise without being overtaken by interpretation. Grounding practices that bring awareness to breath, posture, or weight can begin this return. *Examples*: body scan meditations, the "5-4-3-2-1" sensory grounding technique, or focused attention on bodily temperature and breath rhythms.

- **Restore Containment Through Touch and Pressure**. Touch is often the first language of safety. For many, the absence of attuned touch in early development leaves a gap that later must be repaired through safe and consensual contact, either with self, environment, or other. *Examples*: weighted blankets, therapeutic self-holding postures, deep pressure tools, or somatic movement sequences that restore muscular containment and proprioception.

- **Engage Rhythm and the Vagus Nerve**. The body responds to rhythm. Repetitive, nonverbal acts regulate sensory flow and modulate autonomic tone. This creates safety not only in the nervous system, but in the psyche. *Examples*: rhythmic walking, humming, chanting, bilateral tapping, slow exhalations, or breathwork focused on vagal engagement.

- **Awaken Through Texture, Temperature, and Movement**. Sensorial coherence emerges from contrast, novelty, and felt contact. Engaging multiple sensory channels can anchor fragmented experience and reintroduce the body as a site of knowing. *Examples*: cold-warm water alternation, walking barefoot, holding textured natural objects, or mindful engagement with food textures, scents, and flavors.

- **Support the Body's Physiological Landscape**. The sensorial self is deeply embedded in physiology. Inflammation, nutrient depletion, gut dysregulation, and mitochondrial dysfunction can distort or overwhelm sensory processing. When these conditions are addressed, the sensorial field often becomes more stable and accessible. *Examples*: assessing histamine intolerance, supporting vagal tone, stabilizing blood sugar, or integrating mitochondrial support through nutrition and supplementation.

- **Invite Embodied Expression Without Words**.
Movement, art, sound, and gesture speak where words
cannot. Offering space for spontaneous embodied
expression allows the sensorial to organize in ways that
transcend symbolic processing. *Examples*: intuitive
movement, expressive dance, clay sculpting, sound
toning, or drawing from the body's felt experience.

- **Co-regulate with Environment**. Environments are not
passive, they are co-regulators. The presence of natural
light, calming sounds, soft textures, and nature itself
can reorganize a fragmented sensorial field. *Examples*:
spending time in natural environments, adjusting
therapy space aesthetics, using plant life, water
elements, or natural materials to support grounding.

- **Honor Sensations as Carriers of Meaning**. The
sensorial is not pre-verbal because it lacks meaning, it
is pre-verbal because its language is different. Rather
than asking individuals to describe, invite them to
listen. Sensations can be approached as sacred
messengers. *Prompt*: "If this sensation had a voice,
what might it say?" or "What does this part of you
need, right now, in this moment?"

- **Bridge the Symbolic and Sensorial**. After insight
arises, guide awareness downward and inward.
Symbolic clarity is not enough, it must be metabolized
through the body. *Examples*: After naming a
subpersonality, ask where it lives in the body. Pause
with sensation. Invite stillness. Let integration arise
from contact, not concept.

- **Embody Presence**. As clinicians or companions, our own embodiment matters. Slowness, softness, and somatic attunement are not techniques, they are states that transmit safety. Presence is not something we do. It is something we become. *Practice*: Before beginning work, attune to your breath. Feel your feet. Soften your tone. Let your body signal that it can remain with another, even in their most dysregulated state.

When the sensorial is honored, the body becomes more than a site of symptoms, it becomes a home. Reclaiming this layer offers the possibility of integration not through force, but through felt connection. The sensorial speaks not in ideas, but in pulses, textures, rhythms, and warmth. When we learn its language, we touch life directly.

Conclusion

The sensorial self marks the first emergence of form from the unitive field. The earliest contours of identity drawn not with language, but with sensation. Here, selfhood is not thought, but felt—etched into skin, rhythm, and resonance. Through containment, compassion, and repetition within a relational field, the body begins to organize experience into coherence. Boundaries soften into shape, and a proto-self begins to rise not in isolation, but in mutual process. These early patterns become the foundation for how we regulate, relate, and remember not just psychologically, but physiologically. In this way, the sensorial phase is not simply a developmental stage, it is the somatic architecture of becoming. A reminder that before the self speaks, it listens; before it knows, it feels; and before it constructs meaning, it rests in the rhythm of being held.

Key Takeaways: The Sensorial

- The sensorial self emerges from the unitary field through self-organization, shaped by rhythmic synchrony and resonance in the early relational environment.

- Repeated sensory experiences (e.g., touch, tone, movement) lay the foundation for early patterning, forming sensorimotor schemas, affective templates, and implicit relational memory.

- Edges and boundaries begin to form not cognitively but somatically, through contrasts in sensation, offering the first felt sense of "me" and "not-me."

- Containment is essential to early coherence; it helps regulate sensory overwhelm, support differentiation, and establish a stable inner container for experience.

- The psyche at this stage is fragile and surface-based, like a soap bubble, organized at the level of skin and rhythm, vulnerable to rupture without consistent holding.

- Self-generated sensations (e.g., rocking, flapping) may arise as primitive methods of cohesion in the absence of external containment, strategies of survival rather than pathology.

- Compassion serves as the energetic tone of containment, enabling experience to be held, felt, and integrated. It transforms overwhelm into coherence.

- Without compassion, containment may harden into suppression. With compassion, it becomes receptive presence capable of holding contradiction, intensity, and vulnerability.

- Subpersonalities and inner parts later emerge from these early affect-somatic patterns. Compassion is the only quality capable of bridging their divides and fostering internal coherence.

- Physiological systems (nervous, immune, adrenal, gut-brain axis) begin organizing in response to sensory and relational input, embodying implicit memory in metabolic, immune, and stress patterns.

- Practical applications span from responsive infant caregiving (through rhythm, attunement, and repair) to adult healing practices that restore sensation, boundary, and somatic presence.

- The sensorial self reminds us that before the self is known, it is felt. Before story, identity, or symbol, there is sensation. The body is the first language of the soul.

As the sensorial field stabilizes, its rhythms shaped through touch, tone, and presence, something within begins to stretch beyond the immediacy of contact. The body, once the sole container of experience, now reaches inward to hold what is no longer present. A softness once felt is remembered. A gaze once given is imagined.

Slowly, the infant begins to form internal traces of the field, impressions that persist even when sensation fades. These traces are not yet thoughts, but the beginnings of symbols, bridges between what was and what is, between presence and absence. The psyche does not leave the body; it begins to speak through it differently. This is the moment when the wave of self, once fluid and surface-bound, begins to crest with image and memory. And in that first glimmer of "other," the symbolic self begins to take shape not in rupture, but as a new layer of coherence unfolding from the sea of being.

CHAPTER SEVEN

The Symbolic: The Architecture of Meaning

"The limits of my language mean the limits of my world."

— Ludwig Wittgenstein

From the rhythmic surface of sensation, something new begins to stir. The infant, once fully immersed in the ebb and flow of felt experience (rocked by waves of contact, tone, and movement) now begins to sense that some of these waves have a source. Patterns once experienced as texture alone begin to take on intentionality. Warmth arrives when fed. Pressure arrives when held. The sea is no longer only a sensation; it begins to ripple with meaning. This is the beginning of symbolic life.

Differentiation Within the Field

Just as a wave starts to differentiate from the body of the ocean, still continuous with it, but shaped by wind and depth, the infant begins to perceive difference: between self

118

and other, sensation and source, presence and absence. The field remains whole, but within it, textures begin to signify, and experiences begin to carry trace. What was once purely relational rhythm becomes representational trace. A softness is not just soft, it begins to stand for something.

This marks the slow emergence of the symbolic, not as a leap away from the sensorial, but as its unfolding. A new layer of coherence begins to form, where inner experience can be represented rather than merely enacted. The world begins to take shape in image, in memory, in early gesture. And with this, the possibility of meaning, continuity, and eventually, language, begins to rise, like a new tide from the ocean of being.

As sensory contours become more stable and coherent, the infant begins to link these patterns to sources, to something, or more precisely, *someone* beyond themselves. This is the earliest glimmer of separation: the recognition that certain textures, tones, or sensations arise *from elsewhere*. A softness coincides with feeding. A pressure comes with being held. What was previously a seamless sea of sensation now begins to reveal currents of origin, waves that seem to move toward the self from another direction.

This is the emergence of the object, first as a sensory-affective trace, then gradually as something with a sense of otherness. It is not a cognitive understanding, but a felt differentiation within the field: *this is not me*. The field itself has not broken, it has begun to differentiate from within. What was once pure state becomes signal; what was once texture becomes intention. Sensation begins to imply relationship.

Absence as Catalyst: The Seed of Symbol

In this subtle but profound shift, objects become more than touch, they become "other". They are felt as patterned presences that return, respond, or sometimes fail to arrive. This differentiation is not static; it is dynamic, shaped by the rhythm of appearance and disappearance. Experiences now come and go. And it is this impermanence, the reality that comfort, contact, and presence are not always there, that deepens the infant's awareness of separation.

This impermanence is not just loss; it is the opening into memory, image, and representation. It marks the beginning of inner life, of the psyche learning to carry something within that is no longer outside. The significance of this coming and going, of rhythm interrupted and resumed, will deepen as we move forward. It is the pulse of absence that makes symbol formation possible.

Separation and the Birth of the Inner Image

The experience of separation, the dawning awareness that the caregiver is not the self, is one of the most profound thresholds in early development. It is both a necessary milestone and a potential source of deep distress. In the earliest stages, the infant lives within a field of continuity where needs are met through rhythmic synchrony, sensations blend into a seamless flow, and the boundary between self and other remains unformed. The infant does not know the caregiver *as anything other than the pattern of being with them.*

But as perception sharpens and sensory experiences become more consistent and patterned, the infant begins to register absence, a delay in feeding, a break in gaze, a touch

120

that does not come. These micro-disruptions begin to reveal the limits of bodily expression as a means of control, and the presence of an "other" whose actions are not fully predictable. A realization begins to unfold: comfort comes from outside, and that outside does not always respond.

This awareness can evoke longing, frustration, even fear. But it also marks the beginning of something vital: the birth of mental representation, and the emergence of selfhood. The infant begins to form an image, however rudimentary, that the caregiver still exists, even when not physically present. This image becomes a bridge across absence. The infant no longer lives entirely in the now of sensation, but begins to carry traces of what *was* into what *is*.

The Folding of the Field: From Rupture to Symbol

And with this, symbolic thought begins to stir. A memory, an object, a rhythm, any of these can now *stand in* for what is missing. The soothing tone of a voice, the scent of a blanket, the image of a caregiver's face, these become more than sensations; they become symbols. They carry the presence of what is absent. This is the quiet beginning of representation.

The gap between presence and absence becomes the space in which imagination, memory, and language take root. In this opening, the psyche learns to bridge distance, not by eliminating it, but by folding it inward. The symbol is born not from resolution, but from tension: the ache of separation transfigured into meaning.

In this way, separation is not a break in the field, but a fold within it, a turning inward, a layering of coherence. It marks the beginning of inner life as distinct from immediate experience. The field of being does not fragment, but curves, bending back on itself to reflect, remember, and reach. This folding gives rise to symbolic function, the capacity to hold what is not here and to relate across time, space, and absence.

It is both a rupture and a bridge, the necessary tension through which the unitive fluidity of early life becomes structured, meaningful relationship. What was once pure presence now holds trace. Meaning is born in the wake of loss, and with it, the beginning of narrative, of language, of the symbolic self.

Conditions for Symbolic Emergence

This experience, and how it is lived, is shaped entirely by the quality of the previous stages: the strength of the sensorial foundation, the consistency of containment, and the tone of compassion carried through the field.

Once the sensorial ground is secure, and there is a "skin," both psychic and somatic, to hold experience, the psyche begins to unfold in a new direction: it begins to form symbols. These symbols arise not as abstract constructs, but as living bridges between raw affect and meaning, between the inner pulse of sensation and the outer world of relationship. Symbols are not departures from the body, they are its *echoes*, translated into image, gesture, sound, and story.

The Shifts of Symbolic Formation

This symbolic emergence unfolds through several key shifts in the psyche:

From **presence to image**: The caregiver's consistent, attuned presence leaves an imprint. First as felt experience, then as an internalized trace. The warmth of holding becomes a proto-symbol of "mother," not in name, but in *tone*.

From **action to meaning**: The infant cries and is met with nourishment; they reach and are met with gaze. Over time, these bodily gestures are no longer just expressions, they are encoded with significance. A cry "means" hunger. A look "means" recognition.

From **resonance to metaphor**: Once experience is differentiated and held, the psyche begins to associate. A soft blanket no longer only warms, it *represents* the comfort of the caregiver. The object becomes infused with emotional tone, standing in for the relational field itself.

From **affect to language**: Only now can emotional states begin to be named, shared, and symbolized. Words do not arise from thin air, they emerge only when there is an internal container stable enough to represent experience without becoming overwhelmed by it. What was once enacted through the body can now be spoken, held in language, and reflected upon.

The Function of Symbols: Anchoring Continuity

Through all of this, symbols serve as *bridges*. They tether the immediacy of embodied life to shared meaning, making it possible to remember, imagine, and communicate the inner world. Without a stable base, symbol-making is fragile or distorted, like trying to draw on water. But with a coherent sensorial foundation and the scaffolding of containment, the mind gains a surface on which to paint.

In this way, the sensorial ground becomes the canvas, containment becomes the frame, and symbols are the marks, the brushstrokes, through which the field of experience becomes visible, shareable, and transformable.

The primary function of symbol formation is to maintain a sense of continuity in the face of growing separation. In early development, the infant inhabits a world of immediate sensory and affective flow, where regulation comes through rhythm, resonance, and embodied contact. When the caregiver is physically present, the infant is held, not just in arms, but in coherent relational patterning. But as the caregiver begins to leave or becomes emotionally unavailable, the field of resonance is disrupted. The infant must now find a way to stay coherent even when the source of safety is no longer there. It is in this space, between presence and absence, that symbols begin to emerge.

Symbols function as carriers of presence: a blanket, a smell, a rhythm, a mental image, each holds the emotional tone of the caregiver and offers the infant a way to remain connected in their absence. These symbols act as internal anchors, allowing the infant to regulate affect not just through external contact, but through inner continuity.

They also become containers of feeling. Rather than being flooded by raw sensation, the infant can now hold affect within symbolic form, whether through a transitional object, repetitive gesture, or proto-play. These forms do not eliminate intensity, but they render it *representable*, and therefore tolerable.

Symbols are also bridges across time and space. They extend the field of connection beyond the here and now, allowing the infant to carry the caregiver's presence across gaps in contact. What was once only experienced in the immediacy of the body can now be *recalled, anticipated*, even *imagined*.

And as coherence stabilizes, symbols evolve from tools of regulation into vehicles of meaning. They become the medium through which thought, language, and imagination take root. The symbolic self begins to form not as a replacement for embodied experience, but as its extension into the interior world. In essence, symbol formation is the infant's way of saying: "What I once had, I can now hold inside."

It is the transformation of absence into memory, of longing into representation, of rupture into relational possibility. But all of this rests on a foundation shaped by early sensorial patterning. When that ground is unstable, through trauma, neglect, or misattunement, symbolic life becomes strained. The structure of meaning weakens. The ache of absence becomes a wound to core being.

Proto-Language: The Body Speaks First

Like trying to build a lighthouse on shifting sand, the psyche struggles to form a steady light in the storm. Before words ever arrive, the body speaks.

The rhythmic exchanges of tone, gaze, movement, and touch between infant and caregiver become a kind of embodied proto-language, a sensory grammar that conveys presence, emotion, and intention. These patterned interactions lay the foundation for meaning-making, forming the earliest structure upon which symbolic and verbal capacities are built. Within this field, the infant learns not just to respond, but to anticipate, to associate, and eventually, to represent.

Language as Flowering: From Root to Narrative

Language emerges when the child begins to assign shared, conventional symbols (words) to internal states and external objects. This moment is profound. A word like *hungry*, *mommy*, or *mine* does more than name, it gives structure to experience. It allows the child to locate themselves in time (*I was sad, tomorrow I go*), in space (*Where's mommy?*), and in relation (*That's mine*).

But language is not the beginning of meaning, it is the flowering of a root system already deep within the body. It builds upon symbolic function, expanding the child's ability to organize, express, and reflect on inner and outer life. Through words, the child begins to narrate selfhood, articulate desire, manage contradiction, and thread coherence across developmental layers.

The Dual Nature of Language: Resonance and Rupture

Language becomes a bridge, linking the internal relational world to the shared world of culture and communication. But it is a bridge made of tone as much as of meaning. In a supportive relational field, words carry resonance. They reflect back the truth of experience. They help integrate subpersonalities, mend fragmentation, and invite healing. In an unsupportive or dissonant field, however, language can split experience, becoming a mask, a shell, or a veil. Words may name, but not *touch*. They may explain, but not *feel*.

In this way, language is both essential and limited. It maps experience, but it cannot contain the sea. It speaks of the wave, but not the ocean. It points to being, but cannot become it. And yet, all words arise from being. They emerge from the same field that gave rise to sensation, to form, to self. Language is not a departure from the unitary field, it is one of its many expressions. And when spoken with resonance, language becomes an act of re-entry. A way of remembering.

Maintaining Symbolic Flexibility and Coherence Through Flow

Flow is essential to the healthy emergence and ongoing vitality of the symbolic self. As the child begins to organize experience through language, images, relational templates, and internalized meaning, these symbolic structures offer a new level of coherence. They provide continuity across time and space, helping the child make sense of inner states and external events. But what brings stability can also bring rigidity, especially under stress or in the absence of relational safety.

Without flow, the symbolic self may become frozen in form. Words harden into identity. Roles become defenses. Meaning, once alive, becomes a cage. The symbolic scaffolding, meant to support development, can turn into a mask or a fortress, limiting the self's capacity to adapt, feel, and transform.

Flow is what keeps symbolic life responsive and alive. It allows meaning to evolve rather than calcify. It makes space for roles and identities to shift as context changes. It allows affect to move *through*, rather than become stuck *within*. In polyvagal theory, this flexibility mirrors what is known as the neuroception of safety, the body's ability to detect that it is safe enough to remain open, attuned, and receptive to new experience.

This kind of flow also resonates with the Taoist concept of wu wei—effortless action, or *non-forcing*. Wu wei is not passivity; it is attuned responsiveness. In therapeutic or developmental work, it means following the symbolic thread where it leads, rather than imposing meaning too soon. It is an act of trust in the unfolding process, letting the psyche reveal itself according to its own rhythms.

Just as a river flows by following the path of least resistance, flow honors the natural direction of psychic energy. It moves around obstacles, reshapes its bed, softens sharp edges over time. In moments of trauma or developmental arrest, the symbolic self may crystallize around rigid meanings—*"I am unlovable," "The world is dangerous," "This pain is mine forever."* These are not just thoughts. They are frozen symbols of survival.

Flow is what allows us to re-enter these symbols, to feel them, yes, but also to reimagine and re-author them. Through compassionate presence and fluid attention, new meanings arise, ones that are less rooted in defense and more rooted in truth. Truth not as absolute, but as coherent, *felt*, and *relationally alive*.

Flow is what keeps the symbolic self tethered to the ocean it emerged from. It is what keeps symbols from becoming prisons. It is what allows the self to keep becoming.

Physiological Aspects of the Symbolic

From a physiological standpoint, the emergence of symbol formation does not occur in isolation from the body, it is embodied, embedded within and expressed through the developing systems of the child. As the psyche begins to represent experience symbolically, the body becomes a canvas of encoded meaning, a living archive of what has been felt, integrated, or suppressed.

Each bodily system becomes increasingly interwoven with symbolic processes. The hypothalamic-pituitary-adrenal (HPA) axis, responsible for managing stress, may become chronically activated in response to internalized experiences of unpredictability, threat, or emotional abandonment. Over time, these stress responses no longer reflect the present environment, they reflect symbolic traces of the past: a mother who didn't come, a rupture that went unrepaired, a presence that never returned.

Likewise, metabolic rhythms may mirror unmet affective needs, fluctuating in response to emotional deprivation, overstimulation, or inconsistency in relational nourishment. Food intake, energy use, and digestion are not just physiological, they are symbolic enactments of safety, longing, and containment. A child who does not feel emotionally fed may carry this hunger in the gut for decades, unspoken but metabolically remembered.

Autoimmune patterns may reflect a more complex symbolic imprint: the body turning on itself in the absence of clear self-other boundaries, or in the presence of unresolved internal conflict. These physiological processes are not merely malfunctions, they are somatic metaphors, expressions of what the symbolic self could not yet say in words. They are the language of unformulated experience, spoken through inflammation, pain, or dysregulation.

In this sense, the body becomes a map of meaning, a terrain shaped not just by biochemistry, but by affective

129

experience, symbolic representation, and relational patterning. Every system, nervous, endocrine, immune, metabolic, participates in the organization of symbolic life. They carry forward the resonant tones of early experience, and they respond to shifts in meaning with surprising precision.

This is not to reduce emotion to biology, nor to romanticize illness, but to honor the intelligence of the field. The symbolic self is not suspended above the body, it is *expressed through it*. The skin remembers the absence. The breath remembers the rupture. The pulse remembers what could not be held.

And just as symbols can become distorted under stress, so too can the body become a symptom of forgotten meaning. But in the presence of safety, attunement, and flow, both the psyche and the physiology begin to reorganize. Meaning shifts. Rhythm softens. And the field remembers how to cohere.

The body is not the obstacle to integration. It is the instrument through which integration occurs. It is the echo chamber of the symbolic field, speaking, always, in the language of aliveness.

Nurturing the Symbolic

The symbolic layer is the bridge between raw experience and meaning. It transforms impulse into image, sensation into narrative, chaos into pattern. To work with the symbolic is to enter the domain of imagination, language, and metaphor, not to escape the real, but to organize it, translate it, and hold it with greater coherence.

When the symbolic becomes rigid, dissociated, or overly abstract, it loses its integrative function. But when nurtured

130

with awareness, it allows for rich self-reflection, emotional expression, and the metabolizing of experience through symbol and story. Below are practices and clinical invitations that support the restoration and deepening of symbolic functioning.

- **Honor Preverbal Symbolic Expression:** Before language, children communicate symbolically through play, movement, rhythm, and repetition. Support these early symbolic forms with presence and curiosity without rushing to interpret or verbalize.

- **Support Transitional Objects and Rituals:** Items like blankets, stuffed animals, and bedtime stories act as symbolic anchors. They help children regulate and make meaning during transitions. Honor these as vital bridges of continuity.

- **Use Resonant, Attuned Language:** Language becomes symbolic when it carries emotional resonance. Speak with warmth, rhythm, and responsiveness, naming what is felt, not just what is seen. This helps language remain rooted in connection.

- **Create Space for Imaginative Play:** Play is the symbolic psyche in motion. Encourage roleplay, storytelling, and fantasy without correcting logic or imposing structure. Let symbolic imagination unfold freely.

- **Invite Metaphor and Image:** Children often describe feelings through metaphor ("It's like a monster inside"). Welcome these images. Explore them gently without forcing interpretation. Metaphor allows complex emotions to be held safely.

- **Protect Narrative Fluidity:** Early self-stories are exploratory. Avoid rigid definitions or fixed labels. Encourage storytelling that shifts and expands as the child grows, allowing identity to remain flexible and alive.

- **Encourage Creative Expression:** Drawing, music, movement, and ritual foster symbolic integration. Support these without emphasizing outcome. The act of creation itself nurtures symbolic development.

By nurturing the symbolic in these ways, we help the developing psyche weave together experience, emotion, and meaning, laying the groundwork for a coherent and expressive self. In all stages of life, symbolic development is not about learning new words, it's about remembering the truth beneath them. By offering a flowing presence, we keep the symbolic self fluid and alive, capable of holding memory without being frozen by it, and able to imagine new forms of becoming.

Conclusion

The symbolic self emerges as a bridge, linking the sensory immediacy of early life with the layered meaning of human experience. Rooted in the rhythms of resonance and the scaffolding of containment, symbols arise first as tools of regulation and gradually become vessels of imagination, thought, and identity. They allow the child to hold what is absent, make meaning from the invisible, and carry continuity across time and space. But symbols are not merely cognitive constructions; they are emergent expressions of the unitary field's desire to know itself. Each image, gesture, or word is a crystallization of that deeper current, an attempt to metabolize complexity while preserving coherence.

132

Through symbol, the Self does not depart from the field, it expresses through it. This is where the image becomes a vehicle of becoming, offering the psyche a way to process, represent, and reorganize the currents of experience. In this sense, symbolic life is both a developmental milestone and a spiritual unfolding, where the wave of self rises just high enough to begin seeing itself reflected in the sea. A symbol is a mirror that reflects not what we are, but what we are becoming. We are born through the skin, and only later do we dream through words. Now I am who I am in relation to you and how I have known you inside me.

Key Takeaways: The Symbolic

- The symbolic self emerges from the sensorial self, representing a shift from immediate bodily experience to internal representation, memory, image, and meaning.

- Symbols arise as bridges, linking the infant to continuity across time, space, and separation. They carry presence when the caregiver is gone and allow affect to be held rather than overwhelmed.

- Symbol formation depends on earlier stages: Without secure containment and sensorial coherence, symbolic development may be distorted, rigid, or fragmented.

- Early symbols take many forms—transitional objects, gestures, emotional tones, repeated actions, and proto-play. These precede and scaffold the development of language.

- Language emerges from symbolic function, not the other way around. It provides structure, enables narrative, and connects the internal world with the shared social field.

- Language can heal or divide: When used with resonance, it integrates experience and selfhood. When disconnected from felt experience, it can fragment or disembody.

- Flow is essential to symbolic vitality: Without it, symbols may become rigid beliefs or defenses. With it, symbolic life remains adaptive, relational, and open to reimagining.

- The symbolic self organizes experience through story, image, and metaphor—allowing for integration of identity, memory, and emotion across developmental layers.

- Physiology and symbolic life are deeply interconnected: Chronic stress patterns, metabolic issues, and autoimmune conditions may reflect symbolic imprints of relational history.

- The body becomes a living archive of symbolic meaning, shaped by early resonance, disrupted rhythms, and unspoken narratives.

- Symbols are not only constructed, they are emergent expressions of the unitary field seeking to know itself through form, image, and language.

- Symbolic life allows the self to carry memory, metabolize complexity, and continue becoming, while staying tethered to the deeper coherence of the field.

As the symbolic self emerges, the field begins to remember itself in form. Sensation becomes image, rhythm becomes meaning, and presence becomes language. Symbols give shape to what was once only felt. They allow us to bridge absence, carry memory, and begin the delicate work of narrating the self.

But symbols do more than represent, they begin to organize. As they repeat and gather emotional tone, they settle into patterns. These patterns become roles, and these roles begin to structure identity. What was once a fluid act of meaning-making now becomes a choreography of familiar selves. In this way, the symbolic gives rise to the patterned self, the visible crest of the wave, shaped by all the unseen currents beneath it. It is here that we step into the theater of personality, not to lose ourselves in the performance, but to learn how to hold it with grace, curiosity, and coherence.

CHAPTER EIGHT

The Patterned: Experience Becomes Structure

"Every form is a frozen movement."

— Goethe

As the symbolic field deepens, carrying memory, representation, and meaning, its textures begin to take shape in more visible and consistent forms. Internal images give rise to relational templates. Words begin to loop into narrative. The body, too, starts to rehearse its roles. In time, these threads of meaning become woven into stable patterns of being. The child no longer merely feels or symbolizes the world, they begin to inhabit it through identity, through internalized roles, expectations, and stories. What began as rhythm and resonance now moves with choreography.

This is the expression of the patterned layer, a fluid constellation of subpersonalities, relational maps, and meaning-laden roles that shape how the individual meets the world each day. Though it may appear stable on the surface, the patterned self is not separate from the depths it rises from. It is the crest of the wave, reflecting all the currents below. And yet, it is here, on this surface, that most of life is lived, interpreted, and remembered.

Internal Worlds: How Symbols Become Relationships

As the child continues to engage the world through symbols, the self begins to differentiate through the repeated crystallization of internal relational patterns. In early development, symbols serve as stand-ins for the caregiver, helping the child manage the ache of separation by holding a felt sense of continuity. Over time, when these symbols are consistently paired with emotionally charged contexts, like a blanket always accompanying the caregiver's departure, they become more than transitional objects. They begin to carry relational tone, affective rhythm, and embodied memory.

These emotionally laden symbols gradually consolidate into mental representations, not only of the caregiver's physical presence, but of how the caregiver feels, responds, and relates. The child begins to develop internal models of relationship that include not just the *what*, but the *how*: how closeness feels, how distance is managed, how emotion is met or left unmet. These internal models evolve into what psychoanalytic theory refers to as object relations: dynamic, living constellations of self-and-other, each carrying emotions, expectations, roles, fantasies, and behavioral tendencies.

The Rise of Subpersonalities: Adaptive Structures of the Self

These relational patterns are not static. They are fluid yet enduring, shaping how the child begins to interpret self,

137

others, and the world. At a certain point, the child no longer requires a physical object to sustain coherence, rather they begin to draw instead on an internalized object world, an invisible choreography of self and other in the mind that plays out on the stage of life through memory (past) and imagination (future).

This marks a key developmental shift: the movement from external symbolic support to internal psychic structure, becoming the foundation from which personality, relational style, emotional tone, and behavior patterns emerge. This is the beginning of what we now name the patterned self, a layered and dynamic identity woven from early layers and the ongoing dance between presence and absence.

Multiplicity Within: The Function and Form of Subpersonalities

As the child internalizes object relations, each self-other configuration carries with it a unique emotional tone, core need, relational defense, and way of being. These internal constellations are not abstract, they are felt realities, each embodying a distinct mode of self-experience shaped by a particular relational context. For example, the self that feels safe, playful, and loved in one environment may sharply contrast with the self that feels invisible, rejected, or overly responsible in another. These seemingly contradictory experiences challenge the developing psyche's ability to sustain a unified narrative of self and influence the constant unfolding of becoming.

Rather than forcing coherence too soon, the psyche often responds with compartmentalization, not as pathology, but as adaptive wisdom. It forms subsystems of self, each associated with particular affects, memories, strategies, and relational histories. These are the beginnings of what we refer to as subpersonalities, not in the sense of disorder, but in the sense of differentiated modes of being that allow the child to survive, adapt, and maintain continuity in complex and inconsistent environments.

Each subpersonality serves a function. A compliant self that keeps the peace. A defiant self that guards boundaries. A playful self that seeks connection. A withdrawn self that holds pain or shame. These are not roles the child chooses, but formations the field generates in response to lived experience.

Rather than one consistent "I," the self becomes a fluid constellation of self-states, each orbiting a particular internalized relational pattern. Some of these states come forward with ease; others remain hidden, exiled, or fragmented. They may function in relative harmony or exist in tension, without conscious dialogue or recognition of one another. And yet, all are part of the same field. Each subpersonality is not a separate self, but a patterned expression of the one field's attempt to maintain coherence in the face of complexity.

Subpersonalities can be understood as inner characters or modes of being, each shaped by distinct relational experiences and contextual demands. These are not arbitrary fragments; they are patterned expressions of the self, formed in response to the field of early relationships and refined through the symbolic structures that came before. Importantly, subpersonalities do not exist in isolation, they emerge within the broader nested architecture of selfhood, layered within the sensorial, symbolic, and unitive dimensions that still pulse beneath the surface.

Each subpersonality carries its own worldview, need, affective tone, and defense strategy. Some protect. Some seek connection. Others hide in shame, or surge forward in defiance. They are not disorders to be fixed but intelligent adaptations, each one a story the field tells to preserve coherence.

Roles and Identity: When the Inner Becomes Outer

These subpersonalities often become visible through roles, the outward expressions we take on in response to social expectations, relational demands, or survival strategies. Roles are how subpersonalities dress for the world: the caregiver, the achiever, the rebel, the clown, the helper. They are recognizable postures that allow the inner multiplicity to find coherence and function in shared environments.

Each role serves a purpose, often rooted in an early relational context. The caregiver may emerge from a need to secure love through attunement to others. The achiever might organize around the pursuit of worth in performance. The rebel may protect against conformity, while the clown lightens the unbearable with humor. These roles are not chosen so much as shaped—molded by environment, trauma, and the developmental imperative to belong.

Over time, roles can become mistaken for identity itself. We begin to answer to the name the world calls us, forgetting the quiet voices within that were never invited to speak. What began as adaptation hardens into persona. The self becomes edited, curated for acceptability. Yet underneath the visible role remains the fuller field of the self—dynamic, multivocal, and waiting to be re-membered.

To work with roles is not to discard them, but to recognize their function, loosen their grip, and make space for what lies beneath. When we relate to roles with awareness, they can become bridges rather than cages—pathways through which the inner world meets the outer with greater coherence and choice.

Identity as Lens: The Illusion of Sameness

Over time, a few of these roles become habitual, reinforced, and familiar, and from them, we begin to construct what we call identity, a seemingly stable sense of self. The word *identity* comes from the Latin *idem*, meaning "the same." In this light, identity can be seen as an effort to make oneself the same across time and context, a pattern of continuity drawn from multiplicity. But this identity is not the full terrain. It is a narrative built from dominant subpersonalities, a selective composition of inner figures that feel safe, successful, or socially acceptable.

We live our lives according to the dance of our earliest rhythms until we learn a new choreography.

Identity appears solid, but it is context-sensitive. It shifts with environment, relationship, and internal state. It is not a foundation, but a lens. And when that lens becomes rigid, when we over-identify with a particular role or narrative, the fluidity of the self constricts. This rigidity can create profound relational consequences. When we relate from a fixed identity, we no longer meet others from the present moment, but from a rehearsed pattern. The caregiver may struggle to receive care. The achiever may feel threatened by rest. The rebel may resist intimacy that asks for vulnerability. Rather than engaging in mutual discovery, we enact rehearsals of who we believe we are, and who we believe the other must be.

In this way, rigid identification becomes a barrier to coherence. It reduces the self to a familiar storyline, and filters relationship through expectation, defense, and projection. The self becomes scripted, and so do our connections. What was once adaptive becomes obstructive. Wholeness is not possible when large portions of the self are excluded in the name of sameness.

To mistake identity for the whole self is to forget the sea from which the wave has risen. But to remember the sea is to return to coherogenesis, the ongoing process by which the parts find rhythm, resonance, and integration within the whole. It is a return to fluidity, where identity becomes a momentary expression rather than a prison. Here, relationship can be a site of emergence, not reenactment. And the self, once bound by the illusion of sameness, becomes again a living system— responsive, relational, and whole.

Curiosity as a Pivotal Point

Curiosity marks a vital turning point in the unfolding of the patterned self. It is the first movement away from fusion and reactivity, and toward awareness, spaciousness, and choice. Within the patterned layer, subpersonalities often operate as self-protective loops, each organized around a specific belief or survival imperative: *"I must control," "I am unworthy," "I can't trust."* These parts respond not to the present, but to past relational conditions, repeating what once ensured safety or belonging.

Without awareness, they become automatic and constrained,
reactive or proactive roles shaped by earlier contexts, still
looping through the system long after the danger has passed.

Curiosity interrupts this repetition. It softens
identification: *"I am this part"* becomes *"Who is this part?"* It
invites observation without judgment: not *"This shouldn't be*
here," but *"What is this here to do?"* Curiosity allows space to
listen, to feel, to notice. It says: *"There's something here worth*
understanding."

When curiosity deepens into self-inquiry, it becomes
more than a moment, it becomes a relational stance. A practice
of inner contact. We begin to respond, not react: *What are you*
protecting? When did you first appear? What do you need?

In this space, subpersonalities begin to speak rather
than act out. They start to trust the field of presence rather than
defend against it. Self-inquiry is not interrogation, it is a form
of compassionate witnessing that allows inner figures to
reorganize around truth rather than fear.

Over time, curiosity and inquiry become instruments of
coherogenesis, gently reconnecting the inner multiplicity into a
fluid, dynamic whole. Roles soften, identity becomes more
transparent, and a compassionate internal Self begins to be
remembered, one that can hold all parts without becoming any
one of them.

In this light, curiosity is not a cognitive tool. It is a form
of freedom, an expression of self that is not fused to a single
part. It is the voice of presence. And with presence comes
responsibility. Not as burden, but as response-ability: the

capacity to respond from the present moment, rather than reenact the past.

Where the Wave Remembers the Ocean

From one perspective, personality appears to solidify over time, shaped by social roles, internalized object relations, and ingrained schemas. Subpersonalities emerge as functional adaptations to relational patterns, environmental demands, and unresolved trauma. In this view, development becomes a process of consolidation: the layering of identities and strategies that allow the individual to navigate the external world with increasing consistency and competence.

But from another perspective, one rooted in field theory and lived experience, the self is never fixed. Even as roles are assumed and identities appear stable, the patterned self remains a flowing multiplicity: a dynamic choreography of inner figures, each carrying a tone, a need, a memory, a truth. Subpersonalities are not rigid compartments but living metaphors, portals into the deeper field. For instance, the metaphorical view of subpersonalities provides access to the symbolic. And identity, far from being a container, is a transparent lens, a way through which the One, the undivided field of being, perceives itself in varied form.

Together, this reveals a paradox: the patterned self is both necessary structure and graceful illusion. It is the scaffolding that allows for relational coherence, and the mask that can obscure deeper presence. But through the qualities of presence, compassion, flow, and curiosity, one can begin to hold both truths at once. The individual becomes both witness and participant, both ocean and wave, dancing between the roles they play and the timeless awareness from which those

144

roles arise. This is not disintegration, it is coherogenesis: the weaving of multiplicity into meaning, without losing the thread of wholeness.

The Physiology of Pattern

From a physiological standpoint, the emergence of subpersonalities is not limited to psychological expression, it carries somatic signatures, each with its own neurobiological profile. One part may evoke heightened vigilance and sympathetic arousal, elevated cortisol, tight musculature, a narrowed perceptual field. Another may induce parasympathetic collapse—fatigue, dissociation, withdrawal. Still another may seek activation and stimulation, mimicking manic drive or hyperfocus. Each subpersonality is not just a way of being, but a biochemical and neurophysiological state, a distinct rhythm in the body's orchestration.

These internal states are not isolated, they begin to shape the long-term patterning of body systems. The autonomic nervous system may lose flexibility, toggling between extremes of activation and shutdown. The immune system may learn to over-defend or under-respond. Metabolic processes may attune to states of deprivation or overstimulation, reflecting inner narratives of scarcity, urgency, or threat. In this way, the psychic field impresses itself into the body, and the body, in turn, sustains the psychic loop.

Without integration, the body may flip between these states with little coherence. Over time, this lack of physiological coordination can manifest as chronic symptoms or functional syndromes that reflect deeper pattern-level incoherence. With time, this crystallizes into patterned disease states. The body, like the self, fragments in the absence of a containing field.

But with increasing inner coherence, something shifts. As subpersonalities are met with curiosity, they begin to reorganize not just psychically, but physiologically. This is often reflected in re-organization of lifestyle routines, how one relates to and engages with work, exercise, leisure, diet, sleep, and spiritual practices among other domains. The nervous system becomes more responsive than reactive, improving vagal tone and state regulation. The immune system downshifts from hypervigilance. Metabolic systems re-pattern around cues of present-time safety, rather than past conditions.

In this way, the integration of inner parts is not only a psychological or spiritual achievement, it is a physiological recalibration. A return to rhythm. The body, like the psyche, moves toward coherence. The field, once fragmented by survival, begins to breathe as one again.

Practical Implications: Supporting Pattern Integration in Childhood

The patterned self begins to take shape in childhood through emerging roles, relational dynamics, and adaptive subpersonalities. These early structures help children navigate the complexities of family, school, and social environments. Yet, these patterns are often provisional, attempts to bring order to inner and outer experience. Supporting children at this stage means nurturing fluidity, coherence, and compassionate acceptance of their multiplicity as a natural part of development.

- **Name without fixing:** Children naturally shift between roles—helper, rebel, explorer, nurturer. Rather than labeling these shifts as problems or phases, caregivers can validate them as expressions of different needs. This helps children experience multiplicity as normal and safe, not something to suppress or feel ashamed of.

- **Encourage imaginative play with awareness:** Play is how inner patterns first come to life. When a child assigns voices to dolls, pretends to be animals or superheroes, or creates elaborate storylines, they are experimenting with identity. Joining them in their imaginative world, without controlling or correcting it, validates their internal experience and supports symbolic integration.

- **Support inner coherence through relational consistency:** Children form patterned self-states in response to their relational environment. Inconsistent or emotionally unpredictable caregiving can fragment these states, while consistent emotional presence helps different roles relate to one another within a coherent field. Co-regulation and attuned responsiveness create a safe space where inner patterns can soften and become more fluid.

- **Normalize emotional contradiction:** Children often feel opposing emotions at the same time—excitement and fear, love and anger. Rather than pushing them to resolve these contradictions too quickly, caregivers can help children name and explore them: "It makes sense to feel both happy and a little scared." This affirms the complexity of their experience and lays the groundwork for emotional integration.

- **Invite reflective storytelling:** As language develops, children begin constructing narratives about themselves and their world. Encouraging storytelling (through conversation, drawing, or play) allows them to begin weaving experiences into coherent meaning. Gently reflecting their stories back to them, while staying curious and nonjudgmental, supports a sense of authorship and evolving self-understanding.

To support the patterned self in childhood is to meet identity not as something fixed or final, but as a process of experimentation and unfolding. Through presence, validation, and relational safety, children can begin to inhabit their inner world with confidence and curiosity. Patterns are not problems to correct, but invitations to connection, each role a gesture toward wholeness, seeking resonance in the field of relationship.

The patterned self is where the fluid rhythms of development crystallize into form not as finality, but as function. Here, we meet the inner architecture of personality: the subpersonalities, roles, and narratives that help us survive, relate, and make meaning. But these patterns, while adaptive, are not the whole. They are the wave's crest, not its source. When held with a curious presence even the most rigid roles soften, revealing the deeper coherence that has always lived beneath the surface. The aim is not to dissolve the patterned self, but to let it breathe, to allow it to reconfigure in service of wholeness. In this way, identity becomes not a fixed truth, but a living rhythm, a transparent lens through which the One continues its dance in many forms.

Key Takeaways: The Patterned

- The patterned self emerges as the symbolic field stabilizes into internalized relational dynamics, roles, and subpersonalities.

- Subpersonalities are adaptive configurations, each formed in response to specific needs, relational histories, and survival strategies.

- Roles are the outward expressions of subpersonalities, shaped by social and cultural expectations. Over time, dominant roles consolidate into what we call identity.

- Identity appears stable but is inherently fluid, a narrative constructed from select parts of the inner field that change with context.

- Curiosity is a turning point that invites reflection rather than reactivity, helping to transform fixed patterns into dynamic processes of integration.

- Self-inquiry deepens this process, building trust and coherence across internal parts and allowing a compassionate internal Self to emerge.

- Personality is both structure and illusion, necessary for functioning, yet always permeable, nested in deeper layers of selfhood.

- Physiologically, subpersonalities carry unique state patterns, influencing autonomic tone, immune regulation, metabolism, and stress responses.

- Integration of subpersonalities supports physiological resilience, coherence, and adaptive flexibility across body systems.

- Healing at this level is not about erasing parts, but about inviting dialogue, coherence, and relational flow within the inner system.

While the patterned self often feels like the final destination, where personality crystallizes and daily life unfolds, it is, in truth, only the visible surface of a much deeper movement. Beneath the roles we play and the identities we wear, there remains a living continuity, waves shaped by currents far below. To truly understand the self, we must look not only at the crest but also at the depths that carry it.

In the next section, we'll step back to trace the arc that brought us here, revisiting the unfolding layers of the Unitive, Sensorial, Symbolic, and Patterned, each revealing not only key events in development but also unique expressions of presence that continue to move within us. Only by holding all four layers together can we begin to glimpse the whole—an inner ocean, endlessly becoming.

Part III. Turbulent Waters: Seeing Through the Eclipse

Not all that rises finds the light. In this section, we encounter the eclipse, the obscuring of wholeness through trauma, fragmentation, and disconnection. We explore how what is unintegrated becomes shadow, and how that shadow ripples through time as echoes, patterns of suffering, protective structures, physiological dysregulation, and psychiatric symptoms. Through a holistic lens, we begin to see these not as flaws, but as the psyche's attempts at coherence. Each echo contains an invitation: not to fix what is broken, but to recontact what was lost.

CHAPTER NINE

A Coherent Field: Tracing the Arc of Becoming

"We do not become fully human by forming an identity, but by discovering how we are already whole."

— The Arc of Human Experiencing

Across these four previous chapters, we've followed the unfolding of human experience not as a linear ladder, but as an emergent wave rising from the depths of a unified field. Each layer—*Unitive*, *Sensorial*, *Symbolic*, and *Patterned*—reveals a unique morphology of presence, a distinct way in which being begins to take form.

In **The Unitive**, we begin at the ocean floor, where all is potential, undivided, and alive with the pulse of mutual process. There is no self, no other, only field. Here, *presence* is not something we do; it is what we are. It is the unconditioned "I am," a silent awareness out of which all else flows.

In **The Sensorial**, the ocean stirs. Impressions ripple across its surface. Boundaries begin to shimmer into being. The individual feels through touch, tone, rhythm, gathering early edges of self and other. *Compassion* arises here not as a concept, but as a felt sense of attunement that organizes intensity into safety. It is the warmth that wraps the wave to containing it.

In **The Symbolic**, the wave begins to rise. Experience is now remembered, represented, named. Sensations give way to meaning; rhythms give way to metaphor. The self begins to hold absence, carry memory, and bridge space with image. *Flow* becomes essential here as the fluid navigation of emerging structure without becoming trapped in it. Flow keeps the wave from freezing.

In **The Patterned**, the wave crests into recognizable form. Roles, subpersonalities, and inner narratives settle into familiar shapes and measurable particles. We live in these patterns. We learn from them. And we often mistake them for the whole. But *curiosity* arises here as a gentle turning inward, a questioning presence that softens identification and invites the field to reorganize around truth. Curiosity reminds the wave it is still the ocean.

Each of these layers builds upon and contains the others. They are not steps to transcend, but dimensions to integrate. The self is not constructed out of parts, rather it is patterned from the whole. And so, when we speak of development, we are not speaking of improvement, but of unfolding: the field becoming aware of itself in deeper and more differentiated ways. To look at one layer alone is to miss the music of the whole. But to feel them together—presence, compassion, flow, curiosity—is to begin to hear the rhythm of coherogenesis: the self becoming whole, again and again.

Just as each wave carries the movement of the ocean from which it arises, so too does each layer of human experience carry the resonance of what came before. The patterned self does not stand apart from the sensorial, symbolic, or unitive, it expresses them in differentiated form. A gesture, a belief, or a relational pattern is not merely a surface expression, but a condensation of lived sensation, symbolic meaning, and the underlying coherence of being. This is not evidence of regression or pathology, but of continuity. The field, in its movement toward complexity, does not abandon its origins; it elaborates them. What appears as structure at the level of the patterned is often the maturation of qualities once only implicit, felt but unnamed, sensed but unformed. Becoming, then, is not a departure from being, but its creative articulation.

For example, consider a person's tendency to withdraw in the face of conflict not as a symptom to pathologize, but as an echo of a deeper coherence. This patterned behavior may carry the imprint of early sensorial experiences of overwhelm, loud voices, sudden changes in tone, or felt disconnection in the body. It may also reflect a symbolic structure: a silent narrative that says, "Safety is in stillness," or "My presence disrupts." Yet these, too, are expressions of an original intelligence, adaptive, relational, and rooted in the field of being. What appears as a behavioral pattern in adulthood is not isolated or arbitrary; it is the differentiated unfolding of early relational rhythms and implicit meaning. In this way, the patterned self reveals the layered history of coherence, tracing back not to deficit, but to the field's natural process of becoming form.

Seen through the lens of coherogenesis, this movement from field to form is not linear, but rhythmic. The person's withdrawal is not simply a fixed pattern, it is part of a living choreography in which the unitive, sensorial, and symbolic all participate. Wholeness is not something lost and regained, but something continuously expressed in new configurations. The body, the story, and the behavior are each inflections of a deeper continuity. In this way, even the seemingly fragmented reveals a hidden symmetry. Coherogenesis names this pulse of unfolding, where the formless finds shape, and shape remembers the field. It is the rhythm by which the self becomes visible to itself, over and over, as unity takes on form without ever ceasing to be whole.

Having traced the arc of becoming through the unitive, sensorial, symbolic, and patterned layers of the self, and having stepped back to witness the coherence of their interrelationship, we now turn to the subtle forces that move through them all. Beneath the changing forms of identity and experience, certain qualities begin to reveal themselves not as additions to the self, but as expressions of the field becoming aware of itself. Presence, compassion, flow, and curiosity are not bound to any single stage; they arise and return throughout the journey. In this next chapter, we explore these pervading qualities, not as traits to master, but as natural movements within the coherent self, each one helping the field remember its wholeness in real time.

CHAPTER TEN

Pervading Qualities of the Self

"When the self rests in presence, it moves with flow, meets with compassion, and enters with curiosity."

— The Arc of Human Experiencing

Across the unfolding of the unitive, sensorial, symbolic, and patterned self, certain qualities have emerged not as stages, but as enduring expressions of the unified relational field. These qualities—presence, compassion, flow, and curiosity—are not traits to be acquired, but inherent capacities of the Self that surface as the field becomes more coherent. Each arises from the same ground, each supports the others, and together, they form a matrix through which healing, integration, and transformation become possible. Whether within the self or between individuals, these pervading qualities shape the way the field listens, responds, and remembers its wholeness.

Presence is pure awareness—attuned, receptive, and non-reactive. It is the felt sense of being fully here, in this moment, without needing to change or grasp anything. In presence, all things arise and pass, sensations, thoughts, emotions, behaviors, yet something remains unshaken. That something is awareness itself: spacious, steady, and undisturbed. When we rest deeply in the now, we begin to sense this distinction, the impermanence of content, and the constancy of awareness. No matter what passes through, this moment simply *is*. Nothing can alter it. And yet, within it lies the full potential for what comes next. This is the space where reactivity softens and responsiveness is born. It is not passive stillness, but the quiet ground of possibility. Presence is the "I am" before the story, the silent coherence beneath all becoming. It is the still ocean from which all waves arise, and into which they return, unshaken by their motion.

Compassion is presence infused with warmth and care. It is the relational tone of awareness, the way presence touches what it beholds. Compassion recognizes suffering without merging into it or pulling away. It feels with, but does not take over. In this way, it becomes a stabilizing force: offering safety, containment, and the capacity to remain with discomfort without collapsing or controlling. Compassion is not about fixing or changing; it is about holding, creating a space spacious enough for sensations, thoughts, emotions, and behaviors to arise and be met. It is the quality that makes presence inhabitable. If presence is the light that illuminates the field, compassion is the warmth that makes it safe to be seen.

Flow is the flexible, attuned movement of presence. It is presence in motion—responsive but unforced, attuned but ungrasping. Like the Taoist principle of *wu wei*, flow arises when we move with, rather than against, the unfolding of experience. It does not resist what is present, nor does it rush

158

ahead to impose structure. Instead, it listens deeply to the inner field and follows its natural contours. In flow, symbols, meanings, and identities remain dynamic—alive, adaptive, and evolving. Flow keeps structure from becoming rigidity and keeps openness from dissolving into chaos. It is the rhythm by which presence navigates complexity, like a current within the ocean, guiding rather than directing. When flow is present, the psyche breathes, the system softens, and meaning reorganizes without force.

Curiosity is presence turned inward with interest and openness. It is the receptive gaze of awareness that leans toward, rather than away from, experience. Unlike analysis or judgment, curiosity does not dissect, it inquires. It wonders gently, "What is this?" or "What wants to be known here?" In doing so, it dissolves defenses not through confrontation, but through welcome. Curiosity makes space for the unseen and unheard, allowing subpersonalities, unmet needs, and hidden memories to come into view without fear of rejection. It is the soft invitation that encourages the inner world to speak. In this sense, curiosity is the eyes and ears of presence, the way being listens to itself. It is not passive observation, but engaged intimacy, a bridge between inner truth and conscious recognition. Through curiosity, the field becomes more transparent, more honest, more whole.

These four qualities (presence, compassion, flow, and curiosity) are not sequential steps, but mutually reinforcing expressions of the same coherent field. Presence gives rise to compassion by offering space that is stable and non-reactive. Compassion makes curiosity safe, removing judgment and creating a warm container for exploration. Curiosity, in turn, keeps flow alive by inviting discovery and allowing meaning to

159

evolve. And flow nourishes presence, preventing it from becoming stagnant or rigid. Together, they form a dynamic constellation of inner coherence, a relational matrix through which awareness moves, holds, adapts, and listens. When these qualities are alive, the self is no longer fragmented or reactive, but fluid, rooted, and capable of transformation.

In essence, when we meet the moment with presence, receive it with compassion, move with it in flow, and explore it through curiosity, we create a living field of transformation.

Reflection: Pause and feel into this moment. Let your breath rise and fall without interference. Can you sense the presence that is already here? Can you often into compassion for whatever arises? Can you feel the gentle flow of awareness moving through you? Can you meet your experience with a touch of curiosity, asking nothing more than, "What's here now?". Let this be enough. Not to fix. Not to change. But simply to return to the field, to yourself, to what has always been quietly whole.

Qualities of Self: Signatures of the Field Becoming Aware

The qualities often associated with Self (presence, compassion, flow, and curiosity) are not personal achievements, nor are they fixed traits. They are emergent expressions of a deeper coherence: the field becoming aware of itself through human experience. In this sense, these qualities are not *produced* by an egoic self, but *revealed* when the patterned layers soften and the underlying unity of the system begins to reorganize around wholeness.

In a fragmented or reactive state, we may attempt to mimic these qualities as techniques, striving to be present, trying to be compassionate, cultivating flow or generating curiosity. But from the perspective of coherogenesis, these qualities are not imposed from above or efforted from within. Rather, they are *natural signatures*, the felt tones of a system cohering. They arise spontaneously when interference is reduced and the system is allowed to return to its native state of integration.

Like waves on the surface of the ocean, they are not separate from the sea, they are movements of the sea itself. When a person embodies presence, it is not merely an individual being attentive; it is the field resting in itself, undisturbed. When compassion arises, it is the field turning tenderly toward its own suffering. When flow emerges, it is the field in fluid motion, unresisted. And when curiosity awakens, it is the field's innate impulse to explore itself, to bring what is split or unknown back into contact.

These qualities are developmental as well. In the earliest phases of human experiencing, the unitive and sensorial, these qualities are present, though not yet distinct. They exist as background potential, like light behind clouds. As the symbolic and patterned layers form, protective structures may obscure their expression. Yet the qualities remain latent, accessible in moments of safety, openness, and return. As integration unfolds, often through therapeutic or contemplative processes, these qualities reemerge not as learned behaviors, but as recognitions. The system begins to remember what it is.

They are not strategies. They are signals. Traces of coherence. The presence of presence. The glow of being contacting itself.

This reframing has profound implications for the therapeutic encounter. Rather than instructing individuals to "be more compassionate" or "find their flow," the invitation becomes one of allowing, creating conditions in which the field can recognize itself through the body-mind. The clinician, too, shifts from directing change to sensing emergence. In this shared space, what unfolds is not a performance of healing, but a remembering.

A Metaphor: Light Through Water

Consider the image of sunlight streaming into the ocean. When the water is clear and still, the light penetrates deeply, illuminating everything below. When the water is turbulent or clouded, the light remains, the sun has not disappeared, but it cannot yet reach the depths.

- Presence is the stillness that allows reflection.

- Compassion is the warmth of light touching every hidden corner.

- Flow is the movement of currents unimpeded by obstruction.

- Curiosity is the shimmering dance of light seeking the unlit.

These qualities are not added to the water; they are revealed through it when it is ready. In the same way, the Self does not acquire these qualities, it remembers them. They are the way wholeness feels when it begins to touch what has been split.

In this way, the qualities of Self are more than virtues, they are luminous indicators that the field is becoming aware of itself. They are not ends, but emergent effects. Not goals, but

162

evidence. They are how the process of coherogenesis becomes felt.

The Healer as Coherent Field: A Curious and Compassionate Flowing Presence

In the context of psychospiritual work, the healer does not simply *apply* therapeutic techniques; they *become* an expression of the coherent field. Their presence, grounded, attuned, responsive, is not incidental to healing. It is the primary vessel through which reorganization becomes possible.

When a system is fragmented, defended, or dissociated, it cannot easily access its own coherence. The self-protective structures that once ensured survival now obscure the innate qualities of Self. But when such a system enters into relationship with a clinician who embodies presence, compassion, flow, and curiosity not as strategies, but as spontaneous expressions of coherence, something begins to shift.

These qualities do not need to be taught or interpreted. They are *felt*. They register somatically and relationally. A body in chaos begins to settle in the presence of a body at rest. A mind locked in protection begins to soften in the presence of a mind that does not judge. A self frozen in fear begins to thaw in the warmth of curiosity and care.

The healer, then, becomes more than a guide, they become a tuning fork. Their nervous system, their regulated presence, their spacious attention, invite an individual's system into resonance. This is not co-regulation alone, it is co-realization. The healer's coherence helps reawaken the individual's own.

This healing relationship is not directional but mutual. The healer is not above or outside the individual's process but is *with* it, shaped by the same field, touched by the same wholeness. Their curiosity is not clinical detachment but open wonder: "What in you longs to return?" Their compassion is not sentimentality but alignment with life's integrative drive. Their presence is not observation from a distance, but the very condition in which coherence unfolds.

When the healer embodies a curious and compassionate flowing presence, they do not simply reflect or contain the individual's process, they *participate* in the field's movement toward wholeness. They become an extension of the Self-field, meeting the individual not as a fixer of problems but as a co-regulator of coherence.

This relational quality is what allows the therapeutic space to become sacred not in a religious sense, but in the sense of deep contact with the unitary field. In this space, beyond analysis or intervention, the individual begins to feel: *something in me is still whole*. Not because they were told so, but because it is being felt into existence by the field that now holds them.

Conclusion

These pervading qualities are not merely supportive of becoming, they are the very *conditions* through which becoming occurs. They are not goals to reach, but innate aspects of the self that emerge as the field becomes more coherent. Presence, compassion, flow, and curiosity do not fix or force, they allow. They create the inner and outer atmosphere in which healing, integration, and transformation unfold. When these qualities are cultivated, not as techniques,

164

but as ways of being, we return to something ancient and original: a relational intelligence rooted in wholeness. In this light, the self is not a structure to be perfected, but a field to be tended, an ocean remembering how to move with its own rhythms.

Key Takeaways: Pervading Qualities of the Self

- Presence is the unchanging awareness beneath all experience—attuned, receptive, and non-reactive. It is the ground of being from which all else arises.

- Compassion is presence with warmth. It offers containment and safety, allowing difficult experiences to be held rather than avoided or suppressed.

- Flow is presence in motion—adaptive, responsive, and flexible. It prevents the psyche from becoming rigid or stagnant and supports ongoing integration.

- Curiosity is presence with interest. It gently turns toward experience with openness and inquiry, inviting parts of the self to be seen, understood, and integrated.

- These qualities emerge developmentally as morphologies of presence: *Presence* from the unitive self, *Compassion* from the sensorial self, *Flow* from the symbolic self, *Curiosity* from the patterned self

- Together, these qualities form a relational matrix for healing and coherence, both within the individual and between individuals.

- They are mutually reinforcing: Presence makes space for compassion, compassion creates safety for curiosity,

curiosity keeps flow alive, flow supports the continued unfolding of presence

- These qualities are not techniques or ideals, but inherent expressions of the unitary field; natural capacities that arise when the system feels safe and coherent.

- When embodied, they help us meet experience with depth, flexibility, and care; supporting the integration of subpersonalities, the regulation of physiological states, and the return to a deeper sense of wholeness.

While presence, compassion, flow, and curiosity are innate to the self and essential to integration, their expression is not always seamless. As development progresses and the self organizes around experiences of separation, defense, and adaptation, these qualities can become obscured. They may be eclipsed, not lost, but hidden, by the very structures that once helped the self maintain coherence. The journey ahead invites us to turn toward these eclipsed places with the same qualities we have come to recognize: with presence that holds, compassion that softens, flow that adapts, and curiosity that inquires. In the next chapter, we explore how consciousness narrows and fragments, how parts of the self become disowned or defended, and how even in these shadowed spaces, the light of the self continues to shine—simply waiting to be remembered.

CHAPTER ELEVEN

The Eclipse: The Self HIDEs

*"One does not become enlightened by imagining figures of
light, but by making the darkness conscious."*

— Carl Jung

Having explored the coherent unfolding of the self through the
unitive, sensorial, symbolic, and patterned layers, and the
pervading qualities that support integration across them, we
now enter a more elusive terrain: that which falls outside
awareness. If the previous chapters traced the self as it
expresses through rhythm, resonance, meaning, and adaptation,
this chapter examines what gets filtered, fragmented, or hidden
along the way. Here, we consider how consciousness, ever-
present and continuous, becomes partially obscured, shaped by
the very structures it gives rise to. Just as an eclipse
temporarily conceals the light without extinguishing it, aspects
of the self become veiled by unintegrated experience,
protective patterning, or relational overwhelm. In this chapter,

we begin to understand the unconscious not as a separate domain, but as the part of the field that remains outside the current reach of integration. We explore how presence meets this shadowed terrain not to fix or force illumination, but to widen the lens through which the self is seen, felt, and remembered.

Consciousness is not a product of development, it is the primordial field in which development takes place. It is not built over time, but rather, time unfolds within it. In the earliest moments of life, the infant is not separate from this field, but fully immersed within it—unitive, unbounded, and unfiltered. This field is not something the infant has; it is what the infant is. Here, we use the term consciousness to refer to awareness itself—the open, spacious capacity in which sensations arise, relationships begin to take shape, and meaning slowly emerges. This total field of awareness precedes content, language, memory, or form. It is the silent backdrop upon which the drama of becoming is played, ever-present even when obscured.

As development unfolds, the once-unfiltered field of consciousness begins to take on shape. Through ongoing relationship with the environment, patterns form—emergent structures of perception, sensation, meaning, and identity. These patterns become the lenses through which awareness encounters the world. Each developmental layer (sensorial, symbolic, and patterned) acts as a kind of filter, organizing the raw immediacy of consciousness into recognizable forms. But in doing so, they also narrow the field. What remains accessible to conscious experience, the filtered light that continues to reach awareness, is what I refer to as the **foreconscious**. It is the portion of the field that still shines

168

through. The material that comprises these filters, the unprocessed sensations, unmetabolized affect, and implicit patterns that structure experience from beneath the surface, is what I refer to as the **subconscious**. Neither is static, and both are shaped by the evolving interplay between the self and its environment.

This filtering process is not inherently pathological. It is, in fact, a natural outcome of coherogenesis. As the unitive field expresses itself through the developmental layers, each filter emerges in service of coherence. These layers offer continuity, containment, meaning, and structure. Yet they can never fully contain the vastness of the field from which they arise. This is why, even when functioning well, identification with roles or patterns often leaves a person with the sense that something essential is missing, misaligned, or constrained. Like wearing clothes that are too tight, these structures offer form but can restrict the fullness of being. Paradoxically, the very strategies the system uses to stay connected to wholeness can obscure it. The light of consciousness becomes narrowed not by intention, but by the system's sincere attempts to maintain coherence.

While this process of filtering is a natural developmental unfolding, it can be intensified or disrupted by trauma, a theme that will be explored in greater depth later. Trauma amplifies the system's need for protection, often accelerating the consolidation of defensive structures and narrowing the range of experience that can be safely held in awareness. As these structures become more rigid, the system's flexibility diminishes. Consciousness contracts, not just in scope, but in accessibility. Certain sensations, memories, or parts of the self become too overwhelming to process and are therefore disowned or pushed to the edges of awareness. This fragmentation creates discontinuities within the self, gaps between what is lived and what is known. Metaphorically, this process resembles an eclipse: the radiant field of consciousness is still present, but partially or fully obscured by the shadow of unintegrated experience. The light remains, it is simply hidden from view.

What falls outside the reach of awareness, outside the filtered light of consciousness, becomes the content of the **unconscious**. This is not a separate realm, but the portion of the field that can no longer be directly experienced or metabolized. Anything that cannot be safely integrated, whether due to overwhelm, loss, misattunement, or trauma, is set aside, dissociated, or repressed in service of the system's coherence. Over time, these unintegrated fragments accumulate as residues within the field. They show up as patterned tensions in the body, energetic postures of defense or collapse, relational templates enacted without conscious choice, and implicit procedural memories that silently shape perception and behavior. The unconscious is not "elsewhere," it is fully part of the field, but it exists outside the current organizing frame of the self. Like the moon in eclipse, it casts a shadow not because it is absent, but because it is not yet illuminated.

Physiologically, the eclipse of consciousness is mirrored in the body's regulatory systems. As experiences are filtered, defended against, or dissociated, the system adapts accordingly. Chronic stress, for example, can lead to persistent activation of the hypothalamic-pituitary-adrenal (HPA) axis, embedding a sense of vigilance into the body's baseline. Similarly, the autonomic nervous system begins to organize around perceived safety or threat, reinforcing patterns of fight,

170

flight, freeze, or collapse. The immune and metabolic systems, too, respond to these underlying energetic imprints, sometimes inflaming, sometimes shutting down, depending on the story being held just beneath awareness. Over time, these physiological adaptations become somatic expressions of the unconscious, bodily echoes of unintegrated experience. In this way, the eclipse is not just psychological, but cellular. The body stores what the mind cannot yet process, and in doing so, participates in shaping the boundary between the conscious and the unconscious. Healing, therefore, must occur not only in thought, but in tissue, in the rhythms of the breath, the regulation of stress hormones, and the tone of the vagus nerve. As the system becomes more coherent and safe, the physiological imprint of the eclipse begins to soften, allowing the light of consciousness to permeate the body once again.

From the vantage point of the unitive, the self is a unitary field of potential energy—fluid, open, and inherently whole. This energy flows through the unfolding layers of development, shaping itself into form while seeking to preserve continuity and coherence. It moves like a wave through the sensorial, symbolic, and patterned dimensions, each layer an opportunity for the field to articulate itself more fully. Yet this movement is not linear; it arcs back toward its source, like waves returning to the quiet depth of the ocean. When this flow is interrupted (by rupture, trauma, or overwhelming experience) the energy becomes suspended, frozen in place. These frozen currents of unexpressed potential do not disappear; they remain in the field, awaiting metabolization. Healing, then, is less about fixing what is broken and more about thawing what has been held in latency, allowing the wave to move again, the field to reorganize, and the self to remember its original coherence.

Healing is not simply the act of bringing the unconscious into consciousness, but the deeper process of re-establishing relationship with what was once severed. It involves reconnecting dissociated energies with presence, gently repatterning defensive structures held in the body and field, and restoring the natural fluidity of awareness. As the self becomes more permeable, less rigidly defended and more open to experience, consciousness begins to reclaim what was once split off. Integration is not the accumulation of new content; it is a re-organization of the system that reopens the field to itself. The boundary between conscious and unconscious is not fixed—it is porous, alive, and responsive. What is conscious reflects what the system can currently hold without overwhelm. What is unconscious is not gone, but held in latency, waiting for the right conditions of safety, attunement, and resonance to return. This dynamic accessibility is the essence of healing: not forcing what is hidden into view, but expanding the field so that more of what has always been can now be met.

Regardless of how complete the eclipse may seem, no matter how obscured the light of consciousness becomes, the fundamental "I" remains intact at the ground of being. This essential self does not disappear; it simply becomes hidden. To express this, we might say the Self **HIDEs**. That is, each person **H**as a Self that **I**s unfolding potential energy. What it **D**oes is observe, orient, and organize the interrelationship it **E**xperiences. Even beneath layers of defense, adaptation, or fragmentation, the organizing intelligence of the Self persists. It observes from within the field, orients through the developmental filters it has formed, and continuously organizes

172

experience in service of coherence. The challenge, and the invitation, is not to create this Self, but to remember it. To soften the identifications that eclipse its presence. To trust that beneath every fragmented pattern lies a coherent whole, patiently awaiting recognition. The "I" is not lost, it is simply veiled, and always ready to shine through again when the field is open and the system is ready.

Reflective Invitation: Take a moment to pause and feel into your own field of experience. Can you sense the places where light still shines through, the moments of clarity, connection, or truth? And can you gently turn toward the shadows, not with judgment, but with curiosity? What in you has been hidden, not because it is unworthy, but because it has not yet felt safe enough to be seen? Ask yourself: What might emerge if I made more room? What might soften if I no longer forced integration, but allowed it? Let this be your invitation, to meet the hidden parts of yourself not with force, but with the quiet return of light.

The eclipse of the self is not a failure of development, but a natural consequence of the system's efforts to maintain coherence in the face of complexity and overwhelm. Each layer (sensorial, symbolic, and patterned) offers structure and meaning, yet can also obscure the deeper field from which the self arises. What is hidden is not lost; it is simply waiting. Healing does not require bypassing these layers, but softening within them, allowing presence to penetrate what has been hardened, and compassion to hold what has been exiled. In remembering that the self HIDEs, not vanishes, we are reminded that awareness is never absent, only obscured. The work is not to fix, but to reawaken. The "I" at the ground of being remains intact, quietly observing, orienting, organizing, and waiting to be invited back into the fullness of experience.

Key Takeaways: The Eclipse

- Consciousness is the primordial field not created by development, but the space within which development unfolds.

- Developmental layers (sensorial, symbolic, patterned) act as filters that shape awareness and simultaneously obscure parts of it.

- The foreconscious is the filtered light of consciousness that remains accessible; the subconscious is the material comprising the filters themselves.

- The unconscious holds unintegrated experience—sensory fragments, energetic postures, and relational patterns that fall outside current awareness.

- Trauma augments the eclipse, reinforcing defensive structures and narrowing the field of consciousness, but the light remains present underneath.

- Healing involves re-opening the field by reconnecting dissociated energy with presence and reorganizing patterned defenses.

- The boundary between conscious and unconscious is dynamic and determined by the system's current capacity to process experience without overwhelm.

- The self HIDEs, meaning each person Has a Self that Is unfolding potential energy and Does observe, orient, and organize what it Experiences.

- Physiological systems reflect and reinforce the eclipse, embedding unintegrated experience into nervous, immune, and metabolic regulation.

- Integration is not about fixing, but about remembering the original wholeness and allowing the self to reorganize in the light of consciousness.

While The Eclipse revealed how consciousness becomes shaped, filtered and fragmented, through the natural processes of development and the layering of experience, it also exposed a deeper truth: that this fragmentation is not random or meaningless. The narrowing of awareness and the emergence of the unconscious are not simply dysfunctions, but attempts by the system to maintain coherence when overwhelmed.

In this light, trauma can be understood not only as disruption, but as reorganization. The same intelligence that forms a self also forms a defense. What follows now is an exploration of this adaptive brilliance, how the wound reshapes the field, how symptoms echo what was once split off, and how even in the deepest patterns of pain, the self is still reaching for wholeness.

CHAPTER TWELVE

Trauma and the Eclipse

"Every pain carries a seed of becoming. The echo is not the end, it is the beginning of return."

— The Arc of Human Experiencing

If *The Eclipse* reveals how consciousness becomes narrowed through developmental layering, then trauma is the force that intensifies and crystallizes that narrowing. It is not merely a deviation from coherence, but an adaptive strategy the system employs to preserve coherence in the face of what it cannot fully hold. When the intensity of experience overwhelms the system's capacity for integration, the field constricts not to punish, but to protect. In this way, trauma is not the cause of fragmentation, but the amplifier of it. It deepens the eclipse, forming shadows in the field, shaping how experience is perceived, organized, and remembered. These shadows—the dissociated, the unseen, the too-much—become echoes of the original overwhelm, reverberating across the layers of the self until presence is strong enough to meet them again.

Trauma as a Constriction in the Field

Trauma is not defined by what happens to you, but by what happens within you in response. It is the enduring biopsychosocialspiritual reorganization that arises when an experience overwhelms the system's capacity to process, metabolize, or find meaning. In such moments, the coherent flow of the unitary field is disrupted. Mutual process collapses. The resonance that once held experience in rhythm falters. The system, in its intelligence, contracts, splintering experience into fragments, narrowing the field of consciousness, and reorganizing itself around survival rather than wholeness. Even after the event has passed, the imprint remains, a felt sense of threat, disconnection, or fragmentation that continues to echo through body, mind, and field.

Organization Around Disconnection

When an experience arrives too quickly, too intensely, or with too much contradiction for the system to process, the field cannot hold it in coherent flow. The rhythm fractures, the resonance disorganizes, and the self, still seeking coherence, organizes around disconnection. This is not pathology, but profound intelligence. The system adapts to the rupture by shifting into protective patterns. It pulls awareness away from the intolerable (dissociation), reconfigures physiological responses toward vigilance or collapse, and constructs relational or behavioral strategies to avoid reactivation. In short: it does not merely cope, it rewires.

This is the system engaging in self-organization under perturbation. It does what all complex systems do when confronted with overwhelm: it re-stabilizes around new organizing principles. But in trauma, these principles prioritize survival over wholeness. Physiologically, the nervous system encodes defensive postures, sympathetic hyperarousal, parasympathetic shutdown, or alternating states of freeze and fawn. The hypothalamic-pituitary-adrenal (HPA) axis calibrates toward chronic stress. Immune function shifts toward inflammation or suppression. The gut-brain axis, once oriented toward nourishment and regulation, becomes a network tuned to danger.

Psychologically, the self splinters. Parts of experience that were once integrated become sequestered. Internal representations narrow into protective identities: "I must be good," "I must not need," "I am the problem." Subpersonalities carry fragments of experience the larger system cannot yet bear. Behaviorally, avoidance becomes the organizing pattern. The system orients not around fulfillment, but around the prevention of pain. Habits form around what feels safe, numbing, pleasing, controlling, withdrawing. Life becomes shaped more by what is feared than by what is longed for.

Socially and culturally, the fragmentation can be mirrored. Families may collude with a child's adapted self. Institutions may reinforce performance over presence. Cultural norms may celebrate over-functioning, disembodiment, or emotional suppression, deepening the exile of the fragmented parts. Over time, these external reflections weave into the internal map, stabilizing a self that is coherent only in its disconnection.

178

Yet all of this makes sense. The system is trying, with exquisite sensitivity, to keep itself from breaking further. It minimizes energy expenditure, avoids dissonance, and maintains basic coherence, albeit through contraction. But coherence around fragmentation becomes a kind of prison. A logic built on limitation. And that's why healing, when it begins, often feels like a betrayal of the very rules that once kept us safe.

The Cost of Adaptive Coherence

Trauma-based adaptations are not mistakes, they are stabilizations. Each pattern, posture, and subpersonality formed in the aftermath of overwhelm is a gesture of intelligence, a way the system says, "this is how I can stay together." Yet over time, coherence around fragmentation comes with a price.

What was once protective becomes restrictive. The once-fluid field of the self, designed for resonance, expansion, and integration, now narrows into rigid grooves. These grooves are familiar but limiting, like rivers that no longer change course. Possibilities diminish. Patterns repeat. Identity fuses around survival rather than emergence.

This is the paradox of adaptive coherence: it keeps the system intact, but inhibits growth. It preserves structure at the expense of aliveness. The system, organized around what it had to exclude, begins to believe the exclusion is who it is. The self becomes a curated version of what the field could tolerate, rather than a full expression of what it could become.

Physiologically, this manifests in chronic dysregulation. The nervous system remains locked in high-alert or numbed collapse. The immune system may oscillate between hypervigilance and depletion. Hormonal systems struggle to calibrate to present-time safety. The body becomes a library of implicit memory, each cell holding a page of the unspoken story.

Relationally, the cost is intimacy. The parts of the self exiled for protection cannot fully show up in connection. Vulnerability feels dangerous. Needs are suppressed or projected. Relationships may mirror early dynamics, not because they're inevitable, but because the field of perception is still filtered through the eclipse. Others are met not as they are, but as the nervous system anticipates.

Spiritually, the cost is disconnection from the ground of being. The deeper truth, *I am whole, even in my fragmentation*, becomes eclipsed by the illusion of brokenness. The felt sense of the unitive field, once accessible through presence, is now dimmed by layers of defense. The "I am" is still there, but muffled.

And yet, even here, the field is not lost. It is compressed, but not destroyed. The wave has curled in on itself, but its origin is still the ocean. The wound becomes a portal. The symptom becomes a signal. The body's tension, the psyche's repetition, the spirit's ache, these are not enemies to be eliminated, but invitations. Invitations to soften the defenses, to meet the fragments, and to allow the field to reconfigure.

This is the turning point. When survival is no longer the only priority, the system can begin to open again not because the threat is gone, but because the self is ready to meet it differently. The next step is not erasure of the past, but reorganization around a new center: presence, rather than protection.

The Wound as Compass

What if the very place that hurts is also the place that points the way?

In the ecology of the self, nothing is meaningless. Pain is not random. Symptoms, defenses, and repeated patterns are not evidence of failure, but messages from the deeper field, signals that something once severed is now seeking reunion. The wound, then, is not a detour away from healing, but the very doorway through which healing must pass.

This is the paradox of the patterned self: what we most want to avoid is often where life is calling us back. The ache in the chest, the clench in the gut, the unrelenting story in the mind. These are not intrusions. They are beacons. They illuminate the exact edge where wholeness was once disrupted and now longs to return.

When presence meets these wounds, not with strategy, but with openness, they begin to soften. The frozen pattern stirs. The body, which had braced for repetition, senses something new. A different outcome becomes possible not because the past is undone, but because the present is now different. The ocean has moved closer to the wave.

This is the wisdom of coherence: it is never static. Even in contraction, the field listens for rhythm. Even in defense, the system searches for resonance. A trigger is not just a disruption; it is also an opportunity. It is the resurfacing of what the system is now strong enough to feel. In this way, the wound becomes a compass, it orients us toward what is next to be integrated.

Physiologically, this is mirrored in how healing unfolds. Neuroplasticity allows the brain to reshape connections once forged in trauma. The autonomic nervous system, through co-regulation and attunement, learns new rhythms. The immune system, once conditioned for hypervigilance, begins to recalibrate. Even the gut and hormonal systems, those ancient regulators of internal safety, start to shift as the field of awareness expands. Healing is not imposed; it is invited through relational presence, safety, and time.

Spiritually, the wound invites remembrance. Beneath every adaptation is the undivided field that never broke. The ache is a call not just to feel better, but to remember who we are beneath the layering, to return to the unconditioned "I am" that never left, only hid. In this light, healing is not a fixing of what is wrong, but a remembering of what has always been whole.

And so we begin to follow the wound not to indulge in pain, but to read its pattern. We follow it back to the moment it split the field, and we bring presence to that edge. Not to erase the wound, but to allow it to bloom into something new. The crack, as Leonard Cohen reminds us, is how the light gets in. But it's also how the light gets out.

Reweaving the Field

Healing is not a return to a former state, but a reweaving of the field with the threads of what was once cast out. It is not the removal of trauma's trace, but the transformation of its meaning. What once fragmented the self becomes the very material through which coherence is restored.

In this process, presence becomes the loom. Compassion is the thread. Flow is the motion. Curiosity guides the hands. Together, these pervading qualities allow the self to meet its own history not as an enemy to conquer, but as a companion to include. The wave returns to the ocean, not by force, but by relaxing into the pull of something larger.

To reweave the field is to bring awareness to what has been held in the shadows. It is to let the body speak its postures of protection, to let the patterned self share its story, to let the symbols long frozen in trauma dissolve and reform. It is to loosen the tight clothing of false identities and feel again the texture of one's original coherence.

The nervous system no longer needs to pulse between extremes when safety becomes internalized. The immune system, once primed for attack, begins to recognize self from not-self. Hormonal rhythms return to harmony. Even the gut, long shaped by anticipation and vigilance, begins to digest the world as it is, rather than as it was. Physiology reorganizes not through control, but through remembering its deeper design, connection, regulation, flow.

Psychologically, the inner landscape shifts. Subpersonalities, once isolated, begin to speak across silences. Roles soften. Identity becomes more transparent, more reflective of the whole. The patterned self, once rigid, now dances. The symbolic self dreams. The sensorial self reawakens. And the unitive presence quietly holds it all.

This is not a final state, but a living process. The field is never finished. It is always responding, always reshaping, always inviting us into deeper wholeness. Reweaving is the art of becoming again, again and again. And perhaps this is the greatest transformation: to realize that what once felt like exile was always part of the path home.

Echoes of the Eclipse explores how trauma shapes the organization of consciousness not merely as damage, but as an intelligent, adaptive response to overwhelm. What becomes hidden or fragmented in the wake of trauma is never truly lost, only eclipsed, awaiting the conditions for return. Through presence, compassion, flow, and curiosity, the field begins to reweave itself. The wound becomes the compass. The symptom becomes a guide. And healing becomes not a linear correction, but a spiral path back to coherence, one moment of inclusion at a time.

Reflective Invitation

As you move forward, consider this: What patterns in your life feel repetitive, reactive, or overly familiar? Rather than pathologizing them, can you ask: *What are you trying to protect?* What if the very symptoms or struggles you wish to eliminate are actually doorways, echoes of a part of you that long ago made a choice to protect your coherence?

Find a quiet moment. Breathe. Listen inward. Notice where the body tenses or softens as you explore these questions. You may discover that the field is already reweaving, waiting not for you to force change, but for you to *welcome what was once left out*. Let that be the first thread.

Key Takeaways: Trauma and the Eclipse

- **Trauma is not the event**, but the system's reorganization in response to overwhelm and disconnection.

- **The self adapts intelligently**, forming new patterns that preserve coherence even in fragmentation.

- **Physiological systems mirror psychological reorganization**, including nervous system tone, immune function, and gut-brain communication.

- **These adaptations become costly over time**, creating rigidity, disconnection, and limiting the field of awareness.

- **The unconscious is not separate**, but composed of experiences the system could not yet process, held in latency, not absence.

- **The wound is a guide**, signaling where integration is most needed and where presence can meet the excluded parts.

- **Healing is not fixing, but remembering**, a reweaving of the self through relational presence and felt inclusion.

- **Wholeness is not achieved**, it is revealed through the gentle unfolding of what already belongs.

While the eclipse veils the light of wholeness, the shadow it casts does not remain still. It moves, cycling through the body, shaping perception, and organizing patterns of response. What is split off does not simply disappear; it finds expression through repetition.

The psyche, in its devotion to coherence, begins to orbit the fragments it could not yet digest, replaying unresolved themes in search of completion. These loops are not mere echoes of the past, but living imprints that shape how we experience the present. The trauma that was once eclipsed becomes a gravitational center, drawing behaviors, thoughts, relationships, and physiology into a repeating arc. As we now turn to *Echoes of the Eclipse*, we listen more closely to these reverberations, not as symptoms to be silenced, but as the resonant language of a self still reaching toward wholeness. In these echoes, we hear the soul's insistence that what was once split must someday return.

CHAPTER THIRTEEN

Echoes of the Eclipse

"After silence, that which comes nearest to expressing the inexpressible is music."

— Aldous Huxley

Not everything lost in the eclipse remains silent. Though parts of the self may be obscured, exiled, or frozen by trauma and adaptation, the field does not forget. It reverberates. In the wake of eclipse, the self begins to echo.

These echoes (e.g., symptoms, struggles, compulsions, beliefs) are not random. They are patterned waves emerging from the moment where something essential went underground. They carry the shape of what was once whole, now refracted through the lens of protection and fragmentation. What psychiatry often names as disorder, the deeper self may recognize as an uncompleted gesture, an attempt to remember, reorganize, or restore.

From the surface, these echoes may sound like noise. Anxiety, depression, dissociation, rage, obsessions, each a signal distorted by the distance from its source. This noise is a familiar target of reductive approaches, aiming to suppress in order to achieve silence once again. But when we learn to listen differently, we begin to sense that these disturbances are not meaningless. They are messages, peripheral translations of an occluded truth still trying to reach the light of awareness.

The ocean offers us a way to feel into this process. After a disruption in its depths, the ocean does not return to stillness instantly. Waves move outward, overlapping, refracting, crashing. Each wave holds the memory of that original disturbance, not as an exact replica, but as a trace of what once was. This is how the field of self behaves after the eclipse. Disturbance becomes signal. Signal becomes symptom. And symptoms become echoes, calling the self back into coherence.

In this chapter, we will explore these echoes through a different lens: not as pathologies to be eliminated, but as intelligible reverberations of what was hidden. We will trace how the sensorial, symbolic, and patterned layers each carry their own echoes. We will look again at psychiatric diagnosis, not to discard it, but to uncover what may have been missed when we stopped listening. The echo is not the wound. It is the way the wound speaks.

Trauma and the Birth of Echoes

Not all eclipses are traumatic, but all trauma carries the signature of an eclipse.

When overwhelming experience exceeds the system's capacity to feel, integrate, or respond, the field of self protects itself through fragmentation. Some parts are pushed out of awareness, some are numbed or silenced, and others take on exaggerated roles in the name of survival. What follows is not disappearance, but dissociation, not erasure, but distortion. The fullness of self is not lost, only hidden beneath layers of adaptation. This moment, when coherence is obscured by necessity, marks the birth of the echo.

Trauma does not simply create symptoms. It reshapes the entire field of organization. It constricts flow, warps perception, and redirects energy toward vigilance, defense, or avoidance. What once moved fluidly now becomes rigid. What was once integrated becomes compartmentalized. The system begins to echo not from its center, but from its fractures.

The echoes are shaped by many factors. The nature of the trauma. The age and developmental stage at which it occurred. The degree of safety or support available during and after the experience. And perhaps most importantly, the layer of self through which the trauma moved, sensorial, symbolic, or patterned.

A trauma that overwhelms the nervous system before language emerges may echo as somatic dysregulation, chronic pain, or dissociative states. A trauma that disrupts symbolic meaning may resurface in intrusive images, distortions of self-narrative, or compulsive repetition. When trauma impacts the patterned layer, it often gives rise to entrenched beliefs, rigid behaviors, or relational compulsions all organized not around truth, but around survival.

The echo, then, is not a mistake. It is the system's way of remembering what it could not bear to fully hold. And though these echoes may appear fragmented or pathological, they are also invitations. They point toward the place where the self was once eclipsed and toward the possibility of return.

The Language of Echoes

An echo is not a direct repetition, it is a distortion shaped by time, distance, and terrain. So too with the echoes of the self. After the eclipse, experience does not return in the same form it was lost. Instead, it surfaces in the languages of the body, the image, and the pattern. Each layer of human development (sensorial, symbolic, and patterned) carries its own dialect of echo. To hear these expressions clearly, we must learn to listen in kind.

Sensorial Echoes

These are the first to emerge and often the last to be understood. The body speaks in tension, tone, sensation, and dysregulation. Its language is rhythmic, cyclical, and affective and is held in autonomic patterns, inflammatory cascades, and subtle cues of unease. These echoes appear as chronic pain without clear cause, digestive symptoms without organic disease, or shifts in heart rate and breath that mirror forgotten fear.

They may be dismissed as "psychosomatic" or "functional," yet they carry the raw imprint of early experience. Before words were available, before images could form, the nervous system recorded the world in flesh. When trauma touches this layer, it does not leave in silence. It lingers as vibration. As restlessness. As the body's insistence that something remains unspoken.

Symbolic Echoes

When the eclipse occurs after the emergence of language, or when symbolic structures are destabilized by trauma, echoes often take on metaphorical or imagistic form. Nightmares, intrusive memories, disorganized narratives, compulsive fantasies, or unexplained shame arise, not because the story is clear, but because meaning has been ruptured.

These echoes are the psyche's attempt to re-symbolize what was lost. They are fragments of language orbiting a silence too painful to name. A child who once felt invisible may grow into an adult who compulsively seeks recognition. The underlying echo is not attention-seeking, it is presence-seeking. Beneath the symbol lies the longing for coherence. To attune to symbolic echoes is to sense the metaphor beneath the mask, to feel the myth emerging within the symptom.

Patterned Echoes

This layer is where echoes become identity. When dissociation or protection becomes chronic, the adaptive patterns solidify. Echoes move from momentary reverberations into enduring ways of being. Here, the system organizes itself around what it expects to encounter: abandonment, criticism, failure, rejection.

These patterns may manifest as personality traits, relational strategies, or diagnosable syndromes. A person who once lost connection may come to believe they are fundamentally unlovable. A child who once had to parent a caregiver may grow into an adult who feels responsible for everyone's emotional state. These echoes are not chosen. They are inherited from the field, passed down from the place where coherence fractured.

Patterned echoes tend to be the most visible to others and the most hidden from within. They feel like "just the way I am." But beneath these defensive formations lies the same truth as in all echoes: a fragment of the self still searching for home.

Diagnoses as Echoes, Not Errors

What psychiatry calls a diagnosis may be more faithfully understood as an echo, an intelligible reverberation of an experience too large, too early, or too prolonged to be fully metabolized by the self.

To diagnose is, in essence, to name a pattern. Yet when we name without context, without history, relationship, or meaning, we risk mistaking the echo for the essence. Depression becomes a label instead of a signal. Anxiety becomes a dysfunction rather than a response. Psychosis becomes a defect rather than an ungrounded metaphor. The field is flattened. The music is transcribed into static. But echoes are not noise. They are patterned, purposeful, and rich with information, if we are willing to listen.

What if instead of seeing psychiatric symptoms as fixed pathologies, we saw them as living memories in symbolic form? What if diagnoses were not verdicts, but invitations, each one pointing to a place in the self where the light of coherence was once eclipsed?

A diagnosis of panic disorder may mark an echo in the sensorial layer: a nervous system trapped in cycles of unprocessed fear. Obsessive-compulsive disorder may arise

192

from symbolic echoes, rituals and thoughts trying to restore an order that was once shattered. Borderline personality structure may represent patterned echoes: a system caught between longing for connection and fearing annihilation, shaped by chronic relational trauma. None of these are errors. They are the system's best attempts at adaptation and continuity, until something deeper is possible.

This reframing does not deny the reality of suffering. Nor does it reject the utility of diagnostic categories when used wisely. But it calls us to a deeper view: one that sees symptoms not only as problems to manage, but as stories trying to be heard.

To work with an echo is to become a kind of translator. Not one who silences the sound, but one who listens with curiosity: *What is this trying to say? What layer does this belong to? What history lives here?* In this light, healing becomes less about suppressing symptoms and more about reestablishing resonance, restoring a felt continuity between the self and its lost expressions.

Echoes as Invitations

Every echo is a call, not back to the past, but toward coherence.

When we shift from asking *what's wrong with me?* to *what is this trying to show me?*, the echo ceases to be a problem and becomes an invitation. An invitation to listen where we once dissociated, to feel where we once froze, to make meaning where meaning was once torn away.

Symptoms are not the enemy of wholeness; they are the messengers of its absence. They arise where something vital went unmet, where contact was lost, where the self fractured in

193

order to survive. When we relate to them with resistance, we deepen the divide. But when we meet them with presence and curiosity, we begin to close the gap between surface and depth.

Each echo carries a specific tone, shaped by the original wound and the system's response to it. Some call for safety. Others for expression. Some ask to be witnessed, others to be re-integrated. The task is not to eliminate the echo, but to respond to what it asks. This is how coherence begins, not through force or control, but through resonance.

This is not merely a psychological process. It is an energetic one. The field of the self is always seeking balance. When an echo arises, it is the field's way of drawing attention to an area of unresolved charge or blocked flow. To respond skillfully is to participate in this rebalancing, to become an active partner in coherogenesis.

Therapeutically, this means approaching symptoms not with strategies to suppress, but with presence that allows transformation. A panic attack may become a portal into ungrieved terror. A compulsive behavior may reveal a symbolic structure protecting against helplessness. Even silence, withdrawal, or numbness may contain echoes of a time when collapse was the only protection possible.

What matters most is the quality of relationship we bring to the echo. When it is met with attunement, patience, and enough safety, it begins to soften. It begins to tell its story. And in telling it, the field begins to remember itself.

The Ocean Listens Back

The echo is not a one-way phenomenon. Just as a wave returns from the depth as a signal, it can be met—heard, received, and transformed. The ocean does not merely echo; it listens.

In the presence of attuned awareness, the system that once fractured can begin to reorganize. The pattern that once shouted through symptom can soften into signal. What was once a chaotic reverberation becomes part of the coherent rhythm of the whole. This is not because the echo disappears, but because it is no longer isolated. It is no longer treated as a problem, but welcomed as part of the sea. In this sense, healing is less like erasing and more like harmonizing.

The field of the self is dynamic. It does not require perfection; it requires resonance. When we meet an echo with presence, especially when that presence is held in relationship, it is as if the echo finally reaches the surface and finds response. Not rejection. Not diagnosis. Not interpretation. Not reactivity or proactivity. But response: an embodied yes to the truth of the sound.

This is what depth-oriented psychotherapy, contemplative practice, and integrative healing modalities attempt to facilitate. They offer a rhythm of listening that invites the echo back into flow. They help restore what the eclipse disrupted. Not by returning to the past, but by allowing the past to complete itself in the present.

In this way, the echo becomes the beginning of coherence. Not a relic of damage, but the first note in a song remembered. And in listening, the ocean—vast, layered, and undivided—reclaims its voice.

Conclusion: Reverberations of Return

The echoes that follow an eclipse are not signs of failure. They are signs that the self is still speaking.

Each symptom, each struggle, each repetition is a reverberation of something unfinished, something still alive beneath the surface. When we learn to hear these echoes not as noise but as signal, we discover that what we feared were signs of brokenness are in fact calls toward wholeness.

To walk with the echoes is to walk with care, to trust that the self remembers, even when memory is silent. It is to allow that what seems chaotic may be carrying order in disguise, an order not imposed from the outside, but emerging from the deepest rhythms of becoming.

In this way, healing is not the end of echoes, but a change in their meaning. They no longer call out from isolation. They begin to harmonize with the larger song of the self. They become waves returning to the ocean, not erased, but integrated. No longer trapped in repetition, but free to resolve.

The eclipse may have hidden the light, but the echoes reveal its shape. They show us where to look, where to listen, and where to love again. And as the field listens back, a new rhythm emerges. Not of fragmentation, but of coherence. Not of protection, but of presence. Not of silence, but of return.

Key Takeaways: Echoes of the Eclipse

- After trauma or fragmentation, aspects of the self that were eclipsed do not disappear, they echo.

- These echoes are not random or pathological, but meaningful reverberations of unmetabolized experience.

- Each developmental layer (sensorial, symbolic, patterned) gives rise to distinct echoic expressions: *Sensorial:* somatic symptoms, autonomic dysregulation. *Symbolic:* intrusive thoughts, disrupted meaning, metaphorical expression. *Patterned:* rigid behaviors, personality traits, diagnostic identities.

- Psychiatric diagnoses can be viewed not as errors, but as echoes, adaptive responses to prior eclipses of coherence.

- Healing occurs not by suppressing echoes, but by listening to what they are asking—through resonance, presence, and re-integration.

- Echoes are invitations to reestablish contact with hidden aspects of the self and initiate a return toward wholeness.

- The field of self "listens back" through conscious presence, allowing echoes to soften and reorganize into coherence.

- Echoes, when embraced rather than silenced, become the first tones of healing, resonating not with fragmentation, but with return.

The echoes do not arise in a vacuum, they emerge within structures carefully crafted to keep the self intact. Where the eclipse once fractured coherence, the human system adapts. It protects, constrains, reorganizes. What begins as a temporary survival strategy becomes a lasting architecture of identity and behavior. These structures, formed in the name of safety, can become prisons of repetition. In the next chapter, *Circles of Survival*, we will explore how these adaptive formations crystallize into roles, beliefs, and relational patterns that shape our lives, often long after the original danger has passed. It is here, within these circles, that the echoes live. And from here, that the journey of reorganization must begin.

CHAPTER FOURTEEN

Circles of Survival: The Loop of Repetition

"We repeat what we do not repeat."

— Christine Langley-Obaugh

Every human being carries within them an unfinished story.

These are the stories that never had an ending, moments that were too overwhelming, too fast, too confusing to be fully processed when they happened. And so, the body held them. The psyche tucked them away. And the system reorganized around the rupture, not as a failure, but as a creative act of survival. But what is not metabolized does not disappear. It waits.

It returns not as memory, but as pattern. As tension in the body. As emotional intensity. As a repeated dynamic in relationships. As compulsive behavior. These repetitions are not accidents. They are the system's attempt to complete what was never completed. To make meaning of what had none. To restore coherence where fragmentation once took root.

From the outside, this might look like self-sabotage or "being stuck." But from the inside, it is the loop, the circle of survival, repeating over and over again, trying to find the missing piece that would let it rest. It is the psyche's way of asking: *Can I finish this now? Can I finally be seen here?*

In this chapter, we explore how these loops form, how they are held in body and behavior, and how they shape the landscape of a person's life—physiologically, psychologically, and relationally. We'll look at how the repetition compulsion emerges from the interplay of developmental rupture and the system's intelligent reorganization, and how the loop moves between reactivity and proactivity in search of resolution. And finally, we'll see how the loop is not an enemy to be fought, but a message to be understood—a map that, once decoded, can point the way back to wholeness.

Repetition as Self-Organization Around Fragmentation

When experiences fail to be fully integrated, especially those involving rupture, unmet need, or trauma, the psyche does not simply forget or move on. Instead, what cannot be digested becomes embedded in the field of the body as implicit patterns of sensation, affect, and expectation. These undigested fragments exist outside narrative memory. They are not stories, but unspoken impressions that live beneath words and cognition.

From the perspective of coherogenesis, the system must still organize itself, even in fragmentation. It does so by looping. Without adequate containment or symbolic representation, overwhelming experiences remain frozen, sensorial residues that are neither metabolized nor fully repressed. The psyche, seeking resolution, unconsciously re-enacts aspects of the original situation. These repetitions are not masochistic. They are not flaws. They are the system's intelligent attempt to recreate the conditions for a different outcome, to generate a context in which what was once too much can finally be held.

This is the essence of repetition compulsion: a looping strategy aimed at coherence. It is an attempt to integrate what lacked a witness, to symbolically master what was once unendurable. But because these patterns operate beneath awareness, they often bypass conscious choice. Instead of responding freshly to the present moment, the individual relives the past—through relationships, choices, habits, and internal narratives. Each repetition is the psyche's call for resolution, repeating the unanswered question until it finds a new answer.

Reactive and Proactive Self-States: Two Poles of the Loop

In the wake of unintegrated experience, the psyche often polarizes into two broad adaptive tendencies: *reactivity* and *proactivity*. These are not merely emotional responses, but entire modes of being—affective tones, physiological states, and patterned behaviors. They form a loop: an inner pendulum swinging between collapse and control, helplessness and hyperfunction.

Proactive states emerge when the system attempts to stay ahead of pain. This includes over-control, perfectionism, people-pleasing, chronic hypervigilance, and compulsive caretaking. These self-states are constructed around anticipation, efforts to prevent rupture by shaping the environment. But these strategies are often rooted in early survival adaptations, not current truth. Over time, they become rigid, exhaustive, and unsustainable.

Reactive states emerge when proactivity fails. When the system cannot maintain its anticipatory control or when triggers bypass its defenses, the unresolved material floods in. This is where collapse, rage, withdrawal, dissociation, panic, or somatic overwhelm surface. Reactivity is the fall after the over-functioning climb. It is the return of what the proactive state could not hold off.

This looping dynamic creates a double bind. The proactive state tightens in an effort to stay safe. The reactive state emerges when that effort fails. And so the cycle continues not because the self is broken, but because the self is still searching for the conditions in which it can finally be held, seen, and reorganized.

This looping is not merely psychological. It is physiological. The nervous system learns the loop: alternating sympathetic arousal and parasympathetic collapse. The HPA axis is entrained by chronic stress anticipation and crash. The gut-brain axis follows suit, with motility, appetite, and microbiome balance mirroring emotional tone. Over time, the loop becomes a lifestyle—internalized as identity, shaped by old events, but mistaken as one's nature.

The Lifestyle of the Loop

Over time, the repetition compulsion doesn't just manifest in isolated relational patterns or emotional responses, it becomes an architecture for living. What began as an unconscious loop of unresolved experience begins to structure lifestyle itself. The loop becomes the blueprint not only for how we relate to others, but for how we eat, move, rest, strive, and search for meaning. The result is a life shaped around avoidance, survival, or compensation rather than wholeness. We begin to live according to the pattern, not the present.

The loop does more than shape behavior, it sculpts identity. Over time, the repetition of survival-based responses becomes internalized as personality. When asked who they are, many describe their compulsions: "I'm a perfectionist," "I'm always busy," "I can't sit still," "I need to take care of everyone." These aren't expressions of essence but adaptations, roles rehearsed so often they've become mistaken for the self. The system orients around the loop as if it were truth, organizing experience to confirm its necessity.

This can be clearly seen when we examine lifestyle through the lens of the **WELLNESSs** framework:

Work (Occupation, Academics, and Health Maintenance): Work and productivity often become proxies for safety or worth. A hyperactive loop may drive overworking, people-pleasing, or perfectionism. A hypoactive loop may lead to avoidance, procrastination, or disorganization. Even health-related tasks, like attending appointments or taking medications, may be shaped by the loop's narrative (e.g., "I don't deserve care").

Exercise: Movement may become compulsive, driven by anxiety or body shame, or avoided altogether due to trauma, disconnection, or fatigue. The loop distorts movement into something to endure or control, rather than a means of inhabiting and honoring the body.

Leisure (Recreation, Recovery, Relaxation, Fueling): Play, rest, and restoration often become inaccessible. In proactive loops, individuals may feel guilty when not being productive, while reactive loops may collapse into numbing or disengagement. Leisure is no longer a space of joy but a battleground between exhaustion and permission.

Love (Relationships): Subpersonalities forged in early patterns, such as the appeaser, the defender, or the invisible one, emerge in adult relational roles. These roles aim to prevent abandonment, manage conflict, or control intimacy. Relationships become organized around protecting old wounds rather than fostering genuine connection. One may over-function to stay needed, under-function to avoid rejection, or replay cycles of attachment and rupture.

Nutrition: Eating patterns often mirror the loop's efforts to regulate the internal state. Proactive loops may impose rigid control (e.g., restrictive diets, over-reliance on supplements), while reactive loops tend toward chaotic or emotionally driven eating. Food becomes a coping mechanism rather than a source of nourishment.

Environment: The physical and sensory environment can reflect and reinforce inner fragmentation. A cluttered, chaotic space may mirror disorganization and overwhelm; an overly sterile or controlled space may represent attempts to manage anxiety or unpredictability. The loop seeks environmental alignment with its internal narrative, either amplifying vigilance or numbing awareness.

Sleep: Rest may feel unsafe. Hyperaroused systems (proactive loops) often experience insomnia or restless nights, while hypoaroused systems (reactive loops) may retreat into dissociative sleep marked by excessive fatigue, nightmares, or difficulty waking. The body isn't resting, it's surviving through shutdown or alertness.

Substances: From caffeine and sugar to alcohol, medications, and illicit drugs, substances are often used to buffer the extremes of the loop, whether anxious overactivation or depressive collapse. Though offering short-term relief, these strategies tend to deepen the loop over time, reinforcing dysregulation and dependence.

Spiritual Practice: Disconnection from wholeness often brings about spiritual disorientation. Some pursue transcendence as a means of escape, while others avoid spiritual engagement altogether. Practices meant to foster presence may become infused with bypassing or rigidity. Authentic spirituality—a felt sense of meaning, presence, or sacredness—is distorted by unresolved internal loops.

Each of these lifestyle domains becomes an echo of the unresolved inner pattern. What was once a survival-based inner loop becomes an outer rhythm that shapes everyday behavior, often invisibly. The nervous system, subpersonalities, beliefs, and habits all conspire to maintain a predictable inner world, even if it's painful. When this predictable inner world is shaken, reactivity emerges as a means to restore these rhythms.

When viewed through this lens, lifestyle is not merely behavioral, it is a somatic biography of the self's attempt to protect, preserve, and make sense of fragmentation. These patterns do not emerge from failure or weakness, but from the profound intelligence of a system trying to survive.

Physiological Resonance

Because this loop emerges from a survival response, it leaves an unmistakable imprint on the body. Repetition compulsion is not just a psychological cycle, it is a full-bodied physiological rhythm.

The autonomic nervous system adapts to the loop by narrowing its window of tolerance. In proactive states, sympathetic arousal dominates: elevated cortisol, heart rate variability suppression, shallow breathing, chronic muscle tension. The body prepares for action and threat, even in the absence of danger.

In reactive states, sympathetic arousal peaks and often shifts to parasympathetic dominance, particularly in dorsal vagal collapse. This results in fatigue, disengagement, low motivation, and disrupted immune function. The system toggles between these states with little capacity for regulation. This is not a failure of willpower, but a reflection of the nervous system's training in unrepaired threat.

Other physiological systems follow suit:

- The **endocrine system** adopts a rhythm of hyperproduction followed by crash, affecting metabolism, energy, and reproductive function.

- The **immune system** becomes sensitized, triggering inflammatory responses even to minor stimuli, or suppressing reactivity altogether.

- The **digestive system** responds with slowed motility, bloating, or food reactivity, especially when the gut becomes the body's holding place for unprocessed stress.

In this way, repetition becomes embedded, not only in behavior and thought, but in the biological infrastructure of the self. The body learns the loop. And because the body holds memory more deeply than the mind, breaking the cycle requires not only awareness, but a new pattern of being in the body itself.

The False Promise of Completion

At the heart of repetition compulsion lies a paradox: the drive to resolve what was never resolved by recreating the original conditions of rupture. The psyche longs to master what overwhelmed it, to turn a wound into a story, a trauma into meaning. But in the absence of new awareness or containment, this reenactment rarely leads to integration. Instead, it reinforces the very pattern it seeks to complete.

This is the false promise of completion, the unconscious hope that "this time it will be different," that a partner will finally stay, a parent will finally approve, a goal will finally soothe the ache. But the loop is not designed to resolve. It is designed to preserve coherence by avoiding the original pain. Without presence, compassion, flow, and curiosity, each reenactment becomes a deeper entrenchment. Like trying to fill a well with a sieve, no amount of repetition can substitute for the integration that never originally occurred.

Completion cannot be found by continuing to act within the loop. It is like remaining on stage, endlessly performing a role in a play whose script was written long ago. True healing begins when we step off the stage and, perhaps for the first time, glimpse the projector casting the scenes, the pulleys behind the curtains, the mechanisms that have kept the drama running. It is only by exiting the performance, by returning to the missing feeling, unmet need, or unresolved moment and offering it the presence it once lacked that the system can update its map of safety and reality. In this turning toward what was hidden, we no longer rehearse the past, we rewrite it.

Interrupting the Loop

Interrupting the repetition compulsion is not an act of force, but an act of awareness. The loop is driven by automaticity. To interrupt it is to bring what is automatic into the light of conscious choice and response-ability.

This begins with **recognition**: noticing the pattern without judgment. Where do I feel stuck? Where am I chasing something old? What part of me is trying to protect something younger, more vulnerable?

Next is **deceleration**. The loop moves fast, emotionally, cognitively, behaviorally. Slowing down allows space for curiosity. It's in the pause that we can recognize the familiar pull and choose not to follow it.

Then comes **reconnection**. This means re-engaging with the body, breath, and present moment. It means finding regulation through co-regulation or self-regulation. The nervous system must feel safe enough to allow new responses to emerge.

Finally, **represencing**: choosing a different action, a different thought, a different way of being, no matter how small, that affirms life, connection, and coherence. This isn't about perfection or immediate resolution. It's about choosing response over repetition.

Every interruption is an act of integration. It says to the loop: "You do not define me. I am here now."

Closing Reflection and Invitation

Each of us carries circles within, patterns spun from unspoken pain, unmet needs, and unwitnessed moments. These loops of repetition are not flaws. They are intelligent survival maps, drawn by a self trying to preserve coherence at any cost. But survival is not the same as wholeness.

The moment we recognize the loop is the moment we begin to step out of it. Not by condemning the parts that formed it, but by welcoming them back into the living field of presence. Integration does not erase the past. It reclaims it. You are not your loop. You are the space in which the loop is seen, felt, and transformed.

So, I invite you to pause the next time a familiar pattern arises. Feel into it. Ask it what it wants you to know. Offer it presence. And choose not perfectly, but intentionally to interrupt the circle. This is not the end. It's the beginning of a new path.

Key Takeaways: Circles of Survival

- Repetition compulsion arises when experiences remain unintegrated and symbolically unresolved, especially after trauma or unmet needs.

- The psyche seeks coherence by reenacting past wounds, hoping unconsciously for a different outcome.

- These loops become embodied, showing up in nervous system patterns, physiological rhythms, subpersonalities, and lifestyle choices.

- Through the WeLLNESSs framework, we see how loops shape domains of living: relationships, work, eating, sleep, spirituality, and more.

- The false promise of completion perpetuates the loop, true healing comes from presence, not reenactment.

- Interrupting the loop requires slowing down, recognizing patterns, regulating the nervous system, and choosing new responses.

- Loops are not broken by shame or effort, but by presence, compassion, and curiosity, the same pervading qualities that define wholeness.

- Integration is not fixing, but welcoming back what was left out.

The loops we live, our patterns of reaction, protection, and survival, are not only personal, but are often named, pathologized, and categorized within systems of diagnosis. Yet these diagnoses, while offering language and structure, often fail to capture the deeper logic of these loops. They overlook the origins, the contexts, and the layered adaptations that give rise to them. As we shift from viewing these patterns as isolated pathologies to recognizing them as coherent responses within an unfolding developmental field, a new possibility emerges: understanding diagnosis not as a static label, but as a doorway. *Beyond the Label* invites us to reimagine psychiatric diagnosis through this holistic lens, where even our most painful symptoms point not to disorder, but to unintegrated coherence—waiting to be seen, heard, and held.

CHAPTER FIFTEEN

Beyond the Label: Reframing Psychiatric Diagnosis

"We are not disturbed by things, but by the views we take of things."

— Epictetus

In modern psychiatry, diagnosis is often considered the first step toward understanding. It provides a shared language for clinicians, a means of accessing treatment, and a framework for organizing distress. Yet for many individuals, receiving a diagnosis feels less like clarity and more like containment, a naming that reduces their lived experience to a static label. It offers a category but rarely offers meaning. It identifies symptoms but often misses story. It tracks dysfunction but fails to capture coherence.

The Diagnostic and Statistical Manual of Mental Disorders (DSM), now in its fifth edition, has become the dominant tool for psychiatric classification. It defines mental disorders through clusters of symptoms that must be observed for a certain duration and interfere with functioning. This checklist model has brought standardization and research utility, but it also carries significant limitations: heterogeneity (people with the same diagnosis may share few symptoms), overlap (the same symptom may appear in multiple disorders), and a lack of etiology (it tells us what but not why). It often fails to account for context and physiological dysregulation. And it leaves out the most important question: *what is this symptom trying to express?*

From the perspective of the coherent self, as explored through the unitive, sensorial, symbolic, and patterned layers, diagnosis in the DSM is like looking into a fractured mirror. Each shard reflects a part of the experience, but none shows the whole. The symptom is real, but it is not the source. The diagnosis is descriptive, not explanatory. In this model, psychiatric symptoms are not isolated problems but expressions of a system attempting to maintain coherence in the face of fragmentation.

This chapter proposes a new view: one in which diagnosis becomes a trailhead, not a destination, a pattern of disruption pointing toward a deeper story of survival, disconnection, and the longing for wholeness. It reframes symptoms not as errors but as intelligible, meaningful signals of a system doing its best to adapt. It sees depression, anxiety, psychosis, and other conditions not as fixed diseases but as reflections of how the self has organized around the experience of overwhelm, rupture, and unmet need. What if the goal of diagnosis was not classification, but connection?

The Problem with the Map: Limitations of the DSM

The DSM offers a map, but not the territory. Its categories are based on surface observations, clusters of behaviors, emotions, and thoughts that co-occur frequently enough to justify a label. But when we look more closely, we find a model that catalogues symptoms without understanding origins, that labels complexity without offering coherence.

Symptoms are not fixed entities; they evolve as the individual evolves. What begins as panic may later appear as fatigue. What was once externalized through anger may become internalized as shame. Medication regimens often shift accordingly, not necessarily because the original diagnosis was incorrect, but because the system is in motion. From a coherogenetic lens, this movement is not random but purposeful: the human system is always attempting to restore balance, to metabolize what could not yet be integrated. Each change in presentation is not a sign of failure, but an expression of the psyche's ongoing dialogue with wholeness.

A core limitation is heterogeneity. Two people diagnosed with the same disorder, such as major depressive disorder, may share only one or two overlapping symptoms. One person might present with irritability, insomnia, and guilt, while another exhibits psychomotor retardation, hypersomnia, and hopelessness. The diagnostic label suggests sameness, but their inner worlds and histories may be entirely different.

Next is comorbidity, the high rate of individuals meeting criteria for multiple disorders. Trauma survivors, for instance, often receive a cascade of diagnoses across time: anxiety, depression, PTSD, borderline personality disorder, dissociative identity disorder. From a DSM lens, this looks like

213

complexity or treatment resistance. From a holistic lens, it looks like a system organized around fragmentation, expressing itself across layers: sensorial dysregulation, symbolic injury, patterned roles of protection and defense.

Then there's lack of etiology. DSM diagnoses are agnostic to cause. They do not differentiate between a depressive state resulting from nutrient deficiency, thyroid dysfunction, unresolved grief, chronic invalidation, or developmental trauma. Yet these origins call for very different approaches to healing. Without understanding why a pattern exists, we cannot effectively support its transformation.

The DSM also fails to account for context. It tends to locate the problem within the individual, ignoring the relational, cultural, physiological, and environmental ecosystems in which suffering arises. It does not ask: *What happened to you? What did you have to become in order to survive? What has not yet been heard, held, or metabolized?*

In this way, the DSM medicalizes survival, turning adaptive responses into pathologies. But what if anxiety is not a disorder, but the body's attempt to stay alert in a world it perceives as unsafe? What if depression is not a defect, but the collapse that follows chronic hypervigilance and relational aloneness? What if psychosis is not madness, but the symbolic overflow of a system trying to metabolize what has never been named?

To be clear, this is not a dismissal of diagnosis. There is value in shared language, in naming suffering, in finding common ground for treatment. But diagnosis must evolve. It must become a doorway, not a destination. A question, not a conclusion. A mirror that reflects wholeness in disguise.

Trauma as the Hidden Organizer

Beneath the surface expressions of many psychiatric diagnoses lies a deeper architecture, trauma. Not necessarily trauma in the narrow sense of catastrophic events, but in the broader, developmental sense: disruptions in attunement, unmet needs, misattunement, abandonment, neglect, violation, and overwhelm. These experiences do not always leave visible scars, but they shape the internal landscape of the self.

Trauma reorganizes the field. It shapes the flow of energy and information within the system. From the perspective of a holistic model, trauma is not simply something that happened in the past. It is a current pattern of organization, a system-wide adaptation that emerges in response to a perceived or actual threat to coherence. It shows up as disconnection, rigidity, fragmentation, or over-identification with protective roles. These are not symptoms to be eliminated, but intelligences to be understood.

In this view, psychiatric diagnoses are clustered echoes of how the self has reorganized around disconnection.

- **Anxiety** often reflects a nervous system on high alert, scanning for danger, living in the aftermath of uncertainty or relational unreliability.

- **Depression** may be the consequence of chronic emotional suppression, loss of connection, or internalized despair after failed attempts at relational repair.

- **ADHD** may express the adaptive need to move, shift, and orient in an environment that was overstimulating or unsafe to settle within.

- **Bipolarity** can reflect alternating states of mobilization and collapse, symbolic of a self trying to assert agency after periods of immobilization or powerlessness.

- **Personality disorders** reflect patterned adaptations in how the self learned to survive relationship (through control, withdrawal, merging, or splitting) often beginning before memory.

- **Psychosis** may be an overflow of symbolic and affective content that could not be contained or symbolized in earlier layers, an attempt at coherence when the symbolic field was ruptured.

This model suggests that rather than being discrete diseases, these diagnoses are expressions of where and how the self is organized. What layer it is functioning from, where development was disrupted, and how the system is attempting to maintain continuity under duress.

Trauma is often the hidden hand shaping these structures. Not in a simplistic, reductionist way, but as a field-level influence, distorting how sensations, symbols, meanings, and roles are woven. The DSM often treats these distortions as primary disorders. But they are secondary organizations around a primary rupture: the eclipse of presence, the freezing of potential, the loss of relational safety. To work only at the level of the label is to treat the echo without listening for the original sound.

A Model of Meaning: Reweaving Wholeness through Coherence

In contrast to models that classify and separate, this holistic framework seeks to integrate and contextualize. It does

216

not ask, *"What diagnosis fits?"* but rather, *"What has happened, where did the thread fray, and how is the self now trying to reweave coherence?"* This shift marks a departure from symptom-focused categorization toward a process-oriented understanding of meaning.

At the heart of this model lies the idea of coherogenesis, the unfolding of the self through dynamic self-organization in response to inner and outer conditions. Every symptom is part of a greater pattern, an adaptive attempt at maintaining coherence in the face of overwhelm, fragmentation, or unmet need. What psychiatry labels as disorder, this model understands as patterned compensation.

Rather than fragmenting the person into diagnostic silos, this perspective sees symptoms, behaviors, and traits as layered expressions of the self, each emerging from distinct phases of development:

- Some reflect ruptures in the **sensorial field**—unintegrated bodily experiences, dysregulation, and overwhelm.

- Others reveal disruptions in the **symbolic field**—distorted meanings, frozen narratives, and disembodied language.

- Still others point to rigidifications in the **patterned field**—roles, identities, and defenses locked in survival-mode repetition.

Diagnosis, then, becomes less a matter of naming pathology and more an act of pattern recognition, seeing how and where the self is organized, which layers are accessible or defended, and what is seeking reintegration. It is a map of where the light

217

of consciousness has been eclipsed and where the invitation of healing lies.

This model offers a living diagnostic process rooted in presence, not reduction. It asks clinicians and individuals alike to track patterns, not categories; to listen to the body as deeply as the narrative; and to attune to the field as much as the form. In this way, treatment becomes not a technical fix, but a collaborative unfolding, a return to the ground of being through the relational field.

In practice, this means:

- Shifting from labeling disorders to listening for developmental ruptures and unmet needs.

- Prioritizing coherence over symptom suppression.

- Viewing physiological, psychological, and relational data as interconnected expressions of the same field.

- Facilitating integration through presence, compassion, flow, and curiosity, not simply through correction.

The person is not a diagnostic entity. They are an ocean of lived patterns, shaped by waves of experience, always capable of reorganizing around deeper truths.

A New Kind of Precision: Contextualizing Symptoms and Systems

The promise of psychiatric diagnosis has always been precision: the ability to identify, categorize, and treat specific conditions with clarity and reliability. Yet, in practice, the DSM's categorical approach often leads to the opposite: ambiguity, overlap, and fragmentation. This model proposes a new kind of precision, one that does not rest on rigid categories, but on contextual coherence.

Rather than starting with symptoms and fitting them into predefined boxes, this approach asks: Where did the disorganization begin, and what developmental or relational conditions shaped this response?

Precision, in this model, is not about naming disorders but about tracing patterns across multiple dimensions:

- **Physiological** (e.g., nervous system dysregulation, HPA axis activation, hormonal imbalance, metabolic disturbance, gut-brain imbalance, immune compromise)

- **Developmental** (e.g., disruptions in containment, symbolic representation, identity formation)

- **Relational** (e.g., unmet needs, misattunement, trauma, role rigidity)

- **Experiential** (e.g., states of overwhelm, fragmentation, dissociation, repetition)

For example, what psychiatry might call Generalized Anxiety Disorder becomes, in this view, a repetitive patterned response of hypervigilance, often rooted in disrupted sensorial containment and unresolved relational threat. Depression may be understood not as a chemical imbalance, but as collapsed symbolic energy, frozen affect, or a shut-down physiological state following chronic misattunement, loss, or survival fatigue. ADHD may reflect an oscillation between proactive overfunctioning and reactive disorganization, shaped by a fragmented patterned self lacking integration between internal systems of regulation.

This model honors the underlying intelligence of symptoms, they are not errors, but attempts at coherence within the conditions that shaped them. Such precision calls for attuned listening, not just to what the individual says, but to what their body organizes around, what their patterns of speech, posture, physiology, and emotional tone reveal. It involves mapping across layers:

- Is the nervous system flexible or rigid?

- Are relational templates fluid or defensive?

- Are symbolic systems open to reimagining, or trapped in repetition?

- Is there a felt sense of presence, or is the system still caught in the eclipse?

This is precision without reduction. It is an integrative, non-fragmenting lens that honors the complexity of the person, the intelligence of their adaptations, and the layered nature of their being.

In this framework, healing becomes less about symptom elimination and more about restoring relational, sensorial, symbolic, and physiological coherence. It is not a technical fix, it is a living process of attunement, reorganization, and return.

Wholeness Over Homogeneity: Embracing Variability, Expression, and Depth

In the conventional diagnostic model, sameness is prized. Homogeneity, the idea that people with the same label should look and respond similarly, drives research protocols, treatment plans, and the desire for "clinical clarity." Yet, real

220

human beings are anything but homogeneous. Two people with the same diagnosis may look entirely different, one driven, the other withdrawn; one anxious and hypervigilant, the other flat and dissociated.

This variability is not a problem to be ironed out, it is the very signature of a living system adapting to its unique context. From the perspective of this model, variability is expected, even essential. What is shared is not the specific symptom, but the patterned disruption in coherence and the field conditions that led to it.

This approach replaces the ideal of diagnostic uniformity with a deeper commitment to wholeness. Wholeness is not about being symptom-free. It is about reconnection between parts of the self, between the self and the body, between the individual and their symbolic, sensorial, and patterned world. It is about moving from fragmentation to integration.

A diagnosis in the DSM may stop at the naming of dysfunction. A model of wholeness asks deeper questions:

- What has been lost or split off?

- What is the system attempting to protect or communicate?

- What kind of holding environment is needed to support reintegration?

- How do symptoms reflect not just individual pathology but systemic, cultural, and relational fields?

This model acknowledges that symptoms often carry wisdom. They are metaphors for unspoken truths, protectors of unbearable pain, creative solutions to unmanageable contradiction. Rather than rushing to eliminate them, we are invited to learn from them.

In practice, this means therapy is not a process of containment alone, but of expansion: making room for more of the self to be held, more of the truth to be known. It is a process of cultivating internal spaciousness, where contradiction and complexity are not seen as diagnostic dilemmas, but as signs of a living, dynamic psyche.

Where the DSM seeks consistency, this model honors the living pulse of paradox. A person can be anxious and numb, expansive and defended, functional and deeply wounded. These are not contradictions to resolve, but realities to hold in compassionate awareness.

True precision, then, is not about arriving at the "right" label, but learning to attune to the complexity of the human experience without needing to simplify it. It is about choosing wholeness over homogeneity, depth over tidiness, and complexity over control.

A Living Diagnostic Field: Reconceptualizing the Role of the Clinician

In this model, diagnosis is not a static event but a living, breathing process. An unfolding field of meaning. The clinician is no longer a technician applying predefined criteria to determine what's "wrong." Instead, they are a field participant, co-regulating, attuning, and making meaning in real-time with the person before them.

The diagnostic process becomes a relational inquiry, grounded not in objectivity-as-distance but in presence,

222

compassion, curiosity, and flow. It honors the clinician's subjectivity, not as bias to be eliminated, but as an instrument of resonance. Diagnosis is no longer simply about identifying a category, it is about recognizing the energetic configuration of the self, the coherence of the person's system in context, and the underlying intelligence driving their symptoms.

From this perspective:

- A clinician listens not only for what is said but how it is said, when it is withheld, and how it lands in the room.

- They track nonverbal fields such as tension in the voice, somatic shifts, and pauses in narrative as expressions of deeper organizing patterns.

- They approach every symptom not as pathology to be removed, but as a portal. An invitation to understand the system's attempt at protection, communication, or coherence.

This does not mean abandoning structure. It means using structure in service of connection, not control. Frameworks become maps, not prisons. Guiding curiosity, not foreclosing possibility. Language becomes fluid, evolving in dialogue with the person's own metaphors, meaning-making, and developmental stage.

A living diagnostic field does not ask, "What diagnosis fits this person?" but:

- "What is trying to emerge here?"

- "How has this person organized themselves around unmet need or unresolved rupture?"

- "What layer of self is this symptom arising from (unitive, sensorial, symbolic, or patterned)?"

- "How can I meet them at that layer, not just with intervention, but with attunement?"

In this way, the role of the clinician shifts from diagnostician to witness, collaborator, and guide. Their work is not simply to treat the problem, but to support the unfolding of the person's coherence—across layers, through trauma, within complexity.

When we meet the diagnostic process this way, we open the door not just to more effective care, but to a radical reclamation of the therapeutic encounter itself: not as a place to define what's wrong, but as a sacred space where wholeness is remembered, one layer at a time.

Conclusion

In reimagining diagnosis through the lens of the coherent self, we move beyond fragmented categories and toward a view of wholeness in process. Diagnosis is no longer a label imposed from outside, but a reflection of how the system has adapted, survived, and expressed its unmet needs. Within this model, psychiatric symptoms are no longer fixed traits but emergent properties: signals shaped by trauma, filtered through developmental layers, and patterned through physiology, behavior, and belief.

This perspective invites a shift from pathologizing to understanding, from control to curiosity, and from rigid classification to living context. By considering the whole (layered self, trauma history, physiologic expression, lifestyle patterns, and the presence of consciousness itself) we return diagnosis to its rightful place: as a tool for compassion, integration, and transformation.

Reflective Invitation

As you reflect on your own relationship to diagnosis whether as a clinician, individual, or seeker consider the following:

- What stories have you internalized about what a diagnosis means?

- How might your symptoms reflect unmet needs, unintegrated parts, or earlier ruptures?

- What would it be like to see your patterns not as flaws, but as intelligent adaptations to your environment?

- What layer of your experience (unitive, sensorial, symbolic, or patterned) might be asking for attention?

Pause with presence. Let compassion soften what judgment once held. Allow curiosity to open what has been closed. In this space, the diagnostic becomes dialogic, a co-created inquiry into the truth of what is becoming.

Key Takeaways: Beyond the Label

- Conventional diagnosis (e.g., DSM) tends to be categorical, symptom-focused, and disconnected from etiology, development, and lived context.

- This model views diagnosis as an emergent pattern shaped by trauma, experience, physiology, and mutual process across layered development (unitive, sensorial, symbolic, patterned).

- Symptoms reflect adaptive responses, not fixed disorders. They arise from efforts toward coherence in the face of overwhelm or unmet need.

- Diagnostic heterogeneity and overlap are natural in trauma-informed models, where diverse expressions emerge from shared roots in disconnection and protective reorganization.

- Lifestyle, physiological systems, and relational context are essential to understanding and working with psychiatric patterns.

- Clinicians are participants in a living diagnostic field, engaging with presence, attunement, and inquiry rather than objective categorization.

- Healing begins with coherence, not correction, welcoming all parts of the self, reconnecting to presence, and allowing the system to reorganize around integration rather than survival.

If diagnosis reveals the contours of our fragmentation, it also invites a deeper question: what lies beneath the label? Beyond symptom clusters and surface categories, there are rhythms and disruptions embedded in the body itself, patterns not only of thought and behavior, but of breath, hormone, inflammation, and nerve. The path of return does not bypass the physical; it moves through it. In this next chapter, we turn our attention to the physiological dimension of coherogenesis, to how the body remembers, responds, and reorganizes. For coherence is not solely a psychological integration, but a biological one as well. To heal is to include the body in the story of return.

CHAPTER SIXTEEN

The Role of Physiology in Coherogenesis

"The mind is not confined to the brain but is distributed throughout the body."

— Antonio Damasio

In a coherogenic framework, physiology is not a separate layer; it is an expression of the same field of unfolding experience. Just as a person may develop symbolic meanings and patterned behaviors to navigate early environments, so too does the body develop physiological responses that reflect those same organizing principles.

The patterned layer is especially significant here, it is where diagnosis congeals. In other words, the bodymind's adaptive responses become structured and repetitive enough to meet criteria that can be named, categorized, and often pathologized. This congealing reflects the point at which protective patterns, emotional, cognitive, behavioral, and physiological, have become stable enough to hold form. It is also where the clinical gaze most commonly lands. It is where symptoms are objectified and named (e.g., depression, IBS, ADHD, etc.). Interventions are matched to the "problem". In this domain, labs often validate a diagnostic category or quantify dysfunction resulting in a top-down focus (e.g., symptom, name, treat). Yet this is only the surface layer of a deeper developmental narrative.

- The body as pattern-bearer: physiology stores and expresses repeated energetic, relational, and behavioral themes.

- Disruption as signal: physiological incoherence is a signpost of blocked energy, unresolved experience, or protective adaptation.

- Lab data as echoes of story: values are not random, they mirror the bodymind's attempt to stay coherent under conditions of fragmentation.

This means interventions must support, not override, the system's own drive toward reorganization.

Functional Testing: A Portal Between Layers

Functional testing occupies a unique space in the coherogenic model. Unlike conventional diagnostics, which often focus on disease states and categorical pathology (e.g., major depression, hypothyroidism), functional testing reflects emerging patterns of incoherence before full-blown disease manifests. This includes markers of mitochondrial strain, dysbiosis, neurotransmitter imbalance, detoxification burden, hormonal shifts, and more.

As such, functional testing exists in a liminal space:

228

- It touches the patterned layer when its findings begin to correlate with stable symptom clusters.

- It gestures toward the sensorial by revealing disruptions in the lived processes of digestion, sleep, energy production, inflammation, and stress response.

- It may indirectly reflect symbolic burdens such as nutrient depletions or hormonal patterns emerging from long-held psychological or relational roles.

Functional labs, then, are best understood as mirrors of the terrain, offering glimpses into how early or ongoing experiences have shaped the body's internal landscape. They reveal the bioenergetic cost of symbolic or patterned survival strategies. They track how unresolved or unintegrated experience echoes into physiology before it becomes disease. And they operate across the threshold between sensorial and patterned organization.

Functional labs are like tide pools exposed between waves revealing what lives just beneath the surface of a patterned self, before it returns to the vastness of embodied flow. They offer temporary glimpses into the invisible choreography of adaptation beneath diagnostic form.

Rethinking Laboratory Testing

In this model, lab interpretation becomes less about "normal" vs. "abnormal" and more about attuning to the narrative of the system.

- High cortisol may not simply indicate stress, but a hypervigilant patterned self that never felt safe.

- Low free T3 may suggest not just thyroid dysregulation, but chronic withdrawal from embodied presence.

- Low DHEA and flat cortisol could reflect long-standing energetic collapse consistent with early freeze states or symbolic depletion from adaptive over-functioning.

Clinicians ask not just "What is wrong?" but "What is trying to happen here that is being blocked?" and "What layer of the self is calling for coherence?"

Likewise, understanding this liminal role prevents the misuse of functional tests as just better "diagnostics". Instead of reinforcing fragmentation (e.g., low DHEA = adrenal fatigue = supplement "X"), the clinician can listen more deeply:

- Where is the body trying to reorganize?

- What unconscious pattern might be exhausting this system?

- How can I support re-patterning without bypassing deeper layers?

Labs are not external impositions, but relational tools that help re-tune a complex field toward its own deeper order. For example, the standard view on an elevated c-reactive protein is "inflammation" and the treatment aim is to suppress it. From the view of coherogenesis, the system is signaling a prolonged, unresolved demand; perhaps sensorial, symbolic, or patterned. The inflammation is not the root problem, it is pointing toward a deeper misalignment.

Pharmaceuticals as Temporary Resonators

Pharmaceutical agents, too, are reframed in this model. Instead of being seen as permanent fixes or mere symptom suppressors, medications are viewed as temporary supports that stabilize the system enough to allow for deeper coherence to emerge.

Appropriate use includes:

- Reducing noise in a fragmented system so presence can be accessed.

- Modulating activation when a person is stuck in sensorimotor overwhelm.

- Supporting symbolic access (e.g., emotional integration) when depression or anxiety are too intense.

Caution is exercised when medications risk overriding the bodymind's signal or sustaining an artificial balance that prevents deeper healing. The goal is always to support the natural intelligence of the system, not silence it.

Nutraceuticals as Terrain Modulators

Nutraceuticals are similarly recontextualized not as replacements for pharmaceuticals or band-aid solutions, but as modulators of terrain. They gently influence the physiology to support the conditions necessary for re-patterning and reintegration. Their use may be guided by the phase of development and the active layer of self-expression. What matters most is that these tools are chosen not to chase numbers, but to support coherence.

231

From Intervention to Resonance: A Clinical Reorientation

Every tool (lab, pharmaceutical, or supplement) becomes a point of contact between clinician and field. The aim is not to correct, but to co-attune. The practitioner listens with the same quality of presence that guides therapy: sensing the system's direction, honoring its intelligence, and offering only what facilitates the next unfolding.

Clinical Guiding Questions:

- What is this lab result pointing to in the larger field of experience?

- What layer (sensorial, symbolic, patterned) is most activated or blocked?

- How can this intervention support, not bypass, coherence?

- Is the system ready to reorganize, or does it need stabilization first?

Conclusion: Listening Through the Body

In the coherogenic view, physiology is not secondary to mind, nor merely the substrate of symptoms. It is a voice in the chorus of becoming. Functional data, pharmaceuticals, and nutraceuticals are instruments, not solutions. When used wisely, they amplify the system's own music, guiding it back to a resonance that was always possible, but often forgotten. In this way, the clinician becomes not an engineer fixing parts, but a facilitator of coherence, helping the bodymind remember itself as whole.

The body, in all its complexity, is not merely a vessel for experience, it is a participant in coherence, a living system through which the Self pulses and responds. As we've seen, physiology does not sit outside our stories of trauma and transformation; it carries them, expresses them, and, when conditions allow, helps to reweave them. But integration is not achieved by understanding alone. Beyond insight and intervention lies a deeper invitation: to descend into presence. Part IV marks a shift, not away from physiology, but through it, toward a more intimate encounter with the layers of human experiencing. Here, we begin the return. Not as a retreat to what once was, but as a re-inhabiting of what has always been. Each chapter is a tide, revisiting the patterned, symbolic, sensorial, and undifferentiated layers, not to analyze, but to touch them from within.

Part IV. Returning Tides: Descent Into Presence

As the wave completes its arc, we turn inward not regressing, but returning. This descent is not a fall, but a restoration. Through practices of awareness, relational presence, and inner reorganization, we revisit the patterned, symbolic, and sensorial layers—now as portals rather than prisons. Guided by coherence and compassion, we reconnect with the vitality of experience, loosen fixed identities, and reawaken embodied presence. What was eclipsed begins to shine again, not through force, but through the gentle rhythm of return.

CHAPTER SEVENTEEN

Pathways of Return

"Your conflicts, all the difficult things, the problematic situations in your life are not chance or haphazard. They are actually yours. They are specifically yours, designed specifically for you by a part of you that loves you more than anything else. The part of you that loves you more than anything else has created roadblocks to lead you to yourself. You are not going in the right direction unless there is something pricking you in the side, telling you, "Look here! This way!" That part of you loves you so much that it doesn't want you to lose the chance. It will go to extreme measures to wake you up, it will make you suffer greatly if you don't listen. What else can it do? That is its purpose."

— A.H. Almaas

After the eclipse, when the light of the self has been obscured by layers of defense, adaptation, and fragmentation, it is easy to believe that wholeness is lost. But the field never forgets.

Part IV. Returning Tides

Beneath every disturbance, the ocean still pulses. Even in the moments of greatest confusion or pain, life continues to deliver exactly what is needed. This is often not what is desired, but what is required for the reawakening of coherence. Just as waves rise and crash to stir the still depths, so too do symptoms, conflicts, and ruptures emerge not as punishments or errors, but as invitations. They are the pathways of return. Each difficult experience, each uncomfortable pattern, is the field expressing its longing for reintegration. These moments do not arrive to exile us further from the self, but to gently, or sometimes forcefully, show us the next doorway inward. The self, even when eclipsed, is never absent. And life, in its mysterious intelligence, conspires always to bring us back to it.

We are often taught to fear symptoms, to suppress conflict, to seek relief from discomfort as quickly as possible. But from the perspective of the unitary field, these disturbances are not random intrusions, they are patterned expressions of unintegrated experience. They are messages shaped by the intelligence of the system, surfacing precisely because they are ready to be met. A panic attack may not be an enemy, but the return of a long-banished part of the self pleading for attention. Chronic fatigue may carry the voice of a suppressed truth, whispering through the nervous system that something essential has been abandoned. A conflict in relationship may reenact an early relational wound, not to harm, but to offer a chance for recognition and repair.

Seen through this lens, symptoms are not merely problems to be solved, but signals to be interpreted. They emerge from the same ocean of consciousness as joy, insight, and intuition. The difference lies in our response. When met with resistance, these patterns tend to entrench. When met with
238

presence, compassion, flow, and curiosity, they begin to soften. They reorganize. They reveal the part of the self that was hidden beneath them. In this way, the content of the eclipse becomes the guide home. The very thing that obscures the light becomes the path by which it returns.

Healing does not happen in isolation, nor is it the product of sheer will. It is the unfolding of mutual process, the dynamic, co-creative dance between the self and the world, the inner field and the outer context. Just as early development was shaped in relationship, so too is reintegration. Every moment, every interaction, every pattern that surfaces is a participant in this dance. The universe, in its profound coherence, arranges the exact circumstances needed to evoke what is unresolved. Life becomes a mirror, not only of who we are, but of what we are ready to remember.

In this way, life itself acts as a co-therapist. Karen Horney, a prominent psychoanalyst, acknowledged that life itself can be a potent therapist, offering opportunities for self-discovery and change. A challenging relationship may bring forward an unintegrated attachment pattern. A period of creative stagnation may call attention to a neglected aspect of self. Even so-called setbacks such as loss, illness, and failure can serve as initiations. These are not random obstacles, but gestures from the field, presenting the next opportunity for coherence. The relational field is always working on behalf of wholeness, even when its messages are difficult to receive. When we begin to trust this process, our relationship to experience shifts. We stop asking, "Why is this happening to me?" and begin to wonder, "What is this showing me?" The system reorganizes not through force, but through attuned participation in what is already arising.

239

Part IV. Returning Tides

The path of return is not walked through strategy or control, but through orientation. Presence, compassion, flow, and curiosity are not tools to fix the self; they are how the self remembers itself. When a symptom or conflict emerges, presence allows us to pause and stay with what is rising without immediately reacting or retreating. Compassion enters as the tone of that space, warming the encounter with softness instead of resistance. It holds the space for coherence to reassemble itself. It tells the body and psyche, "This too belongs."

Flow, then, is the movement that follows attunement. Rather than rushing to interpret or resolve, flow responds moment-to-moment, sensing when to lean in, when to soften, when to rest. It adapts without grasping, just as the ocean receives each wave without holding or pushing. And curiosity, perhaps the most delicate of the four, opens a gentle doorway to inquiry: "What is this part of me trying to say?" "What is this pattern protecting?" In the presence of these qualities, the content of experience begins to shift. These moments become portals instead of problems. What was once a burden becomes a message. What was once fragmented begins to reintegrate.

These qualities are not something we must acquire, they emerge naturally when the field feels safe enough. They are the native postures of the unitary self. And when we meet our inner world in this way, experience ceases to be something that happens to us, and becomes something that unfolds through us. Even our defenses, when held this way, begin to relax not because they are defeated, but because they are finally understood.

Each moment of meeting ourselves with presence initiates a subtle repatterning. What was once automatic (reactivity, defense, contraction) begins to reorganize. But this reorganization is not imposed from the outside; it emerges from within, catalyzed by mutual process. The field doesn't require us to force change, it asks us to participate in the unfolding with enough awareness that the next configuration can arise. Repatterning is not about becoming someone new, but allowing the self to reorganize around truth rather than fear, coherence rather than fragmentation.

Physiologically, this process is mirrored in the body's adaptive systems. As we meet experience with less threat and more attunement, the autonomic nervous system begins to shift. Sympathetic hyperarousal (fight, flight, vigilance) gives way to the possibility of ventral vagal regulation: safety, engagement, rest. The hypothalamic-pituitary-adrenal (HPA) axis recalibrates, lowering chronic cortisol output as the system learns that what was once overwhelming is now containable. Immune activity may become less reactive, and metabolic rhythms may re-synchronize with present-moment cues rather than past survival imprints.

Repatterning is not just psychological, it is cellular. Implicit memory, held in musculature, posture, breath, and tone, is gradually rewritten through new experiences of coherence. A conflict once met with shutdown might now be met with firm yet grounded assertion. A trigger that used to induce panic might instead elicit a pause, a breath, a softening. These micro-adjustments accumulate into new trajectories of becoming. Over time, the self no longer orients through avoidance, but through receptivity. It does not grip its old shapes, but flows toward what is emergent. This is the body remembering that it is safe to feel, safe to soften, safe to be.

In this way, the path of return is not a regression to an earlier state, but an evolution toward greater complexity, fluidity, and coherence. It is the nervous system reattuning to the frequency of presence. It is the psyche loosening its grip on old stories. It is the field re-opening not through force, but through resonance.

In the words of Rumi, "This being human is a guest house. Every morning a new arrival. A joy, a depression, a meanness, some momentary awareness comes as an unexpected visitor. Welcome and entertain them all! Even if they're a crowd of sorrows, who violently sweep your house empty of its furniture, still, treat each guest honorably. He may be clearing you out for some new delight. The dark thought, the shame, the malice, meet them at the door laughing, and invite them in. Be grateful for whoever comes, because each has been sent as a guide from beyond."

So consider this: what if every moment is the next step on your path of return? What if your symptoms are not signs of failure, but messages from the self? What if your conflicts are not obstacles, but guides? What if the present moment, whatever it contains, is exactly what you need to meet, to remember who you are?

In the unfolding of this moment, can you pause? Can you welcome it, whatever it is, with presence? Can you hold and feel it with compassion? Can you move with it in flow? Can you turn toward it with curiosity? The invitation is not to fix, but to feel. Not to escape, but to return. And in that return, the ocean of your being waits—unchanged, undivided, and whole.

The path of return is not a straight line, it is a tide. It moves in and out, sometimes clear and calm, other times turbulent and disorienting. But always, it moves. Beneath every crashing wave of conflict, every swirl of emotional pain, every tight knot of reactivity or illness, there is still the ocean. The Self has never been lost—only covered, filtered, eclipsed by the necessary layers of becoming. Now, with presence, compassion, flow, and curiosity, we begin the return.

This return is not a going back, but a going through. Through the layers of our lived experience, through the stories and strategies that once protected us, through the symptoms and ruptures that cry out for integration. And in going through, we find the water beneath the wave. We find that what once seemed like disruption was guidance in disguise. We find that healing is not the erasure of pain, but the widening of the self to hold it with tenderness.

We begin to trust that life itself is not against us, it is speaking to us, always. Every pattern that emerges in the present moment is not random, but precise. It is an intelligent invitation from the field, asking not for perfection, but for presence.

Key Takeaways: Pathways of Return

- **Life as a Guide**: Every conflict, symptom, or emotional disturbance can be seen not as a failure or disruption, but as a *message*. An invitation from the field to return to coherence and wholeness.

- **The Role of Mutual Process**: Healing unfolds within the dynamic relationship between the self and environment. Life becomes a co-therapist, presenting the exact conditions needed for reintegration through mutual process.

- **Symptoms as Signals**: Symptoms, defenses, and repeating patterns are not random. They are *patterned residues* of experience emerging because the system is ready to metabolize and reorganize them.

- **The Repatterning Path**: As the system meets experience with presence, new patterns emerge. This reorganization is mirrored physiologically: shifting nervous system tone, HPA axis activity, immune function, and metabolic rhythms toward regulation.

- **Presence, Compassion, Flow, and Curiosity**: These qualities are the native postures of the unitary self. They allow experience to be *held, felt, moved through, and understood*, initiating the reorganization of mind, body, and field.

- **Integration over Erasure**: Healing is not the removal of difficult experience, but the reinclusion of what has been split off. Integration is *re-opening the field*, not controlling its contents.

- **The Ocean Remains**: Beneath every wave of experience is the unchanging ocean of self: still, whole, and waiting. The path of return is a movement from fragmentation to fullness, guided by the intelligence of the present moment.

As we have traced the layered pathways of return, through the patterned roles we inhabit, the symbolic structures we carry, and the sensorial ground we rediscover, we begin to sense the movement of coherence itself: not as a destination, but as a rhythm that continually invites us back into deeper contact with life. Yet to walk these paths is not merely to revisit what was lost, it is to recognize how cycles of fragmentation repeat, how the past resurfaces in the present, and how, without conscious interruption, protective adaptations can harden into identity. Before we can fully return to presence, we must learn to break the cycle not by force, but by awareness. It is here, at the edge where repetition meets realization, that the work of transformation begins.

CHAPTER EIGHTEEN

Breaking the Cycle

"Between stimulus and reaction there is a space. In that space is our power to choose our response. In our response lies our growth and our freedom."

— Viktor Frankl (Adapted)

We all live by patterns. These patterns protect us, shape us, and help us move through life. But over time, they become tight. Rigid. Predictable. At first, they offer safety and then, they become the very prison we long to escape.

Many arrive at the threshold of inner work not through inspiration, but exhaustion. Not through clarity, but confusion. Something just doesn't work anymore. A symptom keeps returning. A relationship keeps repeating. A dull ache, an unnamable tension, a whisper that says, *there must be more than this.*

This is where the return begins. Not as a heroic conquest, but as a surrender. A quiet noticing that the path forward is not out, but in. Beneath the adaptive layers of personality lie deeper truths. Buried not because they are lost, but because they are waiting to be reclaimed.

The chapters ahead trace this descent, this sacred return, through the levels of the patterned, symbolic, sensorial, and unitive. But first, we pause here at the edge. This chapter is about recognizing the cycle for what it is, and finding the courage to step out of it, not by force, but by turning toward the very experiences we've been trying to escape.

The Cycle of Fragmentation

At the surface, life often appears functional. We go to work, raise families, engage in relationships, build careers, seek meaning. Yet beneath this surface, many live with a gnawing sense of fragmentation. A sense of being split across roles, expectations, wounds, and longings. We become patterned not just by who we are, but by what we've had to endure.

These patterns, originally protective, crystallize around pain. A child who felt unsafe becomes the perfectionist. One who felt unseen becomes the performer. Another, overwhelmed by chaos, becomes the controller. These identities are not false, they are simply partial. And while they allow for survival, they often do so at the cost of wholeness.

Over time, the system begins to send signals. Tension. Symptoms. Relationship struggles. A sense of hollowness despite outward success. These are not failures to push through, but messages to listen to. The psyche, when forced into repetitive roles, eventually loops. The same fears reemerge. The same relational dynamics recycle. Even healing work, when approached from the same level of consciousness that created the pattern, can become part of the loop.

This is the cycle of fragmentation, not a conscious choice, but a gravitational pull toward familiar pain dressed in new clothes. It's not laziness, resistance, or lack of effort. It's inertia, a deep somatic and symbolic coding that says, "This is what keeps you safe." But safety is not the same as freedom. And protection is not the same as integration.

The invitation, then, is to recognize that these patterned ways of being, while necessary in the past, no longer serve the unfolding of the self. That the cycle is not destiny. And that awareness itself can become the first act of breaking it.

The Call to Return

The cycle doesn't usually break through force. It begins to soften when something in us starts to listen. Sometimes, it's the body that calls us back: fatigue that no sleep can fix, pain without a clear cause, or the tight chest that appears in moments of stillness. Sometimes it's the mind: thoughts looping without resolution, narratives that feel increasingly hollow. Other times it's the heart: a persistent ache, a sudden grief, or a longing that seems larger than the life we're living.

These experiences, though uncomfortable, are not evidence of failure. They are thresholds. Something deeper is pressing through the layers. A signal is arising from beneath the surface pattern calling us to return, not to who we were, but to what was forgotten in the rush to survive.

At first, it may seem subtle: a fleeting sense of déjà vu, a dream that lingers, an emotional reaction that feels disproportionate. Or it may come like a rupture: a loss, a breakdown, a moment of profound disorientation. However it arrives, the call is rarely convenient. It disrupts the known. It asks us to question what we've built, to feel what we've avoided, and to touch places we thought were long buried.

It is not a call to transcend the self, but to descend more fully into it. To return through the very layers we once ascended as we formed a coherent identity. It is the psyche's way of saying: there is more of you. You are not yet whole.

This call is not always met with eagerness. At first, we resist. We double down on familiar strategies. We try to fix the symptom instead of understanding the signal. But something shifts when we stop asking "how do I get rid of this?" and begin asking, "what is this trying to show me?"

This is the beginning of return. The first movement of the spiral inward. A movement not of regression, but of remembrance. A turning sometimes gentle, sometimes wrenching toward the deeper layers of the self that have always been waiting.

Threshold Awareness

There comes a moment sometimes quiet, sometimes piercing when awareness turns inward and begins to witness itself. It's subtle at first. You notice the pattern as it's happening rather than only after it's passed. You hear a familiar internal voice, but this time, you don't obey it without question. You feel an emotion swell, and instead of collapsing into it or pushing it away, you become curious. This shift is not cognitive alone. It's a turning of the whole system (mind, body, and spirit) toward presence. This is threshold awareness.

At this threshold, the "I" that was fused with the pattern begins to step back. Not to reject it, but to see it. To recognize that there is a witness behind the one who reacts, the one who pleases, the one who protects. That there is something constant, a thread of awareness, that remains even as the patterned self moves through fear, joy, longing, or shame.

This awareness isn't analytical. It doesn't need to interpret or explain. It simply *sees*. And in seeing, it creates space. Space to feel without fusing. To name without collapsing. To be with what is, rather than becoming what was.

Threshold awareness does not dissolve the pattern overnight. It marks the beginning of relationship. And from relationship comes compassion. From compassion, choice. And from choice, transformation.

The emergence of curiosity is one of the clearest signs that threshold awareness has arrived. Curiosity is the soul's way of reaching forward, a gentle hand extended into the unknown. It doesn't demand certainty. It asks to *be with*. It signals that the self is beginning to sense a deeper coherence, even if it cannot yet name it.

This moment, though often fleeting, is sacred. It marks the crossing from automaticity into possibility. From conditioned reaction into conscious return. And once it has been tasted, even briefly, the journey cannot be undone. Awareness, once awakened, begins to call itself home.

The Courage to Turn Inward

Turning inward is often misunderstood. It's not an escape from life, nor a withdrawal into solipsism. It is an act of profound bravery, the willingness to meet the unprocessed, the unfinished, the unknown.

At the surface, it can feel like falling apart. Old strategies unravel. Familiar roles lose their clarity. What once brought certainty now feels thin, brittle. The world doesn't change, but how we move through it begins to shift subtly, at first, then unmistakably. This descent is not the failure of healing. It is healing beginning to deepen.

To turn inward is to move toward the parts of ourselves we've exiled: the shamed, the scared, the silent, the strange. It means facing not just the pain we've endured, but the defenses we built to avoid it. This is why the journey can feel destabilizing. The structures of the patterned self were constructed for survival, and loosening them can bring fear: fear of regression, of collapse, of becoming lost. But collapse is not the same as surrender. And being lost is not the same as being in transition.

Many models of healing emphasize growth, ascent, evolution. But real healing often begins with descent. Down into the body, the breath, the tension. Down into memory, sensation, image, and impulse. It's here, in the roots, that we find the pieces we need to become whole. Not by adding something new, but by reclaiming what was left behind.

This reclamation does not happen all at once. It happens in moments, a softening around a reaction, a tear where there was once only numbness, a sudden compassion for a part of self that once brought only shame. To choose this descent requires courage. Not the loud, heroic kind, but the steady, enduring kind. The courage to pause instead of push. To feel instead of fix. To stay present when every instinct says run.

And yet, in this descent, something extraordinary begins to happen. What first felt like disintegration begins to reveal integration. What felt like darkness begins to shimmer with depth. The descent is not the end, it's the doorway. A quiet passage back into the truth of who we are.

The Shape of the Return

The return is not a linear journey. It doesn't proceed in tidy steps or follow predictable milestones. Its shape is spiral, recursive, a deepening, a circling back, a widening of the inner horizon. Each turn of the spiral brings us into deeper contact with ourselves, not to repeat the past, but to retrieve from it what was left unloved, unseen, or unfelt. This movement is not regression. It is reintegration.

To return through the layers of the self (the patterned, symbolic, sensorial) is to follow the arc of our original becoming, but in reverse. Where once we built structures to organize our experience, we now meet those structures with curiosity. Where once we lived scattered across roles, identities, and reactions, we now feel the pull back to the undivided ground of being. Where once we developed language to name our world, we now listen beneath the words to what remains unspoken. And where once sensation overwhelmed us or was cut off entirely, we now touch it with compassionate presence.

Each layer invites a different kind of surrender.

- In the **patterned**, we meet the architecture of adaptation and the chance to choose differently.

- In the **symbolic**, we reengage meaning, metaphor, and imagination not to build identity, but to explore its depths.

- In the **sensorial**, we reclaim the immediacy of embodied experience, letting the body tell its truth without interruption.

- And in the **unitive**, we rest in the silent presence that holds it all not as parts, but as one field.

The return is not a project to complete. It is a relationship to cultivate with the self, with life, and with the unfolding mystery that we are part of. It doesn't promise comfort or clarity at every turn, but it does offer something deeper: coherence. A sense that all the pieces, even the painful ones, belong. In this way, the return is not about becoming someone new. It is about remembering who we've always been, beneath the fragmentation.

Breaking the Cycle

To break the cycle is not to erase the past. It is to stop living as if we are only the result of it. Patterns will still arise. Old voices may still whisper. Pain may still echo. But something has changed, awareness has entered the system. And with awareness comes choice.

When we turn toward the self, not to fix or correct, but to witness and include, the repeating loop begins to soften. What was once unconscious becomes illuminated. The

253

automatic becomes conscious. And from this place, the future is no longer dictated by the past, it becomes a creative unfolding.

Breaking the cycle is not an act of force, but of relationship. It is the ongoing practice of meeting what arises (in the body, the mind, the emotions, the story) with compassion, flow, and curiosity. Not to collapse into it. Not to resist it. But to include it in a larger field of being. This is the work of integration. And integration is what liberates.

From this place, we return not to bypass what we've lived, but to weave it into something whole. The journey ahead does not deny the patterned self, the symbolic architecture, the sensorial base, or the unitive ground. It includes them all, honors them all, and moves through them with consciousness.

This is not a return to what was. It is a return to what has always been: the presence that sees, the Self that holds, the life that pulses beneath the layers. Breaking the cycle is not the end of the story. It is the first step in telling a new one.

Key Takeaways: Breaking the Cycle

- **Patterns form around protection.** We adapt to survive: shaping roles, identities, and behaviors that keep us safe but limit our fullness.

- **The cycle of fragmentation is sustained by unconscious repetition.** Symptoms, relational dynamics, and existential fatigue signal the presence of loops: not failure, but opportunity.

- **The call to return often arises from disruption.** Illness, breakdown, or longing initiate a turning point: an invitation to descend into deeper layers of the self.

- **Threshold awareness marks the beginning of change.** When we witness our patterns with curiosity, space opens between reaction and presence. Awareness is the first integration.

- **The descent inward requires courage.** Letting go of patterned structures feels like collapse, but it is the beginning of deeper healing and re-integration.

- **The shape of return is spiral, not linear.** We revisit earlier structures (the patterned, symbolic, sensorial) not to regress, but to reclaim what was left behind.

- **Breaking the cycle comes through conscious relationship.** Awareness, inclusion, and compassion allow us to integrate the past and create something new.

- **The return journey is not about becoming someone else.** It is about remembering, reclaiming, and embodying the wholeness that has always been present beneath the fragmentation.

Breaking the cycle begins with recognition, with the quiet yet radical act of turning inward and noticing the loop. But awareness alone does not dissolve the pattern; it invites us to trace its origins. The survival strategies we inherit are not random. They are shaped by experience, encoded in relationship, and rehearsed through time until they become structure. To move forward, we must look back not to dwell, but to understand. In the next chapter, we revisit the patterned self not as pathology, but as adaptation, a map of where we've been and a compass for where coherence might emerge.

CHAPTER NINETEEN

The Pattern as Portal

"Until you make the unconscious conscious, it will direct your life and you will call it fate."

— Carl Jung

The patterned self is often misunderstood. We speak of habits, roles, defenses, and identities as if they were fixed, obstructive structures to be dismantled. But the patterned layer of human experience is not the enemy of growth, it is the very architecture through which the self once learned to endure, adapt, and survive. It is the trace of an earlier intelligence, encoded in behavior and belief, formed in the face of rupture.

In the initial exploration of *The Patterned*, we traced how experience crystallizes into form. How the repeated tensions of life coalesce into recognizable constellations of thought, feeling, and action. These patterns, though limiting, are also preserving. They protect what the system was not yet ready to feel, know, or integrate.

But in the arc of return, something shifts. What once preserved now constrains. The same patterned expressions that once stabilized the self begin to generate suffering. Symptoms emerge. Disconnection deepens. Life begins to whisper, or scream, for something more.

It is here, at this inflection point, that *The Patterned* becomes not just a structure, but a portal. Patterns reveal. They replay. They reconfigure relationships, repeat choices, resurface feelings, and generate circumstances not to punish or imprison, but to illuminate. In this way, the return journey does not bypass pattern; it must pass through it, with new eyes.

This chapter invites us to re-enter *The Patterned* from a new vantage: one that honors its origin, listens to its messages, and uses its very structure as the scaffolding for transformation. If the first encounter with *The Patterned* was to recognize its grip, this second encounter is to recognize its guidance.

Life as Mirror: Lifestyle as Revelation

Life speaks in patterns. Not only through internal thoughts or emotional reactions, but through the shape of one's days: the rhythm of sleep, the food one chooses, the way one moves or avoids movement, the dynamics of relationships, the handling of time and money, the rituals of work and rest. Lifestyle, often overlooked as mundane, is in fact a living transcript of inner organization.

At the patterned level, repetition compulsion does not only manifest in dramatic or destructive behaviors. It expresses itself subtly across the spectrum of ordinary life. When asked who we are, we often describe our compulsions: "I'm a professional", "I'm a parent", "I'm a student". Among these compulsions, the subtle signs of protective organization manifest. A persistent fatigue, a recurring conflict at work, an inability to say no, a chronic tension in the gut, each may reflect a deeper patterned narrative encoded in the tissue of daily choices.

When life is approached with curiosity rather than judgment, these lifestyle expressions become revelatory. They expose the subterranean architecture of the self not to shame or fix, but to illuminate the protective intelligence behind them. A disordered eating pattern may trace back to early disruptions in relational attunement. A drive toward overachievement may echo a forgotten belief that love must be earned. A preference for isolation may carry the imprint of unspoken grief.

As these echoes surface, the repetition reveals its hidden function. The same pattern that once organized the self around survival and continuity now begins to point toward reorganization. What once maintained distance from pain now becomes the doorway to integration.

Values emerge in this process not as abstract ideals, but as living currents shaped by absence as much as presence. The conditions we lacked in early development (safety, recognition, warmth, freedom) create *formative voids*: spaces in the psyche where something essential was never fully registered or metabolized. These voids are not merely deficiencies; they are energetic contours that give rise to yearning. The absence of nurture may give rise to a deep longing for care and connection. The absence of choice may ignite an inner drive for autonomy and agency. These longings crystallize into values, felt senses of what matters, born from the tension between what was missing and what is possible. These become what we refer to as drives or desires.

Lifestyle, then, becomes the terrain of value expression, the outer architecture shaped by inner scaffolding. But this expression diverges depending on the level of awareness. When values arise from unintegrated voids, they are often enacted through *compensatory patterns*, strategies aimed at covering or controlling the felt lack. These patterns might include overachievement to mask unworthiness, hyper-independence to defend against vulnerability, or people-pleasing to avoid rejection. They are not inherently "wrong," but they reflect an unconscious attempt to resolve an unmet need through patterned behavior rather than integrated presence.

In contrast, coherent enactments are conscious expressions of values grounded in integration. Here, the same yearning for care might be expressed not through clinging or rescuing, but through attuned connection. The desire for agency is no longer driven by a fear of helplessness, but manifests as empowered choice. Coherent enactments are flexible, present, and responsive. They arise when the original void has been touched with awareness, held with compassion, and reorganized through meaning and embodiment.

To meet these patterns with awareness is to begin the return. Life itself, especially in its most ordinary rhythms, becomes the clinician, the revealer, the reflector. Every daily encounter becomes a potential mirror, offering glimpses of what seeks coherence beneath the crust of habit. In this way, values are not imposed but discovered, not enforced but remembered as signals from the deeper field of the Self, shaping form in the direction of wholeness.

When the Mirror Cracks: From Lifestyle to Trigger

Even our most intentional, values-based lifestyles are not immune to disruption. Life interrupts. Plans unravel. Relationships challenge. And in these moments, something unexpected surfaces, reactivity. The sharp word, the tight chest, the urge to withdraw or retaliate. It may feel as though we've failed, lost progress, or regressed. But this, too, is a mirror, revealing what lies beneath the surface of habit and intention.

Reactivity often arises when our lifestyle activities are rooted in compensatory patterns rather than coherent enactments. While both may appear aligned with values on the surface, the distinction lies in origin. Coherent enactments are flexible, flowing expressions of integrated values. Compensatory patterns, on the other hand, are structured around unconscious attempts to shield or soothe the pain of a formative void. These patterns can feel like alignment, but they are often rigid, conditional, and fragile. And when these patterns collapse, something deeper is revealed: the vulnerability behind the pattern.

When a lifestyle built on compensation falters, when the structure that keeps the void at bay begins to crack, reactivity is the signal. The protective edifice collapses, and the raw material underneath is exposed. Anger, panic, shame, collapse. These are not random disruptions. They are patterned responses to the reactivation of old pain, the unmet need returning with fresh urgency. The trigger, in this sense, is not a problem to eliminate but a pointer, a flare signaling where coherence has not yet been embodied. Part of the system is asking to be seen, felt, and integrated.

In these moments, we are invited to come to our senses, literally. Rather than fueling the story or amplifying the reaction, we can turn inward. What sensations are arising? Where in the body is the tension held? What images or memories flicker at the edge of awareness? This simple act of returning to sensation opens the door to curiosity and with it, the possibility of reorganizing reactivity into response. Rumi said, "Don't turn away. Keep your gaze on the bandaged place. That's where the light enters you."

"Coming to your senses" becomes a practice of *repatterning*. Instead of reinforcing the old compensatory route through numbing, avoiding, and controlling we bring presence to the activation itself. This presence does not fix the void, but it makes room for the original unmet need to be felt and integrated. The system is not broken; it is *trying to reorganize.* Reactivity is not failure; it is *a flash of inner truth,* revealing the unmet longing that shaped the pattern in the first place.

Seen in this way, triggers are not disruptions of growth, but part of its rhythm. They show us where values have been organized around unconscious defense rather than conscious choice. They invite us into the body, into sensation, into the very place coherence longs to form. And in doing so, they offer us something more precious than protection: the chance to heal the pattern from the inside out.

The Eclipse Within: Repetition as Remembering

Beneath every patterned response lies something unfinished. Something that could not be fully felt, processed, or understood at the time of its emergence. To protect against overwhelm, the system does not discard these fragments, it stores them. It encases them in adaptive structures: in roles, in habits, in symptoms. These structures orbit the unintegrated material, not unlike planets circling an unseen sun. This is the eclipse.

The eclipse is not a total erasure of experience, but a partial obscuring. A filtering. Consciousness narrows to protect itself, and what is pushed into shadow does not disappear, it becomes formative. It organizes behavior from behind the veil. It sets the rhythm for repetition. And it waits.

Repetition is not just the compulsive re-living of old wounds. It is the echo of something that longs to be remembered. To be seen, not as pathology, but as signal. As a communication from a self once overwhelmed. In this way, the patterned repetition is not only the result of trauma, but the mechanism through which trauma seeks repair.

The eclipse creates a paradox: what has been hidden exerts influence, yet escapes recognition. So, the same choices are made. The same relationships unfold. The same physiological symptoms arise. They are not punishments. They are invitations. Invitations to bring light to what lies just beyond the threshold of awareness.

At the patterned level, repetition becomes the language of the unconscious. It speaks not in words, but in circumstances, in moods, in bodily sensations. And it speaks persistently, until met. To view repetition as remembering is to shift from shame to compassion, from resistance to listening. The clinician, too, must hold this view: that the repetitive is not

263

resistant, but reverent. Reverent of a truth that once could not be held. And now, perhaps, can.

The Spark of Return: Curiosity as Catalyst

There comes a moment, sometimes fleeting, sometimes sustained, when the patterned response is met not with automaticity, but with attention. A pause opens. A question stirs. *Why do I always do this? What is this trying to show me?* In that moment, something breaks through the repetition: not a solution, but a signal. Curiosity. The first quality of return.

It does not emerge from effort or analysis, but from a subtle shift in presence. When consciousness reflects back on itself, when the observer within turns toward the pattern with openness rather than judgment, curiosity arises. Not as an emotion, but as a movement of awareness. It is the embodied question that precedes transformation.

Unlike fear, which contracts, or shame, which conceals, curiosity expands. It makes space. It softens the boundary between parts of the self that were previously divided: between the protector and the wounded, the conscious and the eclipsed, the known and the forgotten. It is the quality of coherence beginning to take form.

At the patterned level, this quality is essential. The return does not happen through force, but through contact. Through the gentle, sustained interest in the self's own structures. Curiosity moves the system from rigidity to responsiveness. It allows the previously automatic to become intentional.

For the clinician, curiosity is both a sign and a tool. It signals readiness. Its emergence suggests that the Self is
264

beginning to sense its own shape, to tolerate the mystery of its own complexity. It is a moment to be honored, not rushed. The therapist's own curiosity, held without agenda, becomes a mirror, reinforcing the legitimacy of inquiry without collapsing into interpretation.

Curiosity invites the system to speak. It asks not *What's wrong with me?* but *What's here?* It doesn't demand immediate answers, it trusts that something meaningful lies beneath the surface of what repeats. And in this trust, it begins to loosen what once held the self together in fixed form.

In many ways, curiosity is the first thread of coherence being pulled back through the eclipse. It marks the beginning of light returning to pattern. And it cannot be manufactured, but it can be noticed, nurtured, and followed.

Multiplicity Within: Subpersonalities and Systems

To revisit the patterned self is to encounter a paradox: what once seemed singular begins to reveal itself as plural. Beneath the surface of a cohesive identity are many voices, many positions, many selves. Each with its own history, tone, and strategy for survival. These are the subpersonalities: the internal figures who took shape to hold what consciousness could not yet bear.

At the patterned level, these subpersonalities are not disordered, they are ordered. Each part arose from a specific context, bearing a specific function. One may carry vigilance. Another withdrawal. Another the performance of worth. Still another, the rage that no one else could express. These parts are not symptoms to be eliminated, but intelligences to be welcomed. They hold the patterned adaptations of a life that learned, over and over again, how to protect what mattered most.

This is the heart of subpersonality work: not to reduce the Self to fragments, but to recognize the Self as relational within. The healing is not in choosing one part over another, but in making space for the dialogue between them. The task is to reintroduce the parts to each other not with force, but with curiosity and care.

The exploration of these internal relationships mirrors what is happening somatically as well. The physiological body, too, reflects multiplicity. The nervous system, immune system, endocrine system, and gut-brain axis are not separate entities, they are interwoven domains in constant communication. Just as the inner child and the inner critic may remain estranged until brought into contact, so too might adrenal imbalance remain misunderstood without recognizing its dialogue with inflammation, micronutrient depletion, or circadian rhythm disruption.

At this level, laboratory and diagnostic testing are not just tools for measurement, they are instruments of insight. They provide a map of the physiological conversation that mirrors the psychological one. Functional diagnostics reveal the terrain upon which internal patterns play out: gut permeability echoing boundary violations, cortisol rhythms mirroring hypervigilance, immune activation reflecting the body's memory of injury or intrusion.

The clinician's role here is not only interpreter, but facilitator of reconnection: between parts of the psyche, and between systems of the body. Healing at the patterned level requires honoring complexity. It asks us to recognize that no
266

single narrative or lab result tells the whole story. It is the relationships (between parts, between systems, between past and present) that illuminate the path forward. Multiplicity is not a problem to be solved. It is the nature of the patterned self. And when seen through the lens of coherence, it becomes the very ground upon which integration takes root.

Mapping the Field: Exploring Interrelatedness

Healing does not occur in isolation. It arises through relationship within the psyche, across physiological systems, and between the individual and their environment. At the patterned level, the return to wholeness is not simply a matter of identifying discrete problems, but of discerning the relational field in which those problems are embedded. Patterns do not exist alone; they cohere with other patterns, forming a living matrix that reflects the whole.

To explore this interrelatedness is to shift from linear thinking to systems perception. One part leads to another. One symptom links to a belief, which links to a behavior, which links to a physiological state. It is this network of connection that must be illuminated, not merely the nodes themselves.

Within the psyche, subpersonalities do not act in isolation. A harsh internal critic may be in constant tension with a frozen child part, while a vigilant protector stands guard between them. The suffering is not just in the presence of these parts, but in their disconnection, the lack of mutual recognition. Healing begins not by silencing one or elevating another, but by fostering relationship between them. The clinician helps to *map the field*, listening not only to individual voices but to the space between them.

The same is true within the body. Systems communicate in subtle, recursive loops. A pattern of sleep disruption may not be a problem of sleep alone—it may reflect dysregulation in cortisol rhythm, itself influenced by inflammatory cytokines, which in turn relate to gut permeability or early-life stress. When these patterns are seen in isolation, the treatment remains superficial. But when they are seen in relationship, the coherence of the whole system begins to emerge.

Lifestyle domains offer further clues. A rigid dietary pattern may reflect both a metabolic imbalance and a deep need for control. A chronic injury may persist not only due to biomechanics, but because it sits in the same relational field as unresolved grief. The individual's relationship to work, leisure, substance use, and spirituality is not incidental, it is expressive of internal structure. And that structure is relational.

This mapping of parts, systems, and behaviors is not about control. It is about listening. It is about developing a felt sense of how the whole system moves, constrains, compensates, and communicates. It is a process of holding the fragments long enough to see their design.

To explore interrelatedness is to begin weaving coherence. It does not require immediate resolution. It requires presence, attention, and willingness to dwell in complexity. It is in this dwelling that the pattern begins to soften, and the field begins to reconfigure.

Modalities and Methods: Tools for Patterned Reorganization

The return journey through the patterned self is not walked alone. Alongside the innate movement of consciousness toward wholeness, there are practices, therapeutic modalities, and diagnostic tools that can assist in deepening, clarifying, and supporting this phase of reorganizational healing.

At the patterned level, the work is relational and systemic. It involves recognizing, mapping, and reshaping internal and physiological patterns that were once adaptive but are now limiting. Some therapeutic modalities are particularly well-suited to meet individuals at this depth not by imposing a new structure, but by helping to illuminate the one already present.

Internal Family Systems (IFS) is foundational here. IFS honors the inner multiplicity of subpersonalities or "parts," offering a non-pathologizing and compassionate framework through which these parts can be seen, understood, and invited into relationship. It supports the emergence of Self-energy (spacious, curious, and integrative) precisely the quality needed for transformation at the patterned level.

Schema Therapy offers another lens, particularly helpful for identifying entrenched cognitive and emotional patterns rooted in unmet core needs. Its structured, experiential approach helps to reparent internalized beliefs and behaviors with a focus on developmental repair.

Psychodynamic and Object Relations therapies deepen the exploration of how internal relationships mirror early relational templates. These modalities help individuals

269

see how current behaviors and affective patterns are repetitions of early object-relational dynamics. They also provide language and holding for the unconscious drivers of repetition compulsion.

Somatically attuned modalities like *Hakomi* and *Sensorimotor Psychotherapy* bring in the wisdom of the body. They allow the patterned self to be explored not just through story or insight, but through sensation, movement, and memory held in the tissue. They emphasize mindfulness in motion, and help individuals attune to the subtle signals of interoceptive and relational shifts.

Polyvagal-informed therapies complement this work by illuminating the physiological substrates of pattern: how autonomic state shapes perception, behavior, and relational capacity. These approaches offer clinicians a map of the body's internal surveillance system, and interventions to support safety, connection, and flexibility.

In parallel, **functional diagnostics and integrative lab work** can provide critical insight into patterned physiological disruptions. Cortisol panels, gut microbiome analysis, hormone mapping, nutrient levels, and inflammatory markers may offer data that mirrors the internal terrain, shedding light on inter-systemic dysregulation that holds or reflects deeper psychological patterning.

Importantly, these modalities are not prescriptive. They are invitations, tools that can deepen presence, clarify the field, and support the unfolding movement of return. They are not ends in themselves, but facilitators of awareness.

Each therapeutic tool, each lens of understanding, is most powerful when held within a larger orientation: that of coherogenesis. The clinician does not seek to fix the pattern, but to understand its intelligence, to support its softening and reorganization, and to hold space for what is ready to emerge through its unraveling.

From Pattern to Possibility: The Path Forward

Patterns, once seen as barriers, become bridges. Their repetitive nature, their friction and constraint, are not signs of dysfunction but signals of readiness. They call attention to where the self has become too narrow, too guarded, too rehearsed. And in doing so, they offer a profound invitation: to move from survival into presence, from protection into possibility.

To revisit *The Patterned* is not to deconstruct the self, it is to listen more deeply to its design. To recognize the intelligence embedded in its form. To honor the beauty in its endurance. What was once automatic can now become intentional. What was once hidden can now be named. What was once fragmented can now be held in a wider field of coherence.

The path forward is not about erasing pattern, but about transforming its function. When met with presence and curiosity, the pattern shifts. It no longer operates as a wall but as a doorway. It becomes a recognizable language through which the deeper Self, the one beyond defense, beyond adaptation, can begin to speak again.

As this chapter closes, the journey turns inward still. The patterned self, when softened, reveals deeper layers of experience: symbolic, sensorial, unitive. These layers, long buried beneath the structure of survival, begin to stir. Each awaits its own moment of return. But none can be reached without first passing through the terrain of *The Patterned* with clarity, compassion, and a willingness to see pattern not as pathology, but as a portal.

This is the promise of coherogenesis: that nothing is wasted. That every adaptation carries within it the seed of return. And that the Self, patterned though it may be, is always seeking its way home.

Key Takeaways: The Patterned as Portal

- **Patterns are portals, not prisons**: The patterned self is no longer viewed as a static structure to dismantle, but as a dynamic and intelligent formation that both preserved the self and now offers a path to its transformation.

- **Lifestyle reveals the inner architecture**: Daily habits, across movement, food, sleep, money, relationships, serve as expressions of internal adaptations. These domains reflect encoded patterns shaped by early voids and attempts to preserve coherence.

- **Values emerge through absence**: What was missing in early development, such as safety, recognition, or agency, shapes core values. These values, when enacted unconsciously, become compensatory patterns. When integrated, they guide coherent living.

- **Repetition as remembering**: Patterned behaviors are not just symptoms; they are the psyche's way of keeping unfinished experiences in orbit. Repetition reflects the eclipse of overwhelming material and signals what still seeks integration.

- **Reactivity as revelation**: When patterns collapse, triggers and emotional surges are not failures but signals. They reveal the unmet need beneath compensatory behaviors and invite a return to embodied presence.

- **Curiosity is the first thread of coherence**: The emergence of curiosity marks a pivotal shift, from automaticity to awareness. This embodied quality of presence opens the space for internal dialogue and systemic reorganization.

- **Multiplicity is intrinsic, not pathological**: The self is composed of subpersonalities that hold specific adaptive functions. These parts mirror both psychological complexity and physiological interdependence across systems like the HPA axis, immune function, and circadian rhythm.

- **Relational mapping restores coherence**: Healing at the patterned level involves mapping relationships— between inner parts, between systems of the body, between symptoms and meaning. Coherence arises not from fixing parts in isolation, but from reintegrating the whole.

- **Patterns become bridges to deeper layers**: When held with presence, patterns reveal the unmet needs and values they were built around. They serve as invitations to descend into the symbolic, sensorial, and unitive layers of being.

- **Therapeutic and diagnostic tools support this phase**: Modalities like IFS, Schema Therapy, psychodynamic work, somatic practices, Polyvagal-informed therapy, and functional diagnostics offer frameworks and tools for making the implicit explicit and supporting transformation without pathologizing adaptation.

- **From structure to story, from survival to meaning**: Patterns carry embedded metaphors, roles, and images. To reorganize the patterned self, one must listen beyond behavior, to the symbolic language it encodes. This sets the stage for the next movement: returning to the symbolic, where the self begins to speak through meaning and metaphor.

As we trace the patterns of survival and protection, the grooves carved by past experience, we begin to notice that these patterns are not just behaviors or symptoms. They are also *stories*, implicit narratives carried in posture, perception, and identity. Beneath every reaction lies a representation: a metaphor, a role, an internal image shaped by memory and meaning. To truly understand and reorganize the patterned self, we must move from the structure of habit to the language of the psyche. In the next chapter, we return to the symbolic, to the realm where parts have names, where pain becomes image, and where the self begins to speak not in logic, but in metaphor. This is where coherence deepens, through the architecture of meaning.

CHAPTER TWENTY

Returning to the Symbolic

"All that we are is the result of what we have thought: it is founded on our thoughts, it is made up of our thoughts."

— Dhammapada, Verse 1

"Before your mind creates the world, the world creates your mind."

— Gabor Mate

There comes a moment in inner work when noticing is no longer enough. We've named the patterns, identified the protectors, and mapped the roles we inhabit. But something in us longs to go deeper not just to understand *what* is happening, but to ask *what it means*. This movement marks a return to the symbolic: a shift from proactive and reactive structure to expressive substance, from rigid identity to fluid metaphor, from control to flow.

At this level, Flow emerges as the dominant quality. Flow is not merely an optimal psychological state, it is the felt sense that one's inner life is speaking, unfolding, evolving. When flow is present, the psyche is not pushing or pulling, but revealing. The symbolic is its language.

The symbolic dimension is not abstract. It is deeply intimate. It gives form to feeling through metaphor, image, and narrative. It allows the soul to speak in its native tongue, not through diagnosis, not through explanation, but through symbol. A swamp, a sword, a silence, each reveals something a thousand words cannot.

In this chapter, we explore the power and precision of symbolic work. We will trace the journey from patterned subpersonalities and associated lifestyle organization to symbolic representations, from fixed beliefs to living metaphors. We'll examine how flow as a morphology of presence open the space for symbols to emerge, and how these symbols transform not by analysis, but by contact, meaning, and inclusion.

To work with the symbolic is to engage the architecture of coherence itself. This is not about solving the self, it is about listening to the stories it already tells, and helping those stories evolve. Through this, we invite coherogenesis: the living integration of the many into a meaningful whole.

From Pattern to Poetic Logic: Symbolizing the Subpersonality

Subpersonalities emerge as fragments of self, forged in adaptation. Initially experienced as automatic roles or emotional states, they arise in language as the inner critic, the pleaser, the abandoned child, the protector. At first, these parts may be disruptive, reactive, or confusing. But with awareness or presence, they begin to soften. They become visible not as pathology, but as participants in the inner ecology of the self.

In earlier stages, awareness brings light to these patterns, what was once unconscious becomes known. Naming, differentiating, and witnessing subpersonalities is the first act of healing. "Ah, this part always shows up when I feel vulnerable." This is the movement from fusion to relationship. From here, one can begin to ask, with genuine curiosity, "What are you trying to protect?"

Curiosity opens the door, but flow is what allows the deeper story to be told. Flow, at this level, is the spontaneous and trust-filled movement between parts of the self. It emerges when the psyche feels safe enough to explore. It is neither coerced nor rushed. Instead, it reflects a shift from managing inner states to meeting them. It is here that subpersonalities begin to reveal not only their behaviors, but their symbolic meanings.

Symbolic revelation may come as an image (a frozen child, a shielded heart), a metaphor (a mask, a cage, a tightrope), or a felt sense of story ("I am the one left behind," "I hold what no one else could carry"). These representations are not distortions of reality, they are the psyche's way of encoding meaning. They are poetic truths, lived truths, that speak in the language of the inner world.

This transition from pattern to poetry does not deny the behavioral utility of subpersonalities; it enriches it. The protector is not only a vigilant part, it may also be a knight, a wolf, a watchtower. The inner critic might appear as a drill sergeant, or as a fragile child trying to prevent shame. These symbolic identities carry emotion, history, and wisdom. They want to be seen not eliminated, but honored and transformed.

Importantly, the symbolic dimension allows us to contact the beliefs that animate each subpersonality. These beliefs are often hidden in behavior but can be unearthed in metaphor. "I must earn love to be safe," "If I'm not perfect, I'll be rejected," "Vulnerability leads to danger." These are not just thoughts, they are structured emotional truths, often organized around symbolic images. They are not irrational; they were once essential. They were formed in the crucible of survival.

When symbolic engagement begins, transformation becomes possible. The subpersonality begins to shift. The frozen child becomes the inner artist. The wall becomes a doorway. The mask becomes a mirror. These changes are not imposed, they arise from within, through presence and poetic resonance.

Thus, symbolizing the subpersonality is not about decoding it like a puzzle. It is about meeting it as a character in an unfolding inner myth. And in doing so, we discover that these parts were never enemies to overcome: they were messages, awaiting a listener.

The Language of Metaphor

Metaphor is the native language of the symbolic. It is how the psyche tells its truth without being confined by literal logic. When words fail to describe a feeling, an image often arises. Not as a decoration, but as revelation. A burning house. A tangled forest. A sealed vault. These are not fantasies; they are forms of inner knowing.

Metaphor bridges emotion and meaning. It gathers experience into symbol, giving shape to what was once unformed. In therapeutic work, a metaphor might emerge spontaneously where an individual describes their anxiety as a spinning top, or their grief as a stone in the chest. These images are not symptoms to resolve; they are *symbols to relate to*. When we honor the metaphor, we gain access to the deeper truths it protects.

Some metaphors carry personal history. Others reveal archetypal dimensions. A protector may not just be a vigilant father figure, it may carry the weight of the ancient warrior archetype. An abandoned child may also hold the mythic resonance of the orphan, the exiled one, the lost heir. Archetypes transcend personal biography and root the self in the shared human story. They offer meaning where there was once only pain. They grant dignity to suffering.

Therapies that cultivate the symbolic (Jungian work, some EMDR derivatives, expressive arts, active imagination, and guided imagery, etc.) all rely on metaphor to engage the unconscious. But metaphor can arise in any modality when there is space for emergence. It does not need to be forced. It comes when flow is present, when the psyche is not interrupted but invited.

Importantly, metaphor does not aim to *explain* away an experience. It invites one to *relate* to it. A metaphor is not something to be interpreted and discarded, it's something to be lived into, dialogued with, shaped over time. "My depression is a cave." What is the cave made of? What lives inside it? What happens when you light a candle in it?

Metaphor, like dream, resists closure. It is living. And in this way, it becomes a vehicle for *coherogenesis*, the spontaneous generation of coherence. In the presence of metaphor, disparate aspects of the Self begin to align not through analysis, but through resonance. The protector and the artist, the warrior and the child, the cage and the key, each becomes part of a larger, fluid pattern. Symbolic images *hold multiplicity* without collapse.

The therapeutic task is not to decode the metaphor too quickly. It is to sit with it, to trust it, to let it speak. To explore what truths it guards and what truths it wants to grow. The psyche will offer its metaphors when it is ready. And when it does, it speaks in a voice older than words and deeper than cognition. A voice not of pathology, but of poetry.

Clinical Bridge: From Labs to Language

In the earlier phases of assessment, laboratory tests and diagnostic criteria serve an essential purpose. They orient us to physiology, patterns, and potential areas of concern. They bring clarity to what might otherwise remain diffuse. At the level of the Patterned, these data points help stabilize and structure the narrative: elevated inflammatory markers, hormonal imbalances, metabolic disturbances, neurotransmitter shifts. They offer a kind of scaffolding, a map of where energy is blocked, where systems are over- or under-active, where compensatory strategies are at play.

But as we move into the Symbolic, a shift in orientation occurs. The data is still relevant, but it no longer holds the same kind of authority. At this stage, it is not simply *what* is wrong that matters, but *what it means*. Numbers alone cannot tell the story of the person. Lab results don't speak in

280

metaphor, but the psyche does. The symbolic invites us to listen not only to the body's chemistry, but to the soul's poetry.

This is not an abandonment of science. It is its recontextualization. The symbolic allows us to ask: *What is the body saying through these patterns?*

- An autoimmune condition may become a symbol of internal conflict, *the self turning against itself.*

- Chronic fatigue might speak to an inner world overwhelmed by vigilance and depletion, *a system unable to rest because it was never safe to stop.*

- Elevated cortisol may not just reflect stress, but a long history of emotional hyperarousal, *a fire alarm that's been ringing for years.*

Even physical sensations, like tightness in the chest or pain in the gut, can be approached symbolically: *What does this constriction represent? What emotion or memory lives here?* Instead of pathologizing the symptom, we can engage it. The question becomes, *"If this symptom could speak, what would it say?"*

This approach invites the clinician and the individual into a collaborative inquiry, one that honors biology and symbolism, structure and soul. The lab result becomes one part of a multi-dimensional map. It is neither reduced to metaphor nor stripped of its physical reality. Rather, it participates in a larger, more coherent narrative.

At this level, treatment may still include medications, nutraceuticals, or dietary changes but the intention is different. These interventions are no longer merely targeted at symptom reduction. They are part of a broader effort to support symbolic coherence. A supplement to reduce inflammation is also an invitation for the system to feel safe again. A medication to stabilize mood may serve as a bridge toward inner listening. Physical healing is welcomed not just for its own sake, but as a space-making gesture *so the psyche can speak.*

Working symbolically doesn't mean projecting metaphor onto every data point. It means remaining open to what the data might reflect in the broader context of the person's story. The symbolic doesn't reject science, it enfolds it into meaning.

Coherogenesis Through Symbolic Integration

Coherogenesis is not a mechanical process. It is a living unfolding, a dynamic organization of meaning from within. Nowhere is this more evident than at the symbolic level. Here, healing occurs not simply through resolution, but through integration by allowing the many voices, images, and truths of the inner world to enter into relationship.

Symbols act as binding threads. They do not explain, they connect. A single image can unite sensation, memory, belief, and affect in a way no diagnostic label can. When a subpersonality and its components are symbolized, it ceases to be an isolated fragment and becomes a part of a larger, unfolding mythos. The psyche is no longer fragmented into symptoms and syndromes, it becomes a story, alive and in motion.

At this level, coherence is not a return to some ideal state. It is not the elimination of contradiction or the removal of pain. Rather, it is the capacity to *hold* contradiction, to *stay present* with pain, and to weave them into a deeper truth. Symbolic coherence is poetic, layered, and alive. It allows us to say: *Yes, this protector arose from fear and it also carries wisdom. Yes, this grief hurts and it also opens my heart.* In this way, symbolic integration cultivates a Self that is not brittle, but fluid. Resilient not because it avoids rupture, but because it knows how to re-form.

Flow, again, becomes essential. It is the quality that allows these internal movements (between parts, between states, between stories) to unfold without obstruction. Flow signals safety. It tells the system, *You can let go of rigidity. You can trust the process.* And when that trust is present, the symbolic begins to move. The frozen child becomes the artist. The wall becomes a bridge. The cage opens, and the bird inside remembers its song.

This is coherogenesis. Not imposed from the outside, but emerging from within. Not by force, but by contact. As symbols evolve, so too does identity. The self becomes less of a fixed structure and more of a dynamic coherence—ever-changing, yet deeply known.

In this space, we begin to live as a whole, not because every part agrees, but because every part is heard. The symbolic doesn't demand perfection, it invites participation. And in that invitation, the many parts of the self begin to find their place. Not as enemies. Not as problems. But as threads in the fabric of a single, coherent life.

Symbols as Bridges: Linking Pattern and Sensation

Symbols are not merely representations, they are bridges. They serve coherence by linking the abstract with the concrete, the invisible with the felt, the known with the emerging. In the context of coherogenesis, the symbolic becomes essential not just as the *architecture of meaning*, but as a *living process* that connects the patterned and the sensorial, those layers of Self that can so easily become estranged from one another. When we engage symbolically, we invite a deeper conversation between automatic structure and embodied presence.

The patterned self organizes through habit, identity, and protective function. It's efficient, but often rigid, replaying roles that once ensured survival but now limit vitality. The sensorial self, by contrast, is immediate and alive: a register of experience in the language of sensation, impulse, and emotion. Without a symbolic bridge, these two domains may remain isolated, leaving sensation unintegrated and pattern unconscious.

Here are several strategies that harness symbolic processes to restore coherence between these layers:

- **Metaphor as Access Point**: Inviting individuals to describe bodily sensations using metaphor ("It feels like a storm in my chest") offers symbolic form to raw experience. This gives structure to the sensorial without prematurely patterning it into a fixed identity.

- **Reframing Pattern as Symbolic Enactment**: Repetitive behaviors and beliefs can be explored not as flaws but as living symbols—archetypal gestures of protection, belonging, or power. An individual who constantly appeases others might be enacting the symbol of "the peacekeeper." Naming it allows the pattern to be witnessed, dialogued with, and transformed.

- **Re-symbolizing the Unspeakable**: Trauma often escapes symbolization, lodging itself in the body and bypassing narrative. Through image, story, dreamwork, or ritual, individuals can gradually re-symbolize dissociated material. This turns implicit memory into something that can be held, honored, and integrated.

- **Symbolic Ritual and Action**: Intentional symbolic gestures (writing a letter and burning it, imaginary release of burden to elements, creating a personal altar, etc.) allow both pattern and sensation to participate in meaning-making. These rituals offer coherent containers for transformation.

- **Dreamwork and Active Imagination**: Dreams offer a space where patterns and sensations intermingle in symbolic form. Engaging these images, especially through active imagination, can bring previously unconscious material into awareness in ways that bypass rational defenses and invite embodied insight.

- **Language as Living Bridge**: Attention to language, especially when individuals move from rigid storylines ("I always have to…") to embodied symbolic expression ("It feels like…"), can guide awareness back toward present-moment coherence. This linguistic shift supports a reintegration of sensing and meaning-making.

- **Tracking the Evolution of Symbols**: Over time, personal symbols may change as coherence deepens.

An individual may begin therapy describing themselves as "a fortress" and later shift to "a garden." These symbolic transformations mirror the reorganization of the system, offering tangible markers of healing.

In each of these practices, the symbolic becomes a site of transformation, able to hold the complexity of experience without collapsing into fragmentation or rigidity. It serves as a translator between the silent language of the body and the stories we carry. And in doing so, it offers the possibility of coherence not through control, but through the deepening of presence across all levels of experience.

Psychotherapy Modalities That Expand the Symbolic

While all therapeutic work touches the symbolic at times, some modalities are designed to dwell there, facilitating metaphor, emotional depth, image, and archetype as vehicles of transformation. These approaches don't merely interpret the symbolic, they *participate* in it. They help create the conditions for symbols to arise, evolve, and integrate. Flow, curiosity, and presence are the soil in which symbolic healing grows.

Internal Family Systems (IFS). IFS offers a structured, relational approach to subpersonality work. It teaches us to approach each part with compassion, curiosity, and non-judgment. As trust builds, parts reveal their roles, burdens, and ultimately their symbolic essence. An "angry protector" may be seen as a burning shield. A "burdened child" might emerge as a collapsed angel. In IFS, healing occurs not by overriding parts, but by helping them unblend and transform within a coherent inner system led by Self-energy (calm, connected, and curious).

286

Jungian Depth Psychotherapy. Jungian approaches are deeply rooted in symbolic language. Dreams, fantasies, myths, and archetypes are not distractions from healing—they *are* the healing terrain. Through active imagination and dreamwork, unconscious material is brought into symbolic dialogue. The shadow becomes a guide. The anima or animus carries missing energies. The Self archetype invites wholeness. Rather than resolving symbols, Jungian work engages them, letting them unfold in their own time and meaning.

Accelerated Experiential Dynamic Psychotherapy (AEDP). AEDP focuses on undoing aloneness and accessing core affect. It may not begin with metaphor, but symbolic resonance often arises through deep emotional contact. An individual feeling "flooded" with grief might describe being "underwater," evoking a metaphor that deepens therapeutic exploration. AEDP's emphasis on transformational affect, emotions that change the self when felt in safety, naturally opens the door to symbolic states and emergent narratives.

Gestalt Therapy. Gestalt draws symbols out of the moment. It invites individuals to *become* different parts of the self (an emotion, an image, a dream character) and speak from it. The chair becomes a parent, the tightness in the chest becomes a voice, the dream tiger becomes an inner fear or strength. Gestalt does not interpret; it animates. Through enactment, metaphors are embodied and transformed.

Hakomi. This mindfulness-centered, body-based modality invites individuals into present-moment experience, where unconscious beliefs and images often surface spontaneously. A hand clenching might evoke a wall. A softening belly might reveal a meadow. In Hakomi, the body becomes a doorway into symbolic meaning. The practitioner is trained to listen for metaphor and support the unfolding without intrusion, trusting the wisdom of the system to reveal what's needed.

Compassionate Inquiry. Developed by Gabor Maté, this approach explores the symbolic underpinnings of belief, behavior, and emotion through relational presence and inquiry. The practitioner gently tracks the individual's language, physiology, and imagery to reveal core stories—often unspoken, often symbolic. A phrase like "I'm carrying the weight of the world" becomes an entry point: *What is this weight? When did it first appear? Who gave it to you?* In this way, the symbolic emerges through attentiveness and shared discovery.

Expressive Arts, Drama Therapy, and Focusing. These modalities invite direct access to the symbolic through movement, sound, art, and sensation. The psyche is not asked to *talk about* itself, it is invited to *create*. Drawing an inner landscape, dancing a dream, sculpting an emotion, these expressions bypass the analytic mind and allow the symbolic to speak in its own language.

What unites these modalities is not their method, but their stance. Each honors the symbolic as real, meaningful, and essential to integration. They do not pathologize metaphor. They *make space for it*, trusting that the psyche knows how to organize itself when it is seen, heard, and invited into coherence.

In working with these modalities, the clinician becomes a witness to myth in motion. A guide, not to fix or impose, but to accompany. To support the individual in discovering that
288

healing does not always look like resolution. Sometimes, it looks like a new story beginning to tell itself.

Living Narratives and Fluid Identity

To return to the symbolic is not to regress into fantasy, it is to awaken into a deeper dimension of meaning. Here, the self is no longer a static entity defined by roles, symptoms, or diagnoses. It is a living narrative, unfolding in time, shaped by presence, image, and relationship. The symbolic invites us to live not just *with* our stories, but *through* them with fluidity, depth, and poetic coherence.

Symbolic integration allows us to hold complexity without fragmentation. A protector is not banished, but invited to lay down its sword. A frozen child is not discarded, but welcomed back as the artist, the empath, the visionary. Beliefs once held as rigid truths begin to soften, becoming perspectives and possibilities. "I must not be seen" becomes "I needed invisibility once, and now I am safe enough to emerge." These transformations are not cognitive, they are soulful. They arise through contact, not correction.

As symbolic dialogue deepens, identity shifts. Not because it is forced to change, but because it is finally allowed to evolve. From rigid scripts to living myths. From trauma-bound truths to emergent meaning. From inherited survival patterns to consciously chosen paths of coherence.

In this space, the self is no longer something to fix or manage, it is something to *listen to*. The symbolic does not provide absolute answers; it offers invitations. Each image, each metaphor, each felt truth is a thread in the greater tapestry of becoming. Ultimately, this is the gift of the symbolic: not resolution, but relationship. Not certainty, but coherence. And in that coherence, life becomes more than manageable, it becomes meaningful.

Key Takeaways: Returning to the Symbolic

- The Symbolic marks a shift from identifying subpersonalities as patterns to engaging their deeper emotional and imaginal meanings.

- Flow becomes the dominant emergent quality—an internal sense of movement, safety, and coherence as the psyche reveals itself.

- Metaphor is the natural language of the symbolic. Through image and archetype, internal experiences are expressed and integrated.

- Core beliefs embedded within subpersonalities are revealed and transformed through symbolic dialogue not by logic, but by presence and relationship.

- Laboratory and diagnostic data are recontextualized as part of the individual's narrative, inviting inquiry into what the body's symptoms symbolize.

- Coherogenesis unfolds through symbolic integration, dissociated parts become threads in a living, evolving inner story.

- Psychotherapy modalities such as IFS, Jungian therapy, AEDP, Gestalt, Hakomi, and expressive arts help evoke and work with symbolic material.

- Identity becomes fluid, less defined by roles or symptoms, and more by a living narrative that honors complexity, change, and inner meaning.

Symbolic insight gives shape to the inner world. Through images, language, and narrative, we come to know our parts, name our pain, and witness the stories that have held us. But there is a limit to what language can hold. At some point, healing asks us to move beyond knowing into *being*, to leave behind interpretation and return to the body, where the truth of experience lives beneath words. In the next chapter, we descend from the architecture of meaning into the ground of felt sense. Here, coherence is no longer constructed, it is contacted. Through breath, touch, and presence, the sensorial reawakens, and with it, the compassionate awareness that holds us in wholeness.

CHAPTER TWENTY-ONE

The Sensorial Reawakened

"Before I could speak, I felt. Before I could name, I knew. I am this skin."

— The Arc of Human Experiencing

Returning from the symbolic to the sensorial is a movement downward and inward, a descent from abstraction and narrative into the raw immediacy of lived experience. It is a turning toward the body, not as object, but as origin: the place where truth pulses beneath the surface of interpretation. This descent is not a fallback to infancy or chaos, but a necessary re-entry into the terrain where coherence must ultimately be grounded.

The symbolic realm, with its metaphors, subpersonalities, and stories, offers profound insight, but insight alone does not integrate. Meaning must be metabolized through the body. Just as air must be breathed to oxygenate blood, symbolic understanding must be felt to transform. Without this descent into sensation, the psyche risks circling above its own pain, narrating its patterns without touching them.

The sensorial invites a different kind of knowing, one that emerges from textures, tones, and rhythms. It is not accessed through language, but through silence. It does not ask, "What does this mean?" but rather, "What does this feel like?" Here, the journey of healing is not conceptual but compassionate: a softening into the body's unspoken truths.

To reawaken the sensorial is to remember that healing does not begin with interpretation, it begins with the willingness to feel. And in that willingness, compassion becomes both the path and the guide.

From Representation to Resonance

The symbolic realm offers clarity and coherence. Through language, metaphor, and narrative, we map the inner landscape, giving name to our parts, meaning to our suffering, and shape to the seemingly chaotic. But as vital as this realm is, it is not the final destination. Insight, while illuminating, is not synonymous with integration.

To truly heal, we must move from representation to resonance, from thinking *about* experience to *being with* it. This is not a rejection of the symbolic, but a loosening of its grip. When symbolic constructs dominate, we may begin to live inside interpretations rather than experience. The map becomes mistaken for the terrain.

The movement into the sensorial begins when thought slows. A pause after insight. A breath held just long enough to feel. For instance, after identifying a subpersonality a gentle invitation might follow: *Where does this part live in your*

293

body? What is its posture? Its weight? Its temperature? Such questions mark the shift from description to embodiment. They invite resonance.

In this movement, de-symbolization becomes a compassionate act. It's not an undoing of meaning, but a returning to the place where meaning was first formed, through sensation. The symbolic often encodes affect. A narrative about abandonment may conceal a deeper layer: a cold hollowness in the chest, a bracing in the gut, or a subtle tremor behind the eyes. By attending to the body's responses, we follow the echo of the symbol back to its emotional root.

In this way, the sensorial does not oppose the symbolic, it completes it. The body becomes the place where story finds form, and where insight becomes felt truth. Resonance, not representation, is the medium through which integration occurs.

The Language of the Sensorial Self

The sensorial realm is the foundation of our earliest knowing. Long before we had words, we had touch. Before identity, there was tone. The sensorial self is pre-verbal and pre-reflective, it does not organize through narrative but through rhythm, texture, pressure, and movement. It is the body's language, the root of meaning before metaphor takes hold.

To reawaken this layer of Self is to shift from the representational mind into the immediacy of perception. This means guiding awareness not toward ideas, but toward sensation. The weight of the body against the ground. The subtle pulsing in the hands. The rise and fall of breath. The constriction in the throat that arrives before tears, or the warmth in the chest that appears before the thought *I am safe.*

The sensorial does not explain; it expresses. It speaks in edges, vibrations, densities. Through interoception, we perceive internal sensations—heartbeat, gut tension, shallow breath. Through proprioception, we sense the body's position and movement in space. Through tactile and visceral awareness, we begin to feel the body as lived territory, not just biological machinery.

In therapeutic practice, this often begins with gentle grounding: *Notice your feet on the floor. Feel the support of the chair beneath you. Sense the breath without changing it.* These simple inquiries return the individual to the present not as an idea, but as a place.

The sensorial self is also the keeper of the unspeakable: the preverbal traces of early attachment, trauma, and vitality. These do not arrive in sentences. They surface in the body's holding patterns, in flinches and freeze states, in warmth or numbness. They often appear when symbolic exploration begins to soften, revealing affective undercurrents hidden beneath the story.

Compassion here means not forcing interpretation, but staying with sensation. Asking not, *Why do I feel this way?* but *What does this feel like in tone, in texture, in movement?* Compassion asks nothing from the sensation, it simply sits beside it.

In this space, even subtle contact becomes sacred. A trembling in the hand. A loosening in the jaw. A breath released. Each becomes a portal through which coherence may re-enter. The sensorial is not merely somatic, it is sacred. It is where the psyche and soma touch.

Cessation of Free-Flowing Energy: The Birth of Fragmentation

In a coherent, regulated system, energy flows freely. Sensations, emotions, impulses, and thoughts arise, move through, and complete their cycles. The body mobilizes for action, then returns to rest. The self remains intact, adaptive, and connected. This is the fluid expression of vitality, life moving in rhythm with life.

But this coherence is fragile. It is shaped not only by what happens, but by how the system perceives what happens. When a stimulus, internal or external, overwhelms our capacity to stay connected, the flow of energy ceases. It might be a physical threat, a relational rupture, or an existential fear. The trigger matters less than the system's assessment: *I cannot safely stay in contact with this.* That assessment happens beneath awareness. It's not a thought, it's a felt determination. The bodymind decides: *This is too much. I must protect myself.*

And so, the natural response of crying, reaching out, fleeing, and defending is interrupted. The energy that was mobilized to respond cannot complete its course. It gets held. Not just as memory, but as physiology: in breath patterns, muscle tone, posture, autonomic states, and implicit beliefs. The system, once open and flowing, now reorganizes around protection.

This is not dysfunction. It is adaptation. The system does what it must to survive. But in that moment, something is sacrificed. A part of the Self becomes frozen in time, wrapped around the unprocessed experience. The rest of the Self moves on, building strategies, beliefs, and identities to accommodate the fracture. These are the roots of internal fragmentation.

Symptoms, reactivity, dissociation, and emotional triggers are not arbitrary, they are echoes of this original interruption. They signal where energy remains stuck, where the body still braces against the past, where the psyche holds its breath. The unconscious doesn't forget, it waits.

The invitation to healing is not to rip these protections away, but to return to them with more resource, with a slower pace, with compassionate presence. Not to force movement, but to offer conditions where movement might resume. Integration is not something we do to the body, it is what the body does when it feels safe.

And so, the frozen places begin to thaw. A shiver, a tear, a memory that surfaces. Not because we pushed, but because we stayed. In this way, compassion becomes the solvent. It dissolves the rigidity of defense, not by breaking it, but by witnessing it with warmth and patience.

The Physiology of Compassionate Contact

The sensorial self does not emerge on command. It reveals itself when the system feels safe enough to allow it. This threshold of safety is not intellectual, it is physiological. The nervous system, more than the brain, determines whether we are available for experience or bracing against it. Compassion is what helps bridge this threshold. It is not just a feeling but a condition, a relational and internal stance that signals: *You are safe enough now to feel what could not be felt before.*

297

Neurophysiologically, this safety is mediated through the autonomic nervous system. In particular, the ventral vagal complex, associated with connection, calm, and social engagement, must be accessible for the sensorial self to come forward. When we are in this state of regulation, we are able to orient to the present, take in nuance, and stay with sensation without becoming overwhelmed.

But when the system perceives threat, we lose this access. We may shift into sympathetic arousal (fight or flight) or drop into dorsal vagal shutdown (collapse, numbness, dissociation). In either case, the body protects by moving away from felt experience.

Here, polyvagal theory offers an essential map: we must *pendulate* between activation and resource, contraction and support, so the body does not overwhelm itself in the act of healing. The task is not to plunge into the pain, but to create the physiological conditions that allow pain to emerge and complete its course without overwhelming the system again.

Candace Pert's work in *Molecules of Emotion* underscores the profound connection between the mind and body through molecular messengers, specifically neuropeptides. These molecules, released in response to emotional experiences, travel throughout the body, linking physical sensations with emotional states. This dynamic supports the notion that emotions are not merely mental constructs but are embedded in our physiology, with the body playing an active role in emotional processing. Pert's findings align with polyvagal theory, reinforcing the significance of somatic awareness in therapeutic settings. By engaging with bodily sensations, we activate the neuropeptides that facilitate emotional release and integration, highlighting the essential role of compassionate contact in fostering healing through the mind-body connection.

Therapeutically, this might look like:

- Tracking the breath to notice subtle shifts in arousal.

- Naming cues of safety: warmth, grounding, a calm voice.

- Gently orienting to the environment: "What are three things you can see right now?"

- Supporting interoceptive awareness without pushing: "What's happening inside your chest? Can you stay with that?"

These invitations are not diagnostic, they are devotional. They say to the body, *You matter. You will not be rushed.*

This is where compassion becomes more than kindness, it becomes regulation. It is being with an experience to hold space or create a container for metabolization. The body is the only thing that can do the work of processing sensations and it can only do so in the present moment. The compassionate presence of the therapist (or the emerging inner witness within the individual) serves as a co-regulating force. Eye contact, vocal tone, and breath rhythm all contribute to a felt sense of "I am not alone in this and it won't last forever." This is reflective of the compassionate presence of a parent co-regulating with a child.

And from this place, the sensorial self may begin to thaw. Raw sensations move. Subtle sensations surface. Numbness softens. The body begins to tell the truth it once had to silence. Not because it was analyzed, but because it was met with enough warmth and patience to finally speak.

Modalities of Re-Sensitization: Compassion in Practice

Reawakening the sensorial self is not accomplished through insight alone. It is a process of gently guiding awareness into the body, into the textures of experience that language cannot reach. Many psychotherapeutic modalities already engage this realm, though each does so through its own unique lens. What unites them is the use of compassionate presence as the medium through which embodiment, and thus integration, occurs. Below are several modalities that exemplify this work as invitations offered *with* the individual guided by curiosity, patience, and care.

Somatic Experiencing (SE). Developed by Peter Levine, SE focuses on tracking internal states and discharging held survival energy. It emphasizes pendulation, moving between sensation and safety, rather than direct immersion in trauma. SE encourages awareness of interoceptive and proprioceptive signals. It utilizes titration to stay within the window of tolerance. Compassion enters through pacing: nothing is forced; the body sets the tempo.

Hakomi. A mindfulness-based, body-centered therapy developed by Ron Kurtz, Hakomi rests on the principles of nonviolence, loving presence, and unity. Individuals enter a mindful state where unconscious material can arise through body cues. The therapist follows the body's lead, tracking microexpressions, shifts in breath, posture, and tone. Healing arises from *being with*, not fixing, offering a field of compassion in which core material can reorganize.

Focusing. Developed by Eugene Gendlin, focusing introduces the concept of the felt sense, a bodily knowing that is unclear yet meaningful. Individuals are invited to turn inward and describe what is sensed but not yet verbalized. Words emerge slowly from the body, not imposed upon it. The therapist's presence serves as a compassionate companion to the unfolding process.

Eye Movement Desensitization and Reprocessing (EMDR). Though often associated with trauma reprocessing through bilateral stimulation, EMDR also engages the body directly. Body scans are used to identify residual activation after reprocessing. Individuals are encouraged to notice where distress lingers somatically. The desensitization process often leads to a spontaneous sense of peace, lightness, or release, deeply sensorial shifts.

Internal Family Systems (IFS). IFS recognizes that parts of us hold trauma in the body. While the model focuses on subpersonalities, its depth comes when those parts are approached **somatically**. The therapist might ask, "Where do you feel that part in your body?" Somatic bridges are used to communicate with protectors and exiles. When a part feels seen and accompanied with compassion, it often softens, revealing its stored emotional or sensorial content.

These approaches differ in method but converge in intention: to reestablish contact with the living, sensorial body and to do so without force, without analysis, and without bypass. Instead, they extend a compassionate invitation to the body's truths, allowing them to emerge in their own time.

In clinical practice, these modalities can be adapted and integrated. What matters most is the stance behind the intervention: Is this being offered with reverence? With attunement? With respect for the body's pace? If so, it is likely to deepen the individual's capacity to feel and thus to heal.

Mutual Process and the Sensorial Field

The sensorial is not solitary. It is shaped, sustained, and restored through relationship. Long before we had words, we lived in the field of another's nervous system, soothed by voice, held by compassionate presence, regulated by breath and touch. To return to the sensorial is to return to the *mutual process* that first gave it form.

In psychotherapy, this mutual process is not just theoretical, it is biological. Mirror neurons fire when we witness another's movement or emotion, allowing us to *feel with*. The therapist's body becomes part of the individual's perceptual field, and vice versa. The breath of one influences the breath of the other. A softening gaze invites a softening jaw. A grounded tone slows a racing heart.

This is the sensorial field. An unspoken, intersubjective space in which healing occurs through co-regulation, not explanation. Within this field:

- The therapist's own regulation serves as an anchor for the individual's nervous system.

- Microadjustments in posture, tone, or breath subtly communicate safety.

- Silence becomes a shared container, not an absence.

The therapist's presence is not neutral, it is sensorially expressive. It can invite or inhibit, soothe or startle. And when offered with compassion and embodied attunement, it becomes a medium through which previously unfeelable experience may now be felt.

This mutual process also helps restore ruptured relational templates. Where once touch may have harmed, proximity may have overwhelmed, or emotion may have gone unseen, the sensorial field reintroduces connection as safe. Not conceptually, but physiologically. The individual's body begins to learn: *This time is different.*

In this way, therapy becomes less about what is said and more about what is sensed. The therapeutic relationship functions not just as a secure attachment, but as a sensorial re-patterning environment, one in which the individual learns to tolerate, interpret, and eventually trust the language of their own body again.

Through this mutual process, compassion is not merely extended, it is exchanged. The individual is not simply receiving care, but participating in a field of care, where both nervous systems influence and inform each other. In this space, the body remembers what it once had to forget: that it can exist, feel, and connect, all at once.

Integration: Compassion as Ground, Not Strategy

To return to the sensorial is not to regress, but to reconnect. To descend from abstraction into the pulse of embodied life. It is here, in the textures of sensation, that coherence begins to take root. Not through explanation, but through presence. Not by force, but through the gentle touch of compassion.

Throughout this chapter, we have traced the path from symbolic representation to sensorial resonance, from mental

303

knowing to bodily truth. We have seen how trauma interrupts the free flow of energy, how the nervous system protects by fragmenting experience, and how healing begins not with confrontation, but with consent given by the body when it feels safe enough to feel again.

Compassion, in this context, is not a technique. It is not a strategy layered on top of suffering to make it more bearable. It is a quality of presence emergent from the ground of being: the spacious warmth that makes sensation survivable, the gaze that makes pain visible, the tone that says, *you don't have to go through this alone.*

As the symbolic and patterned layers are softened by curiosity and flow, the sensorial self begins to speak again not in words, but in pulses, shifts, and subtle stirrings. And as it does, new coherence becomes possible. Dissociated parts begin to re-enter the field of awareness. Previously held energy finds movement. And the self, once fragmented around protection, reorganizes toward connection. In this process, compassion is both the guide and the goal. It makes room for trembling. It allows numbness without urgency. It honors silence. It says: *Even this belongs.*

Ultimately, the sensorial reawakened is not a return to infancy, but a return to innocence where the body is once again trusted as a source of truth. Where feeling is no longer feared. Where sensation is not just tolerated, but listened to, like the first language we ever knew.

And here, in touch with the sacred ground of being, healing is no longer something to strive for. It becomes something that emerges—slowly, tenderly, from within.

Key Takeaways: The Sensorial Reawakened

- **Descent into the Body**: Returning from the symbolic to the sensorial is a downward and inward movement, from narrative and abstraction to the immediacy of felt experience.

- **Compassion as Guide**: Compassion is the dominant quality in this return. It softens defenses and creates the safety needed for sensorial truth to emerge.

- **From Knowing to Being**: Symbolic understanding is important but incomplete without resonance. Integration occurs when insights are felt in the body.

- **The Language of the Sensorial**: The sensorial self communicates through sensation (texture, rhythm, tone) rather than story. It is accessed through interoception, proprioception, and tactile awareness.

- **Cessation and Fragmentation**: Energy ceases to flow when the system perceives it cannot remain safely connected. This interruption births fragmentation, protection, and dissociation.

- **Physiological Conditions for Healing**: The body must feel safe for the sensorial to emerge. Healing unfolds when the nervous system shifts into regulation (ventral vagal state). Compassion regulates and allows for titrated re-entry into held experience.

- **Modality Integration**: Somatic Experiencing: Pendulation and titration of energy. Hakomi: Loving presence and nonviolence. Focusing: Felt sense and body-oriented meaning-making. EMDR: Body scans and dual attention. IFS: Somatic bridges to parts. All modalities honor the pace of the body and the primacy of embodied truth.

- **Mutual Process and the Sensorial Field**: Healing happens in relationship, through shared physiological regulation. The therapist's sensorial presence shapes the field of safety. Co-regulation and mirror neurons play vital roles in restoring embodiment.

- **Integration as Emergence**: Compassion is not a strategy, it is the ground from which healing grows. The sensorial reawakened is a return to embodied coherence, not regression. Through compassionate presence, sensation becomes survivable, meaningful, and sacred.

As we return to the sensorial, we rediscover the body not as a burden but as a vessel of truth. Each breath, each pulse, each subtle tremble reminding us that being is not abstract, but intimate. And yet, even beneath this rich terrain of sensation, something deeper waits. When we rest into the body fully, a quiet unfolds that is not just the absence of noise, but the presence of something whole. Beyond the textures of feeling and the rhythms of the nervous system, we begin to sense the still field from which all experience arises. In the next chapter, we enter this field more directly not through doing, or naming, or feeling, but through simply being. This is the ground beneath all grounds, the unitive presence that holds all layers of the self in silent embrace.

CHAPTER TWENTY-TWO

Resting in the Unitive

"Silence is not the absence of sound, but the presence of everything."

— Gordon Hempton

The journey through human experiencing is often described as a process of becoming—of development, layering, differentiation, and integration. We grow into selves: sensorial, symbolic, patterned. Each layer offers structure, identity, and meaning. Each allows the organism to navigate the world, relate to others, and sustain coherence in the face of complexity. These selves are vital expressions of life's movement toward organization and adaptation. But they are not the whole story.

Integration is often framed as the goal of psychological development: the weaving together of parts into a functional, cohesive whole. And yet, integration can open a doorway rather than close a chapter. For beneath even the most beautifully integrated personality lies something prior. Something untouched by trauma, unlimited by role, unaffected by structure, unchanged by changes, and unformed by time. This chapter begins at that threshold. What lies beyond integration is not more doing, but a profound undoing. A softening. A return.

The sensorial, symbolic, and patterned selves arise from experience, but their source is deeper. Beneath their unique textures and stories is the unitive, what might be called the ground of being. This is not a phase to be developed, nor a state to be achieved. It is a presence that has always been here. A spacious awareness in which all forms arise and dissolve. It is not shaped by identity, but allows identity. It is not the sum of the parts, but the field in which parts appear.

This ground is not conceptual. It is not known by thinking, but felt in the silent spaces between. It reveals itself in moments when the striving stops, when the story falls away, and when we rest not just in body, but in being.

In returning to the unitive, we are not regressing. We are not abandoning the self. We are discovering the formless essence that holds all form. We are returning not backward, but inward and downward, toward the root of our aliveness. Toward presence itself.

The Ground of Being

Beneath the constructed identities, the woven narratives, and the layered adaptations lies a presence untouched by them all. This is the ground of being. Not something we become, but something we uncover. It is the ever-present field from which all forms arise, and to which they all return.

The unitive field is not defined by what can be seen or grasped, but by the spaciousness that allows all things to arise and cohere. As expressed in the 11th verse of the *Tao Te Ching*, it is the emptiness within the wheel, the vessel, the room, that gives form its function and meaning. In the same way, it is the silent presence of Being (the unformed, undivided ground) that gives coherence to all expression. This space is not absence, but potential. A paradoxical nothingness where there is "no thing" and yet, everything. It is the fertile openness from which all phenomena emerge. In resting with the unitive, we begin to recognize that the true nature of wholeness is not the sum of its parts, but the silent center that allows all parts to relate, reflect, and harmonize. Here, usefulness and meaning do not arise from accumulation, but from allowing: allowing presence, stillness, and the mystery of Being to simply be.

In early development, differentiation is necessary. The sensorial gives rise to felt sense and containment, the symbolic brings meaning, the patterned offers structure. Each layer of human becoming serves to maintain continuity, to maintain coherence. Each level scaffolds a workable identity to serve this function. Yet behind the scaffolding stands something more fundamental. Something not born of experience, but rather the context in which experience unfolds.

This ground is not a part or a position. It is not the child self, the protector, the achiever, or the wounded one. It is awareness itself—spacious, still, without edges or conditions. From a nondual perspective, this is not a *thing* we possess, but what we are. Not the experience, but the very witnessing of experience. Not just a subject looking out at objects, but the seamless field in which all subject-object distinctions arise.

In language, we call this presence the Self not to denote another identity, but to gesture toward the unchanging. This Self is not shaped by the past. It is not improved upon by healing. It is whole, even when the system is fragmented. It is here, even when we are lost. It is not a container, but a kind of openness in which all containers appear. Not the voice of a part, but the silence that hears them all.

Accessing this level of being is not a matter of achieving a new state, but releasing our grip on all that obscures it. It is remembered in moments of deep stillness, when the internal dialogues quiet and something wordless begins to shine through. Often, this presence is first recognized not through dramatic epiphany but through an absence. An absence of striving, of story, of separation.

The ground of being is not an escape from reality. It is the foundation that makes reality possible. In its presence, we no longer identify with any single wave, but begin to recognize ourselves as the ocean—vast, open, and undivided.

Awareness as Organizing Principle

When conscious awareness is recognized as the ground rather than one function among many, the entire system begins to reorganize. No longer driven by defense, the psyche loosens its grip on the patterned strategies once required for safety. Rather than operating from protection, the system begins to orient around presence.

This shift is subtle but profound. In the patterned self, identity is held in tension, defined by what it must avoid,

310

achieve, repress or suppress. Responses are reactive, tied to the repetition of past adaptations. Even when these patterns are adaptive, they are still compensatory and rooted in the survival strategies of becoming, not being.

But in the presence of awareness itself, something changes. Proactivity and reactivity diminish. Responses become more spacious, grounded, and choiceful. Identity is no longer a fixed construct, but a fluid expression of the moment. Inner multiplicity, once managed by internal hierarchies, can be held together in a wider field of coherence. The need to defend dissolves as safety is no longer externally secured but internally embodied.

This does not mean the loss of personality. It means the liberation from personality and associated compulsive loops. The "I" is not erased, but revealed as a movement within something vaster. What we previously called "self" is now seen as a constellation of patterns within a deeper intelligence.

From this orientation, even familiar challenges are met differently. Emotions arise but no longer overwhelm. Subpersonalities speak but no longer dominate. The past may still echo, but it no longer dictates. Awareness, by its very nature, holds contradiction without conflict. It offers the internal system a new organizing principle. One that does not control, but includes. One that does not suppress, but listens.

In therapeutic work, this shift is often marked by a new quality of self-presence. The individual no longer seeks solely to fix what is broken, but to relate from a deeper truth. The inner world becomes more transparent, less burdened by secrecy or shame. What was previously exiled or over-identified finds room to breathe. The system begins to organize

311

not around fear or fragmentation, but around coherence, compassion, and clarity. Awareness does not fight for control. It doesn't need to. Its presence is enough.

To relate from the ground of Being is to move from a deeper truth. One that is not conceptual or imposed, but organically revealed through the coherence of presence. In this model, truth is not a fixed endpoint but an ever-deepening emergence: the undistorted pattern arising from the field of lived experience. As fragmentation heals and the layers of the self align, this truth becomes more perceptible not as static knowledge, but as a living current of coherence flowing through sensation, symbol, behavior, and relationship. It is revealed not by effort or analysis, but through attunement to the unitive ground from which all meaning arises. In this way, truth is not something we find. It is something that finds us when we rest into what has always been most real.

The Embodied Realization

Presence is not just a psychological insight, it is a physiological event. When the system organizes around awareness, the body begins to respond in kind. No longer bracing against life, it softens into it. The muscles relax their historical grip. Breath deepens without instruction. The nervous system, once locked in cycles of defense and anticipation, finds new rhythms aligned with safety, stillness, and connection.

This is not a bypassing of the body, but a descent into it. Awareness becomes embodied not through dissociation or detachment, but through full presence with what is. The body, long shaped by trauma and adaptation, begins to entrain not to old imprints, but to now. It becomes an instrument of presence—finely tuned, deeply responsive, inherently wise.

Physiologically, this may manifest as increased vagal tone, greater heart rate variability, and improved regulation across autonomic, endocrine, and immune systems. Allostatic load, the wear and tear from chronic stress, begins to reduce. Hormonal and metabolic processes recalibrate. The body is no longer just a container of the past, but a partner in the unfolding of presence.

At this level, healing is not something done to the body, but something that arises within the body as it comes into coherence with awareness. The therapist or practitioner does not impose change, they help the individual listen. The body, given space and safety, knows how to return to wholeness.

This embodied realization changes the felt sense of identity. One no longer feels *in* a body as much as *of* the body—interwoven, inseparable. The boundary between mind and soma begins to dissolve, revealing a unified field of experiencing. Emotional processes become more fluid. Somatic cues, once muted or chaotic, start to organize into intelligible patterns. There is a sense of "rightness" not because all is resolved, but because nothing is being resisted.

This level of realization redefines regulation. It is not the suppression of distress or the pursuit of a steady state. It is the ability to move with life, to return to presence again and again. It is a flexible, dynamic coherence that arises when the system is no longer defending against itself.

The embodied realization is not the endpoint of development. It is the revelation of what was always available when awareness and body meet without interference. In that meeting, there is rest. Not just for the mind, but for the whole being.

The Unitive Beyond the Body: Environment and Society

To rest in the unitive is not only to feel the body as an expression of wholeness, but to perceive all of life as interwoven. Each organism, each system, each moment arising from the same indivisible ground. From this perspective, the boundary between self and world softens. The environment is no longer something "out there," but a reflection of the same living field that breathes through our cells. Society, too, is not a collection of separate individuals, but a dynamic interplay of relationships, each shaped by and shaping the whole.

When coherence deepens within the self, it reverberates outward: toward how we relate to others, how we move through space, how we care for the environment. The unitive view does not isolate healing within the skin, nor locate wisdom solely in the psyche. It sees the forest as an organ of the planet, the community as an expression of shared consciousness, the climate as a pulse of collective behavior. Just as sensation arises from the body's internal coherence, sustainability arises from the coherence between humanity and the natural world. In both cases, fragmentation leads to suffering; alignment restores vitality.

To live from the unitive is to recognize that every act of presence ripples outward. The way we listen to another, tend the soil, or design a policy reflects our degree of attunement to the whole. This is not idealism, it is interdependence. The more we live in coherence with the deep field of Being, the more we begin to see every ecological and societal structure as an
314

extension of our own internal patterning. And from this place, change becomes possible. Not through control, but through rhythm and resonance.

The Paradox of Return

To return to the unitive is not to go backward, but to fall inward into the ever-present ground from which all experience arises. It is a return not to a developmental stage, but to the timeless dimension that has always accompanied every stage. And in this, there is paradox: we do not become something new, we recognize what has never not been.

This recognition does not discard the differentiated self. It sees it clearly, tenderly, as an expression of something deeper. The sensorial, symbolic, and patterned layers do not dissolve, they are held. They continue to move and speak, but now from within a wider field. No longer mistaken for the whole, they are freed to play their part without carrying the burden of defining the "I."

This paradox extends even to identity itself. In earlier phases of development, identity offers coherence, direction, and continuity. But in returning to the unitive, identity becomes more like clothing. Something worn lightly, changed easily, never mistaken for the skin. The "self" becomes transparent to the Self. What once appeared as a solid object becomes a dynamic expression—ever-shifting, never fixed.

From the outside, little may appear different. Life continues. Emotions still arise. The body still ages. But the inner position has changed. There is less struggle, less reactivity, less compulsion. Life is met with greater intimacy and less grasping. What was once clung to begins to loosen.

What was once rejected begins to be included. The wave begins to remember the ocean.

And yet, even the metaphor of the wave and ocean is incomplete. For the wave is not other than the ocean. The form is not separate from the formless. This is the deepest paradox: the unitive does not replace the differentiated, it saturates it. The more deeply one rests in Being, the more fully one can participate in becoming.

In this way, return is not an erasure of complexity, but its grounding in simplicity. Not a negation of difference, but its holding within unity. This is the coherence that arises when form and formlessness are no longer in tension. We return not to innocence, but to essence. Not to childhood, but to source. And in that return, we find we have never truly left.

Practices that Nurture Presence

While the ground of being is always present, it is not always accessible. The layered adaptations of the differentiated self (protective strategies, internalized narratives, physiological dysregulation) can obscure the direct experience of presence. Yet many psychotherapeutic and spiritual practices have evolved as doorways back to this ground. They do not create presence, but they clear the way for it to be known.

In psychotherapy, certain modalities seem especially attuned to this deeper orientation. Internal Family Systems (IFS), for example, holds that within every person is a Self characterized by qualities like calmness, curiosity, clarity, and compassion. This Self is not a part among others, but the field that can relate to all parts with spaciousness and non-judgment.

316

In practice, IFS helps individuals unblend from over-identified parts and rest in the stable presence of Self-awareness.

Similarly, somatic approaches such as Somatic Experiencing, Sensorimotor Psychotherapy, and Hakomi bring attention to the body not as a problem to be fixed, but as a living expression of experience. These methods slow down the pace of interpretation and invite direct contact with sensation, impulse, and movement. In this embodied space, presence is not theorized, it is felt. Practitioners often model and co-regulate this state, helping the individual entrain to an internal field of safety and coherence.

Mindfulness-based therapies such as Mindfulness-Based Cognitive Therapy (MBCT) and Acceptance and Commitment Therapy (ACT) encourage observation of thoughts, emotions, and sensations without fusion or resistance. Over time, this fosters a witnessing awareness that is distinct from content. The "self-as-context" described in ACT echoes the unitive: a stable field within which all experience unfolds.

Transpersonal and depth-oriented psychotherapies also make space for the ineffable. Jungian analysis, for instance, emphasizes the Self as a central archetype of wholeness, guiding the individuation process. Psychospiritual modalities may include imagery, dreamwork, or altered states to access layers of consciousness beyond the ego's domain. Altered states facilitated by psychedelics has become a more well-received practice to touch the unitive.

Spiritual practices from contemplative traditions mirror these intentions. Meditative practices, particularly in nondual lineages like Advaita Vedanta, Taoism, Zen or Dzogchen, invites the practitioner to rest as awareness itself. The

317

instruction is not to attain something new, but to recognize the ever-present nature of the experiencer. Self-inquiry, asking "Who am I?", does not lead to an answer, but to a silent recognition of that which is beyond the question.

Contemplative prayer, sacred movement, chanting, breathwork, and devotional rituals can all serve as pathways not because they invoke a distant divinity, but because they quiet the noise that hides the nearness of being. These practices orient not around fixing the self, but around resting as Self. When approached from presence rather than prescription, they invite a direct encounter with the unitive, an inner stillness that is both deeply personal and entirely beyond the personal. In this way, spirituality emerges not through adherence to doctrine, but through dissolution of the boundaries that doctrine often protects.

As Eckhart Tolle observes, the more religious we become, the less spiritual we may become. This is because religion, as a patterned construct, can become yet another identity to defend, another structure to maintain. But true spiritual practice carries us beyond structure. It loosens the patterned scaffolding of belief and returns us to the raw immediacy of Being. Here, the sacred is not mediated by hierarchy or institution, but discovered in the simplicity of breath, silence, movement, and presence.

At their best, psychotherapy and spiritual practice converge. They become less about solving a problem and more about revealing what's already whole. The healer or teacher, in this context, is not merely a technician, but a presence-holder, a guide who models coherence and invites the individual to recognize it within themselves. Ultimately, these practices do not take us to the ground of being. They help us stop running from it.

Language, Silence, and the Ineffable

To speak of the unitive is to point toward what cannot fully be said. Language, by nature, divides and defines. It separates figure from ground, self from other, subject from object. But the ground of being is prior to these distinctions. It does not reside within language, it gives rise to it. And so, when we attempt to describe this dimension, we inevitably fall short.

Yet language still plays a role. Metaphor, poetry, and gesture can orient the mind toward what lies beyond it. We speak of the sky, the ocean, the still point at the center of the turning world not to define the ineffable, but to evoke it. These are not explanations, but invitations.

In therapeutic and contemplative contexts, this limitation of language becomes a doorway rather than a barrier. Words may guide the seeker to the edge of experience, but presence begins where words end. Often, it is in the pauses, those spaces between sentences, between breaths, where something deeper is felt. Silence is not the absence of meaning, but its fullness. It holds what cannot be grasped, only known.

In this sense, the symbolic and patterned selves are not abandoned. They become allies in the descent. Language, when softened of its certainty, becomes a raft not the shore itself, but a way across. The mind learns to bow, to surrender its compulsion to understand, and in doing so, becomes transparent to presence.

Paradoxically, as we deepen into the ineffable, our use of language changes. We may speak more slowly, more simply. We may find ourselves drawn to poetry or prayer. We may say less, but feel more. The symbolic becomes quieter. Not silenced, but attuned.

In the presence of another, these shifts are often palpable. An individual may describe "not knowing what just happened," yet feel clearer, lighter, or more whole. What occurred was not cognitive insight, but contact with the real. And the clinician, if attuned, senses that something sacred passed through—unspoken, but known. Ultimately, the ineffable is not inaccessible. It is simply not grasped in the usual way. It is not something we speak *about*, it is what speaks *through* us, when we are quiet enough to listen.

Coherence Through Presence

The journey through the sensorial, symbolic, and patterned reveals the intricacy of human becoming. Each layer adds depth and complexity to our experience of selfhood. Yet as we descend through these layers, gently peeling back what was once necessary, we do not fall into fragmentation, but into wholeness. We return not to a prior version of ourselves, but to that which was never separate to begin with.

This ground of being is not a goal to be reached or a state to be maintained. It is a truth that quietly underlies every moment. It is presence itself—unwavering, unconditional, and undisturbed. When the psyche begins to organize around this presence, coherence arises not from effort but from alignment. Patterns soften, multiplicity finds harmony, and the organism breathes again not just in body, but in being.

To live from this ground is not to transcend the human, but to embody it more fully. It is to allow every part (every sensation, story, emotion, and identity) to be held in something vaster. The wave no longer fears its form when it knows itself as ocean.

In the therapy room, this presence is not taught, but modeled. It is felt in the space between words, in the attuned silence, in the eyes of someone who is not trying to fix you. It is remembered through relationship. Through resonance. Through rest.

The invitation of this chapter, and of this work, is not to escape suffering, but to find the place in which even suffering is allowed. To rest not *after* healing, but as healing. To recognize that what you seek has always been here, quietly waiting for your return. You are not the fragments you've carried. You are not even the one who carries them. You are the field that holds it all. Rest there.

Key Takeaways: Resting in the Unitive

- **Beyond Integration:** Integration of the sensorial, symbolic, and patterned selves is not the endpoint, it reveals a deeper substratum, the unitive ground of being.

- **The Ground of Being:** The unitive is not constructed or achieved; it is the timeless field of awareness from which all experience and identity arise. It is not a self among others, but the Self—as presence, as witnessing, as formlessness.

- **Awareness as Organizing Principle:** When awareness becomes the organizing center, the system shifts from defense to coherence. Identity becomes fluid, multiplicity is held rather than managed, and reactivity gives way to response.

- **The Embodied Realization:** Presence becomes physiological. The body entrains to now, not to trauma. Deep systemic regulation emerges, manifesting as vagal tone, reduced allostatic load, and restored balance across bodily systems.

- **The Paradox of Return:** Returning to the unitive is not regression, but revelation. The differentiated self is included, not negated. Form and formlessness are not opposed, the unitive saturates the differentiated.

- **Practices That Nurture Presence:** Psychotherapy modalities like IFS, somatic therapies, mindfulness-based approaches, and transpersonal work support access to Self-presence. Spiritual practices, meditation, self-inquiry, contemplative ritual, help quiet the mind and reveal the ground already present.

- **Language, Silence, and the Ineffable:** The unitive cannot be fully captured by language. Stillness, metaphor, and poetic gesture point toward it. Silence becomes the carrier of presence.

- **Coherence Through Presence:** Living from the ground of being does not erase the human, it embraces it. Healing becomes the unfolding of what was always whole. Presence is not a technique. It is a return to the truth of what you are.

Resting in the ground of being, we discover a presence that is silent, whole, and undivided. A stillness that holds all things
322

without effort. Yet this stillness is not inert. Like fertile soil, it contains the potential for movement, unfolding, and becoming. When fragmentation quiets and defenses soften, something more essential begins to stir not as a role or an identity, but as life itself moving through us with coherence.

What arises here is not a new self, but a clearer intimacy with the Self as field, consciousness aware of itself, flowing in rhythm with all that is. In the chapters that follow, we enter this living coherence: where presence is no longer just something we rest in, but something we live, express, and become. This is the beginning of the ocean beyond. A rhythm without edge, and a wholeness without shore.

Part V. The Ocean Beyond: Resting in the Rhythm of Wholeness

At the culmination of the journey, we do not reach a conclusion, but dissolve into a deeper coherence. This final section explores what unfolds when consciousness is no longer striving to fix, complete, or become, but simply is. Here, the Self is not something to attain, but the field through which life flows in rhythm. Consciousness becomes aware of itself not as content, but as presence—fluid, playful, and whole.

We explore coherence as a living expression, not a static state. In this space, healing is not the end of suffering, but the release of resistance to what is. Paths remain unfinished, not because they are broken, but because aliveness does not conclude. The ocean no longer surges toward shore, but expands in every direction, an open invitation to rest, participate, and play in the mystery of being and becoming.

CHAPTER TWENTY-THREE

Coherence Through Conscious Awareness

"Consciousness is the womb of transformation."

— The Arc of Human Experiencing

In previous chapters, we traced the unfolding of human experience through layered expressions of the Self—unitive, sensorial, symbolic, and patterned. Along this arc, trauma and adaptation shaped how awareness was filtered, how fragments formed, and how psychiatric frameworks often mirrored our disconnection. Now, we turn inward toward the integrative capacity of conscious awareness.

Awareness is not a passive observer of experience, it is the living field in which healing unfolds. It persists even when identity fractures. It is the one element in the system that remains whole, capable of welcoming what has been exiled and restoring coherence not through force, but through presence.

Part V. The Ocean Beyond

The Self as Field, Witness, and Organizer

The Self, in this model, is not a part to be discovered or constructed. It is the field of being itself, the unitive ground from which all experience arises and into which all returns. The Self is not something we find, but something we *remember* as we soften the layers of fragmentation. It is not a fixed identity or a role, but the coherent unfolding of wholeness through time—being becoming, the ocean shaping its waves.

We encounter the Self not as content within the field, but as the field itself becoming conscious. When awareness stabilizes, when presence includes what has long been excluded, what emerges is not a new part, but the presence that has always been here. This is why the Self is often experienced as a steady witness not because it is separate from experience, but because it is the context within which all experience moves.

In the unfolding of human life, the Self is both immanent and emergent. It is the ground of being expressed through the differentiated layers of experience—sensorial, symbolic, patterned. As it moves through these layers, the Self becomes an organizing principle: not a controller or commander, but a center of gravity around which coherence begins to form. It is the internal leader not by authority, but by resonance.

When trauma occurs, this resonance can be disrupted. The system fragments in service of protection. Experience is split into parts that cannot yet be held together. But the Self, being the field itself, is never lost. It remains present even when the system forgets. Healing does not happen by

328

constructing a stronger identity, it happens when awareness becomes stable enough to include all that has been excluded.

As presence returns, the qualities associated with the Self (compassion, clarity, curiosity, calm) begin to emerge spontaneously. These are not traits to be developed, but the natural radiance of the field when it is no longer braced against itself. The Self is not a role we step into, but the signature of coherence returning to the system.

This is why many modalities describe the Self as both witness and guide. In this model, these roles are unified. The Self is the field witnessing itself and guiding the system not through control, but through resonance. It knows what to include, not because it has a plan, but because it is whole, and wholeness naturally integrates what fragmentation leaves behind.

Physiologically, the presence of the Self coincides with regulation. Vagal tone increases, defensive postures soften, and the brain re-engages its integrative circuits. The heart and breath synchronize. The nervous system, long organized around defense, begins to organize around contact. The coherence of the Self is not abstract, it is *embodied.*

Importantly, the Self does not need perfection to emerge. It arises when striving gives way to allowing. When we stop pushing away parts of ourselves, we discover that what we've been searching for is not ahead of us, but beneath us—already here, already whole.

The Self is not the manager of healing. It *is* the healing. It is the presence in which all parts can return, and the wholeness through which life coheres. As both the field and the witness, it does not act, it *organizes*. And in its silent organizing, transformation begins.

The Healing Intelligence of Awareness

When experiences are overwhelming, the system may dis-integrate splitting sensations, emotions, and meanings into fragments stored in the unconscious or the body. These parts do not vanish; they wait. And it is awareness, especially when offered with compassion, that allows them to return. Awareness is the medium through which the implicit becomes explicit, not through analysis but through contact. It sees without judgment, feels without overwhelm, and invites without force.

Healing begins with this quality of witnessing. In therapeutic practice, this can be as subtle as noticing a sensation, naming a belief, or gently turning toward a part that was once too painful to acknowledge. Awareness allows us to stay where before we had to flee. It opens a relational space in which coherence can emerge, not as sameness, but as harmonized differentiation.

Regulation and Reorganization

Trauma reorganizes the system around defense. The nervous system narrows perception, pulling us into fight, flight, freeze, or fawn. These states, while adaptive in the moment, become rigid when chronically activated. Awareness shifts the equation. When we meet inner experience with presence, we send a signal to the body: "This is safe now."

Conscious awareness engages the prefrontal cortex and quiets threat centers like the amygdala. In polyvagal terms, it supports ventral vagal tone, facilitating states of connection, curiosity, and calm. Physiologically, this translates into reduced

330

inflammation, balanced hormones, improved metabolism, and softer muscular tone. The body no longer organizes around survival, it begins to orient toward wholeness.

And because the body, mind, and spirit are not separate, this shift ripples outward. Behavior becomes less reactive. Identity becomes more fluid. Awareness doesn't change our stories overnight, but it changes our relationship to them. In that shift, the story itself begins to evolve.

Awareness as Integrative Field

In complexity science, coherence is not about uniformity, but about the relational integrity of parts in dynamic interaction. Similarly, awareness does not erase parts, it holds them in relationship. What trauma once fragmented, awareness gently reweaves.

This coherence is felt somatically and seen systemically. Inner protectors no longer silence exiles. Vulnerable parts no longer need to hide. Each thread of experience finds its place in the tapestry of selfhood, not by being made the same, but by being included. Awareness does not force integration, it invites resonance.

Even physiologically, this reconnection is visible. Systems that were siloed, nervous, endocrine, immune, begin to re-synchronize. Emotional shifts emerge not from strategy but from attunement. Healing, in this model, is not the imposition of order but the reemergence of relationship.

Awareness as Non-Doing Medicine

Healing is often misunderstood as something we must do. But awareness introduces us to the paradox of non-doing.

True healing arises not from effort, but from presence. This is not passivity, but active receptivity. It is what Taoist philosophy calls wu wei: effortless action.

When we bring this kind of non-intervening awareness to our inner world, the system begins to reorganize. Defenses soften not because they are dismantled, but because they are no longer needed. The body begins to trust the environment. The mind no longer rushes to predict or protect. In this space, healing unfolds.

This non-doing is biological. In states of attuned presence, vagal tone increases, cortisol decreases, and the entire physiology shifts from vigilance to restoration. The body enters a state of readiness, not for defense, but for repair.

Awareness as Bridge and Guide

Awareness bridges past and present, conscious and unconscious, self and system. It not only sees, it knows where to look. It tracks patterns and invites inquiry: "What is this part protecting?" "What needs inclusion here?" In this way, awareness acts not only as witness, but as guide.

This guiding intelligence is not imposed from the outside. It arises from within, often in the smallest moments: a pause before reacting, a deepened breath, a willingness to feel something we once pushed away. These gestures are not trivial, they are thresholds. They mark the system's readiness to reorganize not around protection, but around coherence.

Living from Presence

To live from presence is not to be without difficulty, but to relate to difficulty differently. In presence, emotions become signals, not threats. Thoughts become passing weather, not identity. Patterns become invitations, not prisons.

This shift transforms physiology, perception, and relationship. We become more attuned, more choiceful. We respond rather than react. And even in conflict, presence allows intimacy because we are no longer fusing the moment with our past. Presence is not a final destination, but an orientation. A returning, again and again, to the space within that can meet what is.

Conclusion

Awareness is not simply a backdrop, it is the integrating force at the heart of transformation. It witnesses without judgment, holds without urgency, and guides without control. In trauma, the self fragments. In awareness, the self re-members.

This is the essence of coherence: not uniformity, but relationship. Not control, but contact. Consciousness doesn't fix the self, it reveals it. And in that revelation, healing becomes not only possible, but inevitable.

Reflective Invitation. Where in your life do you habitually leave yourself? Can you notice these places without judgment? Can you begin, gently, to return to them? Not to change them, but to meet them? In this act of returning you are not fixing, you are remembering. And in remembering, the system begins to trust again. Let awareness be your guide. Not because it has all the answers, but because it knows how to stay.

Key Takeaways: Coherence Through Conscious Awareness

- **Awareness is integrative by nature**: It allows fragmented parts of the system to return to relationship, restoring coherence not through force but through inclusion.

- **The Self is the unitive field expressing itself through the layers of experience**: It is not a fixed identity, but the coherent unfolding of being, a presence that organizes rather than manages.

- **Healing arises when awareness becomes stable enough** to hold what was previously excluded. This inclusion reorganizes physiology, emotion, and identity.

- **The Self is both field and witness**: It is the spacious context within which experience unfolds, and the organizing force that reorients the system toward wholeness.

- **Non-doing awareness is deeply reparative**: It signals safety to the nervous system, reduces reactivity, and enables the system to reorganize around truth instead of protection.

- **Integration is relational**: Awareness bridges inner fragmentation by creating space for sensation, emotion, and memory to return to the flow of lived experience.

- **Presence becomes a way of living**: As awareness stabilizes, life is increasingly lived from responsiveness rather than reactivity, coherence rather than fragmentation.

We've seen how awareness functions as the healing force: restoring coherence, guiding integration, and reawakening the Self as a living field of presence. But something profound begins to unfold as this presence stabilizes. No longer just a lens through which experience is observed, consciousness begins to sense itself as the very ground of being from which experience arises.

What was once a healing relationship between self and parts begins to shift. Awareness, now anchored and inclusive, turns gently toward its own source. This is not an act of doing, but of deepening, a quiet recognition: I am not only aware of experience... I am awareness itself. And with that recognition, we cross a subtle but luminous threshold: the movement from coherence into consciousness aware of itself.

CHAPTER TWENTY-FOUR

Consciousness Aware of Itself: The Mirror of Presence

"I am not the body, not even the mind. I am the witness - the one who sees."

— Sri Nisargadatta Maharaj

There is a kind of awareness that quietly eclipses all others, a turning inward so complete that the usual scaffolding of self drops away. It's often described as one of the most profound and transformative modes of experience available to a human being. Not because of what it reveals, but because of what it *is*.

This is not metacognition, the thinking mind observing its own thoughts. Metacognition still operates within the domain of content, ideas reflecting on ideas. What we're speaking of here is more fundamental. It is the moment when awareness itself becomes the object of awareness. There is no thought to grasp, no narrative to follow. It is not about something. It simply *is*.

In this space, awareness recognizes itself. Not as an observer of objects or sensations, but as the condition for all observation. The experience is quiet, spacious, and strangely self-evident. There is a soft but stable clarity: *I am*. Not *I am this* or *I am that*, but simply *I am*. The quality of this awareness is different from identification or self-concept. It is unstructured, unboundaried, unlimited, and free from effort.

Many traditions have pointed to this state. In Advaita Vedanta it is the Atman, the pure, witnessing awareness. In contemplative Christianity, it echoes the presence of the soul before God. In Zen it is the face you had before your parents were born. Others describe it simply as being without grasping. Across all, the message is the same: when awareness becomes aware of itself, a profound stillness is revealed beneath the noise.

And this stillness is not dead space. It is vibrant, alive, and quietly luminous. It does not require proof or performance. It simply abides. To touch this space is to encounter a kind of peace that is not dependent on conditions. It is the field in which all parts of the self are held but none are needed to define it.

Complexity and the Self-Modeling System

In systems theory, there's a critical threshold of complexity beyond which something remarkable happens: the system begins to model itself. It becomes reflexive. A feedback loop is established in which the system doesn't just respond to input, it begins to hold an image or representation of its own functioning.

This self-referential quality lies at the heart of what we call *selfhood*. Consciousness, in its most basic form, is simply experience. But when experience becomes aware that it is experiencing, a sense of "I" emerges. This is not yet identity, it is simply the system becoming aware of itself in motion.

In human beings, this self-modeling capacity gives rise to language, agency, and narrative. But at deeper levels, it also gives rise to stillness. Because the more accurately a system can perceive itself, the less it needs to compensate, defend, or project. As defenses drop, perception becomes cleaner. Energy that was once devoted to managing fragmentation becomes available for integration.

When consciousness turns inward without clinging to content, it begins to reflect itself, like a mirror looking into a mirror. This infinite loop doesn't lead to confusion, but to clarity. The system stabilizes not around a fixed identity, but around the open awareness that contains all identities. This loop, paradoxically, is what creates stillness. Not inertia, but dynamic equilibrium.

In this recursive arc, consciousness begins to rest in its own ground. Not in a particular thought, emotion, or image, but in its own nature. Awareness becomes its own anchor.

And this is more than philosophical abstraction. The lived experience is subtle but distinct: things slow down. Attention softens. There's a kind of exhale across the system. Rather than scanning the environment for meaning or threat, consciousness turns toward itself and finds that it is already whole.

Energy Withdrawal and Resting in Being

Consciousness is often on the move. It moves toward goals, toward others, toward problems to solve or dangers to avoid. Most of the time, our attention is extended outward or fragmented inward, searching, organizing, protecting. We live in the content: stories, identities, emotions, memories, plans. Energy flows into what we perceive and what we believe we must manage.

But something changes when consciousness begins to recognize itself. The outward flow begins to reverse. Attention that was once scattered across the surface of experience begins to fold inward. Not in collapse, but in return.

Energy, no longer caught in identification, settles. There is no longer a need to prop up a self-image, to resolve a storyline, or to defend against a sensation. This is not repression or avoidance. It is inclusion without attachment. Everything is allowed, but nothing is required to stabilize the self.

In this space, a kind of stillness emerges. Not because the world has changed, but because consciousness is no longer chasing it. The system, once driven by effort and organization, now rests in presence. It doesn't mean we stop thinking or feeling, but that we are no longer *located* inside those thoughts and feelings. They pass through, but they do not define.

Many traditions have named this background field. In Advaita, it is the unmoving witness. In Buddhism, it is the unborn or unconditioned. In mysticism, it is union with the divine. The names differ, but the experience is shared: a quiet awareness that holds everything and is held by nothing.

And importantly, this is not dissociation. Dissociation is fragmentation, disconnection from parts of the self or from reality. This is the opposite. It is full inclusion, without entanglement. Everything belongs, thoughts, emotions, memories, the body, but none are mistaken for the totality. There is spaciousness around experience. This is akin to the Sufi saying, "be in the world, not of it". Impermanence is fully realized as the change occurring before you as an unchanging presence.

When energy settles back into the ground of being, something essential is remembered: *I am not any one thing, but the field in which all things arise*. This realization brings not just clarity, but relief. There is nothing left to prove, and nowhere to go. Awareness has come home to itself.

Embodied Awareness

When awareness turns inward and begins to rest in itself, it can sometimes seem as though the body disappears. No longer a solid object, but a spacious field. Sensations become less dense, more fluid. The boundary between self and world softens. But this isn't a departure from the body; it's a different way of being *in* the body.

In many ways, this is a return. A return to the body not as a vehicle to manage or control, but as an expression of presence. When consciousness includes the body in its self-reflection, we experience what might be called *embodied presence*. Not floating above experience, but touching the immediacy of sensation with openness and grace.

The body may feel less like a structure and more like vibration, breath, rhythm, space. Sensations arise and pass like waves across a still sea. Muscles that once braced for impact begin to soften. The nervous system downshifts. The felt sense becomes the ground for knowing. Not as conceptual knowledge, but as direct, living truth.

Trauma, by contrast, fragments this experience. It pulls us out of the body or into parts of it that feel unsafe or disorganized. It becomes the organizing principle in the system. We become protectors, managers, or survivors, orienting around what must be avoided. In this state, embodied presence is lost. The body becomes a battleground or a stranger.

But healing invites a return. Slowly, gently, the body is re-inhabited not as a problem to be fixed, but as a home to be tended. Presence does not force itself into the body; it waits until safety allows re-entry. The morphologies of presence (compassion, flow, and curiosity) blossom. As these qualities emerge more fully, the body becomes less a site of pain and more a field of aliveness.

And something beautiful happens here: when self-aware consciousness embraces the body, fragmentation gives way to coherence. The body is no longer a separate domain but an expression of the same stillness that permeates awareness. We are not just aware *of* the body, we are aware *as* the body. And in this, the boundary between formlessness and form dissolves. This is not transcendence *from* the body, but realization *through* it. The body becomes a mirror, not of identity, but of being itself.

The Healing Field of Presence

When consciousness becomes aware of itself and settles into embodied presence, something profound unfolds: the inner landscape begins to reorganize. Parts that were fragmented, protective, or burdened no longer feel they must hold the center. They are no longer driving the system. Instead, they are seen, felt, and held by something deeper—an awareness that does not judge, react, or recoil.

This shift is not about fixing or changing. It is about *being with*. Not from a place of effort, but from a field that is already whole. This field, this self-aware presence, is inherently healing because it does not divide. It is not at war with any part of the self. It does not rush, and it does not collapse. It simply holds, and in that holding, things begin to soften.

In many trauma-informed therapies, this quality of presence is what makes integration possible. The part that could not speak, the memory that could not be felt, the emotion that was too much. These return not through force, but through the gentle invitation of a witnessing self. The system no longer fears annihilation in the presence of pain. It knows it will be held.

Curiosity emerges here, not as interrogation but as open inquiry. Flow arises as the system begins to move without friction. Compassion deepens, not as a strategy, but as a natural byproduct of inclusion. And presence, true presence, is revealed not as a technique, but as a fundamental expression of being.

This healing field is not a state we achieve, but a truth we uncover. It was always there, beneath the noise of survival. In its light, the parts return, not erased, but re-integrated. They are no longer exiled or exalting. They belong.

This is why consciousness aware of itself is so often the medicine. Not because it has the answers, but because it makes space for what already is. It allows the system to stop performing, stop defending, and simply be. And in that being, wholeness reveals itself not as something to reach, but as something that has always been waiting.

The Paradox of Being

As consciousness settles into itself, familiar structures begin to loosen: identity, narrative, time. What emerges isn't emptiness in the hollow sense, but a spaciousness rich with quiet coherence. There is nothing to hold, no belief or role or goal and yet, everything is held. It is a paradox at the heart of human experience: when you stop seeking, you arrive. When you try to accord, you deviate.

This paradox is not something the thinking mind can resolve. It doesn't compute. But the deeper awareness, the field of presence itself, understands it intuitively. In this space, opposites are not contradictions but complements. Effort and surrender, form and emptiness, silence and sound, all coexist within a greater whole that needs no resolution.

"You" are nowhere to be found as a fixed point, and yet you are more fully here than ever before. There is no edge, and yet there is a clear sense of being. The usual scaffolding of self dissolves, but awareness remains, rooted, open, undisturbed.

This is the paradox of resting in being: you no longer orient from the contents of consciousness, but from its nature. You are not this or that, you are *thisness itself*. The moment is complete, not because it fulfills a need, but because it lacks nothing. There is nothing to push away and nothing to grasp.

And from this spacious place, action may still arise. Words are spoken, gestures are made, life continues. But the movement is not driven by fear or fragmentation, it flows from wholeness. It is what the Taoists might call effortless action: *wu wei*.

This paradoxical presence allows us to participate in life without being overwhelmed by it, to care deeply without clinging, to move through the world without losing ourselves in it. And perhaps most tenderly, it allows us to meet each moment, including moments of suffering, from a ground that does not fracture. The paradox is not a riddle to solve. It is a mystery to be lived.

The Arc Completes

In the journey through differentiation and integration, through sensation, symbol, and pattern, the self discovers its coherence. In transcendence, it begins to glimpse what lies beyond structure. But it is here, in the turning of consciousness back onto itself, that the arc completes. The spiral returns to its source, not in regression, but in revelation.

When consciousness becomes aware of itself, there is nothing left to attain. No higher level to reach, no missing piece to find. The search resolves not in answers, but in presence. The very awareness that once sought becomes the space in which everything already belongs.

This is not an ending, but a new beginning. A return not to naivety, but to simplicity. Not to unconsciousness, but to clarity. From this ground, the full range of life can be met—joy and sorrow, chaos and beauty—not as problems to solve, but as expressions of a deeper wholeness.

Curiosity continues, not to escape the moment, but to deepen into it. Flow unfolds, not to distract from suffering, but to carry us with grace through it. Compassion arises, not as duty, but as the natural radiance of coherence. Presence remains not as practice, but as the quiet truth of being itself.

"You are the unchanging mirror, and all that you see is a reflection in it." - Mooji

In the mirror of self-aware consciousness, the system stabilizes not as a fixed identity, but as a dynamic, living field. The parts are welcomed. The stories are held. The movement of life continues. But now, there is a center that does not collapse.

This is the gift of the arc: not perfection, but peace. Not escape, but embrace. Not certainty, but intimacy with what is.

And so, the journey becomes less about becoming and more about *being*. All along we've described the nature of the layers of human becoming as a means of maintaining continuity. All paths emergent from these layers lead us back to the center. Consciousness, aware of itself, rests in the simple fullness of now. The arc has returned to its source, only to realize that it was never apart.

Key Takeaways: Consciousness Aware of Itself

- **Beyond Metacognition**: This is not thinking about thinking. It's awareness becoming aware of itself, absent of identity, story, or object—simply *I Am*.

- **Self-Modeling and Reflexivity**: In complex systems, consciousness can arc back onto itself. This recursive loop stabilizes presence and reveals the ground of being.

- **Energy Withdrawal and Stillness**: When attention no longer flows outward into content or defense, it returns to stillness. Everything is included, but no longer grasped.

- **Embodied Awareness**: As self-aware presence includes the body, it becomes a field of aliveness rather than a structure. The body is re-inhabited as a spacious, safe home.

- **The Healing Field**: Awareness that holds itself becomes the medicine. Parts can rest. Nothing to fix, only the freedom to belong and reorganize within wholeness.

- **The Paradox of Being**: Nothing to hold, yet everything is held. No fixed self, yet fullness of presence. This field is coherent, compassionate, and at ease.

- **The Arc Completes**: The spiral returns to its origin. Consciousness stabilizes not through becoming more, but by resting in what it has always been.

When consciousness becomes aware of itself, there is nothing left to seek. The impulse to grasp, fix, or define dissolves, and what remains is presence—vast, still, and self-knowing. Yet even here, something begins to move not from longing, but from fullness. Awareness, having touched its own ground, begins to flow again, not as striving, but as rhythm.

In this movement, life is no longer something to control or transcend. It is lived as coherence: presence expressing through breath, gesture, relationship, and unfolding form. In the next chapter, we explore this sacred rhythm: not as something to master, but to join. This is the living pulse of being, ordered yet free, spontaneous yet whole.

CHAPTER TWENTY-FIVE

Living the Rhythm: Daily Life as Coherogenesis

"There is a dance only you can do, that exists only in you, here and now, always changing, always true."

— Gabrielle Roth

We have spoken of coherence, of selfhood, of the field from which all arises. But coherence is not static. It is a rhythm, a pulse of being that moves through experience like a tide. In every breath, every emotion, every thought, there is rhythm.

The movement of life, its expansions and contractions, surges and stillnesses, can be met not as problems to fix, but as music to hear. When we begin to live the rhythm, we stop treating life like a series of obstacles and start encountering it as an unfolding pattern. One that, if followed attentively, leads us toward wholeness. Coherogenesis is not a state. It is a dynamic, rhythmic unfolding—one that we live, not solve. Life moves in waves, not lines.

Listening to the Body's Time

The body doesn't operate on the linear timelines of cognition. It moves in pulses, oscillations, and waves. The nervous system regulates through rhythm, through cycles of arousal and settling, effort and rest, contact and retreat.

To live the rhythm is to reclaim this deeper biological intelligence. It's to know when to pause, when to move, when to digest, and when to release. It's to understand that dysregulation is not failure, but a signal: a beat skipped, a tempo lost.

By syncing our days with the rhythms of breath, food, light, sleep, movement, and relationship, we begin to cohere from the inside out. We stop imposing order and start rediscovering it. Rhythm is the body remembering it belongs to the earth.

The Pulse of Daily Coherence

In everyday life, coherence does not arrive as epiphany. It arrives in small, rhythmic returns:

- A breath before reacting.

- A softening of judgment.

- A moment of presence before reaching for the familiar.

- A gentle curiosity toward discomfort.

These are not mere habits. They are acts of rhythm, reentries into the field of being.

Living the rhythm does not mean perfection or peace. It means responsiveness. It means allowing the qualities of the unitive field (presence, compassion, flow, curiosity) to express through us, not occasionally, but rhythmically. As practices, as postures, as return paths. In a fragmented world, rhythmic coherence is a quiet revolution.

What to Do When the Rhythm Breaks

The rhythm of life is not constant, it breaks, falls out of sync, goes silent. This is not a failure. It is part of the song. Living the rhythm means recognizing that rupture is included in the pattern. It is through rupture that deeper rhythms are revealed.

When coherence is lost, we don't need to rebuild it from scratch. We need to listen for the beat beneath the noise.

Living the rhythm means allowing incoherence to be a call, not a condemnation. It is learning to trust the tide, even as it pulls us away from shore. In essence, reclaiming coherence is more about being than doing. Wholeness is not the absence of rupture; it is the ability to re-enter rhythm again and again.

In Rhythm with Others, In Rhythm with the World

Rhythm is not only internal, it is relational. We are shaped by the rhythms of those we love, the environments we inhabit, and the cultures we participate in. The nervous system co-regulates. The psyche co-creates.

To live the rhythm is to notice:

- The subtle synchrony of walking in step with a friend.

- The way shared laughter regulates the vagus nerve.

- The dissonance that arises in hurried or misattuned spaces.

We can begin to ask, *Is this rhythm life-giving? Is this pace sustainable? Is this interaction aligned with the pulse of being?* Rhythm is a form of care: one we offer ourselves, each other, and the world.

Letting Life Move You

At its core, living the rhythm means allowing life to move through you, rather than trying to move against it.

It's less about doing something new, and more about remembering what was always there:

- The way your body already knows how to settle.

- The way truth feels like alignment, not effort.

- The way presence doesn't require effort, it only requires space.

Letting life move you is not passive. It's participatory. It means dancing with what is. The rhythm of coherogenesis is not something we impose, it is something we become.

Closing Reflection: Becoming the Dance

We do not become coherent once and for all. We become it in motion. Coherogenesis is not a destination, it is a rhythm that becomes us as we learn to let it move through us. To live the rhythm is to become the dance itself: A wave expressing the ocean. A being unfolding into presence. A human life lived in time with the eternal.

Even as we learn to live the rhythm, tuning to the pulses of body, mind, and world, we discover something quietly humbling: the rhythm never ends. There is no final arrival, no permanent coherence to hold onto. Life keeps moving. The Self keeps unfolding. Coherogenesis continues not as a path we master, but as one we continually meet. And so, we turn now to this essential truth: that the journey is not complete, and perhaps never meant to be. In the next chapter, *The Unfinished Path*, we explore what it means to walk forward rooted in presence, open to becoming, and guided by a rhythm that is ever leading us home.

CHAPTER TWENTY-SIX

The Unfinished Path: Trusting the Mystery

"We are not human beings having a spiritual experience. We are spiritual beings having a human experience."

— Pierre Teilhard de Chardin

We often long for closure, for the moment when healing is finished, when we are finally whole, finally free, finally "there." In medicine, in psychology, in spirituality, the promise of resolution can feel like a beacon. We search for it in diagnoses, in practices, in breakthroughs. But as this book has suggested, wholeness is not a final destination. It is a dynamic rhythm, a movement of return. The process of coherogenesis does not culminate in arrival but deepens into presence.

This chapter is not a conclusion. It is a threshold. What has come before has offered a way of seeing the human experience as layered, coherent, and emergent, from the unitive ground of being through the sensorial, symbolic, and patterned unfoldings of self. We've explored how fragmentation occurs, how meaning takes shape, how symptoms arise, and how healing emerges through recontact with the Self. And yet, even after all this, something remains open. That openness is the unfinished path.

To live from the field of coherence is not to be free from struggle, confusion, or repetition, but to remain in relationship with these experiences, to see them not as signs of failure but as invitations into deeper awareness. The unfinished path is not a detour from healing. It is healing, continued.

In this spirit, the journey does not end here. Rather, we turn now to the living spiral of human becoming, where each return is not regression but revelation, where each encounter is a mirror, and where the Self, ever undivided, keeps finding new ways to express wholeness.

Coherogenesis as a Living Spiral

Healing is not linear. Neither is growth, integration, or awakening. While much of modern psychology still leans on hierarchies, steps, or stages, life itself rarely moves in such tidy progression. Instead, the movement of transformation resembles a spiral, each turn returning us to familiar ground, yet from a new vantage. In this way, coherogenesis is not a straight path upward, but a rhythmic unfolding: recursive, layered, alive.

In the spiral of coherogenesis, we revisit old material not because we have failed to resolve it, but because the field is deepening. What once emerged as symptom may now be recognized as symbol. What once felt symbolic might now be sensed somatically. And what was once only partially known may now be held with presence. We are not circling back to the same place, we are meeting it anew, from a greater wholeness.

This is the nature of becoming. As consciousness expands, the field reorganizes. The psyche does not simply aim for relief; it seeks coherence. It orients toward truth, even if truth emerges slowly, through repetition, through encounter, through suffering. The spiral is not a flaw in the system, it is its elegance.

When presence enters the spiral, the motion becomes conscious. What was once reactive becomes reflective. What was once fate becomes choice. This is the grace of a coherent field: it does not resist its own unfolding. It turns again and again toward what has not yet been loved, integrated, or understood. This returning is not regression. It is revelation.

The Incompleteness of Human Experience

To be human is to be incomplete. We are born into limitation—of time, of perspective, of body—and yet within those limits, something infinite pulses. This paradox is not a problem to be solved but a truth to be lived. The desire to finish, fix, or finalize is understandable. But the soul doesn't seek perfection. It seeks participation.

In the framework of coherogenesis, this incompleteness is not viewed as pathology but as potential. The unfinished nature of our experience creates the very space through which coherence can unfold. Wholeness is not the absence of fragmentation, it is the capacity to hold fragmentation within a larger field. Each symptom, each misstep, each disorientation becomes part of the journey back into relationship with Self.

Even the experiences that feel regressive or disruptive, the return of an old pattern, the flare of a long-dormant emotion, are often signs that something deeper is ready to be metabolized. In this view, setbacks are not failures. They are signals of readiness. The field has ripened. Something unseen is now close enough to touch.

And as identity continues to shift, as the symbolic and patterned structures reorganize, the idea of completion itself begins to lose meaning. We no longer measure progress by how far we've moved from pain, but by how fully we can remain present within it. Incompleteness, then, becomes a source of compassion, a softening that allows more of ourselves, and others, to belong.

In this way, the human experience remains open-ended, not because it is flawed, but because it is alive. To be unfinished is not to be broken. It is to be in motion.

The Ongoing Role of Encounter

Life continues to call us forward through encounter. Not only the dramatic or painful ones, but the subtle, ordinary, and often overlooked invitations that surface in daily life. A conversation that stirs emotion. A sensation that won't go away. A dream, a mistake, a silence. Each encounter, whether welcomed or resisted, holds the potential to reawaken coherence.

From the perspective of coherogenesis, these encounters are not random disruptions; they are movements of the field. They carry echoes of past organization and signals of what is ready to reorganize. When met with presence, an encounter becomes a mirror, showing us not just what is, but what is possible. The unfinished path is composed of such moments: openings in the fabric of experience where integration can begin or deepen.

At the patterned layer, we often respond to these encounters with habit—predictable, protective responses that maintain stability. At the symbolic layer, we try to narrate and give meaning, drawing on beliefs, language, and archetypes. At the sensorial layer, the body registers these encounters viscerally, often before we know why.

But beneath all these is the unitive field, the ocean from which all these waves arise. The Self does not react. It receives. It does not defend. It includes. When we become aware of this dimension of our being, even the most painful encounter is no longer something to be escaped, but something to be engaged with compassion and curiosity.

The unfinished path is not a flaw in the architecture of life. It is the very design that allows for creativity, transformation, and return. Each new contact with experience, no matter how familiar or foreign, is a new chance to meet the Self again, as if for the first time.

The Healer's Path is Also Unfinished

It can be tempting, especially in the healing professions, to unconsciously adopt the role of the one who has arrived, the one who knows, who guides, who holds steady ground. Yet to truly accompany another on the path of healing, we must remain in touch with our own unfinishedness. The healer, too, is a field in motion—unfolding, reorganizing, learning.

In the coherogenic view, the healing encounter is not a one-way transmission of knowledge or technique. It is a mutual field of discovery. The individual arrives not just as someone in need of help, but as a living system expressing its own movement toward coherence. The healer meets them not from outside that movement, but from within it as a fellow traveler.

This orientation requires a deep humility. Not a diminishment of the healer's role, but an honoring of its sacred reciprocity. To support another's coherence, we must remain in touch with our own. To help someone meet their fragmentation, we must know what it means to meet our own. The qualities that most powerfully facilitate healing (presence, compassion, curiosity, and flow) are not techniques. They are signatures of an attuned and unfinished self.

When healers hold themselves apart from the process, they risk solidifying their own patterns, clinging to certainty, authority, or perfection. But when they allow themselves to remain in motion, to be affected, to stay open to their own becoming, something remarkable happens: the encounter becomes more real. More human. More healing.

To be a healer on the unfinished path is not to be incomplete in a way that disqualifies, but to be incomplete in a way that includes. It is to become a curious and compassionate presence in the room, not only for the individual, but for oneself.

The Grace of the Incomplete

There is a quiet grace in recognizing that we are not meant to be finished. That our stories remain open. That healing, growth, love, and meaning are not destinations, but movements—waves in an ocean without edge. In a culture obsessed with mastery, progress, and resolution, this truth can feel like a kind of heresy. But it is, in fact, a form of freedom.

To embrace incompleteness is to unhook from the tyranny of final answers. It is to step out of the linear timeline of "once I heal, then I'll live" and into the living immediacy of this moment. This is where wholeness begins not in the perfect arrangement of parts, but in the presence that allows all parts to be here, just as they are.

The grace of the incomplete is that it keeps us soft. It keeps us listening. It reminds us that the soul is not a project to be perfected, but a presence to be encountered. That every ending is also an opening. That the questions themselves are sacred.

In this light, the unfinished path is not something to be overcome, it is something to be honored. It means we still have the capacity to be surprised. To be moved. To be changed. And it means that the Self, in its radiant coherence, continues to find new ways to emerge, express, and belong.

So we do not close this chapter with certainty, but with invitation. May the spiral continue. May the field unfold. May you walk your unfinished path with wonder, not weariness, with reverence, not resistance. And when you forget, may you remember again. That every step forward is a return.

"I have arrived. I am home. In the here, in the now, I am solid. I am free." — Thích Nhất Hạnh

Key Takeaways: The Unfinished Path

- Healing is recursive, not linear, it unfolds in spirals, revisiting familiar themes from new depths.

- Incompleteness is not failure, it is the very condition that allows for coherence, creativity, and transformation.

- Encounters are invitations—each moment, sensation, or relationship can reopen a path to deeper integration.

- Clinicians, too, are in process, their unfinishedness is a resource, not a liability, when held with awareness.

- Grace emerges in openness, embracing the unfinished path leads to humility, presence, and ongoing reorganization.

To walk the unfinished path is to stay in relationship with becoming. It is to allow wholeness to be fluid rather than fixed, to be lived rather than achieved. And in that space, where we stop striving to arrive and begin simply to show up, something playful begins to stir. Not as escape, but as expression. Not as avoidance, but as art. What emerges is not the end of the journey, but the joy of the dance. And so, from this place of open presence, we now turn to what it means to live not in search of coherence, but as its embodiment, in the spontaneous, sacred unfolding of the play of being and becoming.

CHAPTER TWENTY-SEVEN

The Play of Being and Becoming

"That the powerful play goes on, and you may contribute a verse."

— Walt Whitman

What if this life and its pain and poetry, its fragments and flashes of insight, were not a puzzle to solve, but a story to live? What if each experience, each subpersonality, each symptom or pattern, were not detours or mistakes, but lines in a great play, or waves in an endless sea?

This chapter begins not with an ending, but a turning. We've traveled through the layers of the self (the patterned, the symbolic, the sensorial, the unitive) not to escape life's complexity, but to remember its ground. Each chapter has pointed toward one truth: what arises within us is not separate from the field in which it arises. The field is presence. The ocean is consciousness. The play is being.

All the parts we've explored—stories and symptoms, identities and insights—are performances upon a stage that was never solid to begin with. They are gestures of meaning, waves curling into form before dissolving back into formlessness. And yet they matter. Not because they are permanent, but because they are *alive*, and because we are the ones who bring them to life.

This final chapter is not about tying things up neatly. It is an invitation to hold paradox: unity and multiplicity, wholeness and part, silence and story. To see that the journey through differentiation and reorganization was never a departure from the self, but a revelation of what had always been true. The wave never left the sea.

The Field and the Forms: Unity and Multiplicity

Everything we have explored, the differentiated layers of the self, the emergence of symptoms, the movement toward coherence, arises not from separate origins, but from a singular field. This field is not a concept or location. It is the open, aware presence that is always already here. It is the ocean that gives rise to the wave.

Multiplicity is often misunderstood as a problem: too many voices, too many parts, too many patterns. But within this model, multiplicity is seen not as pathology, but as play, the field expressing itself in diverse forms. The inner critic, the abandoned child, the protector, the achiever. Each is a wave of meaning, a configuration of experience arising within the wider ocean of being. They are not separate from the field. They *are* the field, temporarily shaped into form.

This is a shift in perspective that changes everything. If all parts arise from the same ground, there is no fundamental conflict between them, only misrecognition. The work is not to eliminate multiplicity, but to recognize it as an expression of unity.

The field of consciousness does not resist these forms. It includes them. It allows them. It holds them as the ocean holds the wave: with fluid boundaries, without judgment, and without fear of dissolution. The wave may rise with force or fall in silence, but the ocean remains, untouched and unchanged.

To live in alignment with this truth is to stop striving for control and begin nurturing coherence. Not by suppressing difference, but by allowing each part to remember its source. Multiplicity is not something to be overcome. It is something to be understood, included, and integrated so that all parts may bow together toward the same truth: we are many, and we are one.

Remembering and Reorganizing: The Path of Coherogenesis

Beneath every symptom lies a signal. Beneath every pattern, a pulse. What we call pathology is often coherence out of context, an adaptive organization that once served survival but now seeks transformation. In this model, healing is not about correction, but about re-orientation. A turning back toward the deeper intelligence from which all forms arise.

This process is not imposed from outside. It is not manufactured through will or technique. It emerges from within. Life reorganizes itself when given the space and safety to do so. This is coherogenesis, the natural movement of systems toward integration, wholeness, and meaningful complexity.

To remember is not merely to recall the past. It is to re-member, to bring back into belonging what was once fragmented or dissociated. The return journey through the patterned, symbolic, sensorial, and unitive layers is a path of re-membering: each step allowing previously split-off experiences to rejoin the living self. Each subpersonality, each narrative, each bodily sensation is invited back not to dominate, but to participate.

And as these parts are held in consciousness, they begin to shift. Defenses soften. Rigidities unwind. Insight becomes embodied understanding. The system reorganizes not because it has been forced, but because it has been felt, witnessed, and included.

Coherogenesis is not a static endpoint. It is a dynamic process, an ongoing invitation. Just as nature moves toward harmony through diversity, so too does the psyche. The goal is not perfection, but participation in the ongoing unfolding of being.

In this light, healing is not a return to some idealized version of self. It is the ever-deepening alignment of all parts with the field from which they come. It is the movement from fragmentation to fluidity, from survival to meaning, from protection to presence.

Constructed Selves in a Conscious Field

If the ocean is consciousness, and the waves are forms, then the self as we usually conceive it is not a fixed entity, but

364

a constructed expression within the field. In this view, drawn from both Vedanta and constructivist perspectives, the self is not the origin of experience, but its product, an emergent organization of memory, meaning, perception, and protection.

This does not diminish the importance of the self. On the contrary, it invites us to see the self as a living process rather than a static identity. Our personalities, patterns, and narratives are not illusions to be discarded, but configurations of energy and awareness, shaped by culture, trauma, relationship, and time. They are necessary structures, bridges between formless presence and lived experience. But like all structures, they are provisional.

When we identify too strongly with these constructions, suffering arises. We forget that the one who observes the story is not bound by the story. We mistake the wave for the sea. Yet even this forgetting is held within consciousness. Even the most rigid ego formation, the most entrenched symptom or belief, is already arising within the unbroken field of awareness.

To realize this is not to abandon the self, but to relate to it differently. From within the field, we can hold our constructions lightly. We can appreciate their function, honor their history, and gently invite them into reorganization. The self becomes less a fortress and more a vessel—capable of fluidity, capable of holding multiplicity, capable of participating in transformation.

The miracle is not that we can deconstruct the self. The miracle is that we can reconstruct it consciously, again and again, each time closer to coherence, to compassion, and to truth. The field does not reject the form. It plays through it.

Relational Ontology: What Exists is Interrelated

What is real for human beings does not exist in isolation, it exists in relation. There is no sound without a listener, no self without an other, no experience that is not shaped by context. Even our internal world, so often conceived as private or solitary, is made of relational echoes: voices of caregivers, inherited meanings, cellular memory, ancestral imprints, cultural symbols.

Ontology, the study of being, cannot be separated from relationship. The patterned, symbolic, and sensorial dimensions of self are not solitary structures but nodes in a living web, each influenced by the others. The body informs the story. The story shapes the belief. The belief modulates the breath. And all of it unfolds within an environment, within time, within presence.

This view honors complexity. It allows us to hold symptoms, identities, and patterns not as internal malfunctions but as expressions of relationship—between parts of the self, between the self and others, between the self and the world. And because relationships can change, the structures built within them can reorganize.

In this light, healing is not a solitary act. It is a relational emergence. It arises in the space between therapist and individual, between presence and part, between awareness and pattern. What is touched by relationship can be transformed by it.

This interconnectedness also applies to the qualities explored throughout the journey. Curiosity, flow, and compassion are not isolated traits, they are emergent expressions of a deeper presence. Curiosity arises when presence meets mystery. Flow arises when presence meets movement. Compassion arises when presence meets suffering.

Everything is in relationship. And relationship is not a distraction from being, it is the way being becomes knowable, feelable, and transformable. There is no form without field, no self without the other, no healing without connection. To live this truth is to stop seeking solidity and start listening for resonance. Not "Who am I?" but "What am I in relationship to now?"

Qualities of the Field: Presence and Its Expressions

Presence is not just a state, it is the field in which all states arise. It is the ground beneath sensation, the stillness beneath story, the awareness that does not change even as everything else changes. Presence is not something we create, it is something we return to. And when we do, something begins to reorganize.

Throughout this model, we've seen three qualities consistently emerge when the system is no longer dominated by protection, fragmentation, or reactivity. These are curiosity, flow, and compassion. And they are not random traits, they are the natural expressions of presence meeting form.

- **Curiosity** arises when presence encounters the unknown not with fear, but with openness. It is the mind's movement toward coherence, drawn by an inner gravity that wants to understand, to touch, to include.

- **Flow** arises when presence meets movement, when the system is no longer locked in defense but can adapt,

367

respond, and express itself freely. Flow is what coherence feels like in motion.

- **Compassion** arises when presence meets suffering, without turning away, without judgment. It creates space for what is there, just as it is. It is the felt sense of connection, the inherent knowing that what is wounded still belongs.

These are not skills to be practiced in isolation. They are signposts that the field of presence is active within experience. They are how the ocean moves through the wave.

Presence does not eliminate our patterns, it *accompanies* them. It does not dissolve multiplicity, it welcomes it. And through this welcoming, the system reorganizes, not through pressure, but through permission.

When presence is embodied, it becomes the condition for transformation. It holds space for truth, for grief, for joy, for all that was once split off. It does not need to fix what arises, it only needs to be with it. In this way, the qualities of presence are not just therapeutic, they are ontological. They reveal the nature of the field itself.

And as we learn to live from this field, the expressions of curiosity, flow, and compassion become not occasional events, but ways of being. They are not strategies. They are symptoms of coherence.

The Final Turn: From Witness to Player, From Player to Presence

There is a moment, often subtle and unannounced, when the witness becomes the player. When observation yields to participation. When we stop watching the play of our lives from a distance and begin to inhabit it fully, vulnerably, consciously.

And yet there is another movement, equally profound: from player back to presence. A softening of the script, a loosening of the costume. Not to abandon the role, but to remember: we are not only the character, we are also the stage, the light, the silent space holding it all.

This is the final turn: not away from multiplicity, but through it, into a fuller realization of the field in which the play unfolds. It is not a rejection of roles or stories, but a gentle step back into the awareness from which they rise. The actor continues to act, but now with the knowledge that the stage is made of light, and the audience is also the self.

To witness the self as a construction is liberating. To play it consciously is healing. But to remember the presence from which it arises, that is transformation.

This final turn is not an escape from life. It is a return to its essence. It is the realization that nothing needs to be added to make us whole, and nothing needs to be erased to make us free. Every subpersonality, every symptom, every gesture of the self is already arising within the field. And that field is already whole.

We do not become presence. We remember that we are it. The wave returns to the sea not to vanish, but to become the ocean in motion.

Closing Reflection: The Play Continues

The journey through the patterned, symbolic, sensorial, and unitive has brought us here, not to an ending, but to a widening. What began as inquiry into layers of the self now opens into something vaster: the realization that the self was never separate from the field in which it unfolds. The play continues.

There will still be roles. Still be stories. Still be moments of confusion, contraction, and conflict. But now, there is something else, something remembered. A deeper knowing that what arises is not other than what is. That each gesture, no matter how fragmented, is already held within the coherence of consciousness.

You are not the problem to be solved. You are the field in which problems arise and dissolve. You are not the wave trying to return to the ocean, you are the ocean playing as the wave. To live from this place is not to transcend the world, but to participate in it with awareness. To feel the fullness of each moment. To listen with compassion. To move with curiosity. To flow with change. This is coherogenesis, not as an endpoint, but as a way of being.

The model offered here is not a prescription, but an invitation to see more clearly, feel more deeply, and remember more wholly the unity behind all forms. The play goes on. And you, now more fully yourself, more fully the field, are free to offer your verse not as a reaction, but as a response. Not out of protection, but out of presence.

What you do next is not the conclusion. It is the next unfolding of the one, in many forms, still singing.

Epilogue: The Still Point

"You do not need to find the Self. You are the Self, finding."

— The Arc of Human Experiencing

In the end, there is no end. The journey traced across these pages is not a path with a final arrival, but a rhythm, of remembering, forgetting, and returning. It is the quiet breath beneath the storm of experience, the still point around which all transformation turns.

We began in the ocean—unbroken, vast, and whole. From that formless ground, life stirred, shaping sensation, image, meaning, and structure. Identity formed, wounds accumulated, and the light of presence became partially eclipsed. Yet even in fragmentation, something remembered. A pulse beneath the surface. A longing not for perfection, but for coherence. Not to erase the past, but to include it. Not to escape form, but to infuse it with awareness.

This remembering is not linear. It loops. It spirals. It waits patiently for the moment of softening, for the body that

371

begins to feel again, the story that finds new language, the pattern that loosens its grip. In that moment, healing is not something we do. It is something that *happens*, because we have made space for the field of the Self to touch itself again.

There is no final version of you waiting at the end of this arc. No perfected self to construct. No singular truth to attain. There is only this breath, this unfolding moment, this living rhythm of coherogenesis, where the wave and the ocean are never apart, only appearing that way for a time.

So, if you find yourself caught in repetition, in symptom, in confusion or grief—remember: the tide turns. Presence returns. What feels lost may only be hidden. And what has been hidden longs to rejoin the whole.

Let this be your practice, your orientation, your hope: Not to strive toward coherence, but to rest into it. Not to chase meaning, but to become available to it. Not to fix the Self, but to recognize it—everywhere.

The Self is not elsewhere. It is here. In the rhythm of your breath. In the ache of your longing. In the silence between words. In the way the light moves through you when you stop trying.

You are not the broken one seeking wholeness. You are wholeness, remembering itself through the arc of your becoming.

Welcome home.

References

Chapter 1. The Problem of Fragmentation in Modern Psychiatry

1. American Psychiatric Association. (2013). *Diagnostic and statistical manual of mental disorders* (5th ed.). https://doi.org/10.1176/appi.books.9780890425596

2. Bentall, R. P. (2003). *Madness explained: Psychosis and human nature*. Penguin Books.

3. Boyle, M. (2002). *Schizophrenia: A scientific delusion?* (2nd ed.). Routledge.

4. Frances, A. (2013). *Saving normal: An insider's revolt against out-of-control psychiatric diagnosis, DSM-5, Big Pharma, and the medicalization of ordinary life*. William Morrow.

5. Gergen, K. J. (1991). *The saturated self: Dilemmas of identity in contemporary life*. Basic Books.

6. Gøtzsche, P. C. (2015). *Deadly psychiatry and organized denial*. People's Press.

7. Kirmayer, L. J., & Gómez-Carrillo, A. (2019). Healing in contexts of social adversity: Cultural, structural, and epigenetic perspectives. *Transcultural Psychiatry, 56*(4), 626–647. https://doi.org/10.1177/1363461519850295

8. Kirmayer, L. J., & Crafa, D. (2014). What kind of science for psychiatry? *Frontiers in Human Neuroscience, 8*, 435. https://doi.org/10.3389/fnhum.2014.00435

9. Moncrieff, J. (2008). *The myth of the chemical cure: A critique of psychiatric drug treatment*. Palgrave Macmillan.

10. Paris, J. (2015). *The intelligent clinician's guide to the DSM-5* (2nd ed.). Oxford University Press.

11. Pies, R. W. (2007). *The anatomy of sorrow: A spiritual, phenomenological, and neurological perspective.* Rowman & Littlefield.

12. Satel, S., & Lilienfeld, S. O. (2013). *Brainwashed: The seductive appeal of mindless neuroscience.* Basic Books.

13. Scull, A. (2022). *Desperate remedies: Psychiatry's turbulent quest to cure mental illness.* Belknap Press.

14. Van der Kolk, B. A. (2014). *The body keeps the score: Brain, mind, and body in the healing of trauma.* Viking.

15. Wampold, B. E., & Imel, Z. E. (2015). *The great psychotherapy debate: The evidence for what makes psychotherapy work* (2nd ed.). Routledge.

16. Zachar, P., & Kendler, K. S. (2012). The philosophy of nosology. *Annual Review of Clinical Psychology, 8*, 49–71. https://doi.org/10.1146/annurev-clinpsy-032511-143152

Chapter 2. Coherogenesis: A Return to Living Wholeness

1. Almaas, A. H. (2004). *The inner journey home: Soul's realization of the unity of reality.* Shambhala.

2. Capra, F., & Luisi, P. L. (2014). *The systems view of life: A unifying vision.* Cambridge University Press.

3. Dossey, L. (1999). *Reinventing medicine: Beyond mind-body to a new era of healing.* HarperOne.

4. Ferrer, J. N. (2002). *Revisioning transpersonal theory: A participatory vision of human spirituality.* SUNY Press.

5. Gendlin, E. T. (1981). *Focusing.* Bantam Books.

6. Goldstein, J. (1999). Emergence as a construct: History and issues. *Emergence, 1*(1), 49–72. https://doi.org/10.1207/s15327000em0101_4

7. Jonas, W. B., & Chez, R. A. (2004). Toward optimal healing environments in health care. *The Journal of Alternative and Complementary Medicine*, 10(Suppl 1), S-1–S-6. https://doi.org/10.1089/1075553042245953

8. Kegan, R. (1982). *The evolving self: Problem and process in human development*. Harvard University Press.

9. Laszlo, E. (2004). *Science and the Akashic field: An integral theory of everything*. Inner Traditions.

10. Mahoney, M. J. (2003). *Constructive psychotherapy: A practical guide*. Guilford Press.

11. Maturana, H. R., & Varela, F. J. (1987). *The tree of knowledge: The biological roots of human understanding*. Shambhala.

12. Ogden, P., Minton, K., & Pain, C. (2006). *Trauma and the body: A sensorimotor approach to psychotherapy*. W. W. Norton & Company.

13. Parse, R. R. (1987). *Nursing science: Major paradigms, theories, and critiques*. W.B. Saunders.

14. Prigogine, I., & Stengers, I. (1984). *Order out of chaos: Man's new dialogue with nature*. Bantam.

15. Schore, A. N. (2003). *Affect regulation and the repair of the self*. W. W. Norton & Company.

16. Siegel, D. J. (2012). *The developing mind: How relationships and the brain interact to shape who we are* (2nd ed.). Guilford Press.

17. Snow, C. P. (1993). *The two cultures*. Cambridge University Press.

18. Stern, D. N. (1985). *The interpersonal world of the infant: A view from psychoanalysis and developmental psychology*. Basic Books.

19. Thompson, E. (2007). *Mind in life: Biology, phenomenology, and the sciences of mind*. Harvard University Press.

20. van der Kolk, B. A. (2014). *The body keeps the score: Brain, mind, and body in the healing of trauma*. Viking.

21. Wallace, B. A. (2007). *Contemplative science: Where Buddhism and neuroscience converge*. Columbia University Press.

22. Wilber, K. (2000). *A theory of everything: An integral vision for business, politics, science, and spirituality*. Shambhala.

Chapter 3. The Self as Field: Foundations of Coherogenesis

1. Almaas, A. H. (2004). *The inner journey home: Soul's realization of the unity of reality*. Shambhala.

2. Bohm, D. (1980). *Wholeness and the implicate order*. Routledge.

3. Capra, F., & Luisi, P. L. (2014). *The systems view of life: A unifying vision*. Cambridge University Press.

4. Ferrer, J. N. (2002). *Revisioning transpersonal theory: A participatory vision of human spirituality*. SUNY Press.

5. Gendlin, E. T. (1997). *Experiencing and the creation of meaning: A philosophical and psychological approach to the subjective*. Northwestern University Press.

6. Gergen, K. J. (2009). *Relational being: Beyond self and community*. Oxford University Press.

7. Heron, J. (1998). *Sacred science: Person-centred inquiry into the spiritual and the subtle*. PCCS Books.

8. Laszlo, E. (2004). *Science and the Akashic field: An integral theory of everything*. Inner Traditions.

9. Maturana, H. R., & Varela, F. J. (1987). *The tree of knowledge: The biological roots of human understanding*. Shambhala.

10. Newman, M. A. (1994). *Health as expanding consciousness* (2nd ed.). National League for Nursing Press.

11. Parse, R. R. (1992). *Human becoming: Parse's theory of nursing*. National League for Nursing Press.

12. Schore, A. N. (2012). *The science of the art of psychotherapy*. W. W. Norton & Company.

13. Siegel, D. J. (2018). *Aware: The science and practice of presence*. TarcherPerigee.

14. Thompson, E. (2007). *Mind in life: Biology, phenomenology, and the sciences of mind*. Harvard University Press.

15. Wallace, B. A. (2007). *Contemplative science: Where Buddhism and neuroscience converge*. Columbia University Press.

16. Wilber, K. (2000). *Integral psychology: Consciousness, spirit, psychology, therapy*. Shambhala.

Chapter 4. A Map of the Journey: Being and Becoming

1. Bateson, G. (1972). *Steps to an ecology of mind: Collected essays in anthropology, psychiatry, evolution, and epistemology*. University of Chicago Press.

2. Campbell, J. (2008). *The hero with a thousand faces*. New World Library.

3. Cozolino, L. (2017). *The neuroscience of psychotherapy: Healing the social brain* (3rd ed.). W. W. Norton & Company.

4. Damasio, A. R. (2010). *Self comes to mind: Constructing the conscious brain*. Pantheon.

5. Fosha, D. (2000). *The transforming power of affect: A model for accelerated change*. Basic Books.

6. Gendlin, E. T. (1996). *Focusing-oriented psychotherapy: A manual of the experiential method*. Guilford Press.

7. Jung, C. G. (1960). *The structure and dynamics of the psyche* (Collected Works Vol. 8). Princeton University Press.

8. Kegan, R. (1982). *The evolving self: Problem and process in human development*. Harvard University Press.

9. Ogden, P., & Fisher, J. (2015). *Sensorimotor psychotherapy: Interventions for trauma and attachment*. W. W. Norton & Company.

10. Schore, A. N. (2003). *Affect regulation and the repair of the self.* W. W. Norton & Company.

11. Siegel, D. J. (2012). *The developing mind: How relationships and the brain interact to shape who we are* (2nd ed.). Guilford Press.

12. Stern, D. B. (2010). *Partners in thought: Working with unformulated experience, dissociation, and enactment.* Routledge.

13. Turner, V. (1969). *The ritual process: Structure and anti-structure.* Aldine publishing.

14. Van Gennep, A. (1960). *The rites of passage.* University of Chicago Press.

15. Varela, F. J., Thompson, E., & Rosch, E. (1991). *The embodied mind: Cognitive science and human experience.* MIT Press.

Chapter 5. The Unitive: Being Before Becoming

1. Almaas, A. H. (2004). *The inner journey home: Soul's realization of the unity of reality.* Shambhala.

2. Bion, W. R. (1962). *Learning from experience.* Heinemann.

3. Capra, F., & Luisi, P. L. (2014). *The systems view of life: A unifying vision.* Cambridge University Press.

4. Damasio, A. R. (1999). *The feeling of what happens: Body and emotion in the making of consciousness.* Harcourt.

5. Gendlin, E. T. (1997). *Experiencing and the creation of meaning: A philosophical and psychological approach to the subjective.* Northwestern University Press.

6. Klein, M. (1952). Some theoretical conclusions regarding the emotional life of the infant. In M. Klein, *Envy and gratitude and other works, 1946–1963* (pp. 61–93). The Free Press.

7. Laszlo, E. (2004). *Science and the Akashic field: An integral theory of everything.* Inner Traditions.

8. Maturana, H. R., & Varela, F. J. (1987). *The tree of knowledge: The biological roots of human understanding*. Shambhala.

9. Newman, M. A. (1994). *Health as expanding consciousness* (2nd ed.). National League for Nursing Press.

10. Ogden, P., Minton, K., & Pain, C. (2006). *Trauma and the body: A sensorimotor approach to psychotherapy*. W. W. Norton & Company.

11. Parse, R. R. (1987). *Nursing science: Major paradigms, theories, and critiques*. W.B. Saunders.

12. Rogers, M. E. (1970). *An introduction to the theoretical basis of nursing*. F. A. Davis Company.

13. Stern, D. N. (1985). *The interpersonal world of the infant: A view from psychoanalysis and developmental psychology*. Basic Books.

14. Thompson, E. (2007). *Mind in life: Biology, phenomenology, and the sciences of mind*. Harvard University Press.

15. Todaro-Franceschi, V. (2008). Preventing compassion fatigue and reaffirming purpose in nursing. In *Proceedings of the 3rd European Federation of Critical Care Nursing Associations Conference*.

16. Trevarthen, C. (1998). The concept and foundations of infant intersubjectivity. *Intersubjective Communication and Emotion in Early Ontogeny*, 15–46. Cambridge University Press.

17. Wilber, K. (2000). *Integral psychology: Consciousness, spirit, psychology, therapy*. Shambhala.

18. Winnicott, D. W. (1960). The theory of the parent-infant relationship. *International Journal of Psychoanalysis, 41*, 585–595.

Chapter 6. The Sensorial: Where Presence Becomes Flesh

1. Almaas, A. H. (2004). *The inner journey home: Soul's realization of the unity of reality*. Shambhala.

2. Cozolino, L. (2017). *The neuroscience of psychotherapy: Healing the social brain* (3rd ed.). W. W. Norton & Company.

3. Damasio, A. R. (1999). *The feeling of what happens: Body and emotion in the making of consciousness*. Harcourt.

4. Dana, D. A. (2018). *The polyvagal theory in therapy: Engaging the rhythm of regulation*. W. W. Norton & Company.

5. Fisher, J. (2021). *Transforming the living legacy of trauma: A workbook for survivors and therapists*. PESI Publishing.

6. Gendlin, E. T. (1981). *Focusing*. Bantam Books.

7. Kain, K. L., & Terrell, S. P. (2018). *Nurturing resilience: Helping clients move forward from developmental trauma*. North Atlantic Books.

8. Levine, P. A. (2010). *In an unspoken voice: How the body releases trauma and restores goodness*. North Atlantic Books.

9. Miller, R. M. (2008). *Bioenergetic exercises: For patients and therapists*. Bioenergetic Press.

10. Ogden, T. H. (1992). *The primitive edge of experience*. Jason Aronson, Inc.

11. Ogden, P., Minton, K., & Pain, C. (2006). *Trauma and the body: A sensorimotor approach to psychotherapy*. W. W. Norton & Company.

12. Porges, S. W. (2011). *The polyvagal theory: Neurophysiological foundations of emotions, attachment, communication, and self-regulation*. W. W. Norton & Company.

13. Rothschild, B. (2000). *The body remembers: The psychophysiology of trauma and trauma treatment*. W. W. Norton & Company.

14. Schore, A. N. (2003). *Affect dysregulation and disorders of the self*. W. W. Norton & Company.

15. Siegel, D. J. (2010). *Mindsight: The new science of personal transformation*. Bantam Books.

16. Stern, D. N. (1985). *The interpersonal world of the infant: A view from psychoanalysis and developmental psychology*. Basic Books.

17. Treleaven, D. A. (2018). *Trauma-sensitive mindfulness: Practices for safe and transformative healing*. W. W. Norton & Company.

18. Van der Kolk, B. A. (2014). *The body keeps the score: Brain, mind, and body in the healing of trauma*. Viking.

19. Wallace, B. A. (2007). *Contemplative science: Where Buddhism and neuroscience converge*. Columbia University Press.

Chapter 7. The Symbolic: The Architecture of Meaning

1. Almaas, A. H. (2004). *The inner journey home: Soul's realization of the unity of reality*. Shambhala.

2. Campbell, J. (2008). *The hero with a thousand faces* (3rd ed.). New World Library.

3. Corbett, L. (2011). *Psychotherapy and the spirit: Theory and practice of transpersonal psychotherapy*. Rowman & Littlefield.

4. Dickerson, V. C., & Zimmerman, J. L. (1996). *Myths, misconceptions, and a word or two about politics*. In F. Kaslow (Ed.), *Handbook of relational diagnosis and dysfunctional family patterns* (pp. 239–254). Wiley.

5. Haley, J. (1991). *Strategies of psychotherapy*. Triangle Press.

6. Hillman, J. (1975). *Re-visioning psychology*. HarperPerennial.

7. Jung, C. G. (1969). *The archetypes and the collective unconscious* (R. F. C. Hull, Trans.; 2nd ed.). Princeton University Press. (Original work published 1959)

8. Mindell, A. (1985). *Working with the dreaming body*. Routledge.

9. Moon, B. L. (2007). *The role of metaphor in art therapy: Theory, method, and experience*. Charles C. Thomas Publisher.

10. Morgan, A. (2000). *What is narrative therapy? An easy-to-read introduction*. Dulwich Centre Publications.

11. Perls, F., Hefferline, R., & Goodman, P. (1951). *Gestalt therapy: Excitement and growth in the human personality*. Julian Press.

12. Schwartz, R. C. (2021). *No bad parts: Healing trauma and restoring wholeness with the Internal Family Systems model*. Sounds True.

13. Siegel, D. J. (2010). *The mindful therapist: A clinician's guide to mindsight and neural integration*. W. W. Norton & Company.

14. Somé, M. P. (1998). *The healing wisdom of Africa: Finding life purpose through nature, ritual, and community*. Tarcher/Putnam.

15. Thompson, E. (2007). *Mind in life: Biology, phenomenology, and the sciences of mind*. Harvard University Press.

16. Wilber, K. (2000). *Integral psychology: Consciousness, spirit, psychology, therapy*. Shambhala.

17. Woodman, M. (1985). *The pregnant virgin: A process of psychological transformation*. Inner City Books.

Chapter 8. The Patterned: Experience Becomes Structure

1. Almaas, A. H. (2004). *The inner journey home: Soul's realization of the unity of reality*. Shambhala.

2. Beebe, J. (2004). *Energies and patterns in psychological type: The reservoir of consciousness*. Routledge.

3. Bowen, M. (1978). *Family therapy in clinical practice*. Jason Aronson.

4. Clifton, D. O., & Harter, J. K. (2003). Investing in strengths. In K. S. Cameron, J. E. Dutton, & R. E. Quinn (Eds.), *Positive organizational scholarship: Foundations of a new discipline* (pp. 111–121). Berrett-Koehler.

5. Fosha, D. (2000). *The transforming power of affect: A model for accelerated change*. Basic Books.

6. Gendlin, E. T. (1981). *Focusing*. Bantam Books.

7. Haley, J. (1991). *Strategies of psychotherapy*. Triangle Press.

8. Heller, L., & LaPierre, A. (2012). *Healing developmental trauma: How early trauma affects self-regulation, self-image, and the capacity for relationship*. North Atlantic Books.

9. Kalsched, D. (2013). *Trauma and the soul: A psycho-spiritual approach to human development and its interruption*. Routledge.

10. Levine, P. A. (2010). *In an unspoken voice: How the body releases trauma and restores goodness*. North Atlantic Books.

11. Linehan, M. M. (1993). *Cognitive-behavioral treatment of borderline personality disorder*. Guilford Press.

12. Mahoney, M. J. (2003). *Constructive psychotherapy: A practical guide*. Guilford Press.

13. Ogden, P., Minton, K., & Pain, C. (2006). *Trauma and the body: A sensorimotor approach to psychotherapy*. W. W. Norton & Company.

14. Porges, S. W. (2011). *The polyvagal theory: Neurophysiological foundations of emotions, attachment, communication, and self-regulation*. W. W. Norton & Company.

15. Schwartz, R. C. (2021). *No bad parts: Healing trauma and restoring wholeness with the Internal Family Systems model*. Sounds True.

16. Schore, A. N. (2003). *Affect regulation and the repair of the self*. W. W. Norton & Company.

17. Stern, D. N. (1985). *The interpersonal world of the infant: A view from psychoanalysis and developmental psychology*. Basic Books.

18. Thompson, E. (2007). *Mind in life: Biology, phenomenology, and the sciences of mind*. Harvard University Press.

19. van der Kolk, B. A. (2014). *The body keeps the score: Brain, mind, and body in the healing of trauma*. Viking.

20. Winnicott, D. W. (1965). *The maturational processes and the facilitating environment: Studies in the theory of emotional development*. International Universities Press.

Chapter 9. A Coherent Field: Tracing the Arc of Becoming

1. Bohm, D. (1980). *Wholeness and the implicate order*. Routledge.

2. Cooperstein, M., & Kaeufer, J. (2002). *The field: Kensington Conference Series*. Imprint Academic.

3. Friedman, H. L., & Davidson, R. J. (2000). *The coherence of the social domain: Self-organization of consciousness through group dynamics*. In D. J. Sussman (Ed.), *Advances in consciousness research*.

4. Gendlin, E. T. (1979). *Focusing*. Bantam Books.

5. McGilchrist, I. (2009). *The master and his emissary: The divided brain and the making of the Western world*. Yale University Press.

6. Mitroff, I. I. (2004). *Smart thinking for crazy times: The art of solving the right problems*. King's Well.

7. Rosen, S. (1990). *The self-aware universe: How consciousness creates the material world*. Tarcher/Putnam.

8. Ruiz, M. (1997). *The four agreements: A practical guide to personal freedom*. Amber-Allen Publishing.

9. Siegel, D. J. (2012). *The developing mind: How relationships and the brain interact to shape who we are* (2nd ed.). Guilford Press.

10. Varela, F. J., Thompson, E., & Rosch, E. (1991). *The embodied mind: Cognitive science and human experience*. MIT Press.

11. Wheatley, M. J. (2006). *Leadership and the new science: Discovering order in a chaotic world* (3rd ed.). Berrett-Koehler.

12. Wilber, K. (2000). *Integral psychology: Consciousness, spirit, psychology, therapy*. Shambhala Publications.

13. Wilber, K. (2006). *Integral spirituality: A startling new role for religion in the modern and postmodern world.* Shambhala Publications.

Chapter 10. Pervading Qualities of the Self

1. Brown, B. (2018). *Dare to lead: Brave work. Tough conversations. Whole hearts.* Random House.

2. Brown, M. (2007). *The presence process: A journey into present moment awareness* (Rev. ed.). Namaste Publishing.

3. Damasio, A. R. (1999). *The feeling of what happens: Body and emotion in the making of consciousness.* Harcourt.

4. Fosha, D. (2000). *The transforming power of affect: A model for accelerated change.* Basic Books.

5. Goleman, D., & Davidson, R. J. (2017). *Altered traits: Science reveals how meditation changes your mind, brain, and body.* Avery.

6. James, W. (1890/1983). *The principles of psychology.* Harvard University Press.

7. Kernis, M. H., & Goldman, B. M. (2004). Authenticity, social roles, and well-being. In A. Tesser, J. V. Wood, & D. A. Stapel (Eds.), *On building, defending, and regulating the self: A psychological perspective* (pp. 13–31). Psychology Press.

8. McAdams, D. P., & McLean, K. C. (2013). Narrative identity. *Current Directions in Psychological Science, 22*(3), 233–238.

9. McGilchrist, I. (2009). *The master and his emissary: The divided brain and the making of the Western world.* Yale University Press.

10. Rogers, C. R. (1961). *On becoming a person: A therapist's view of psychotherapy.* Houghton Mifflin.

11. Ryan, R. M., & Deci, E. L. (2000). Self-determination theory and the facilitation of intrinsic motivation, social development, and well-being. *American Psychologist, 55*(1), 68–78.

12. Siegel, D. J. (2012). *The developing mind: How relationships and the brain interact to shape who we are* (2nd ed.). Guilford Press.

13. Stern, D. N. (1985). *The interpersonal world of the infant: A view from psychoanalysis and developmental psychology*. Basic Books.

14. Tolle, E. (2005). *A new earth: Awakening to your life's purpose*. Penguin Group.

15. Wilber, K. (2000). *Integral psychology: Consciousness, spirit, psychology, therapy*. Shambhala Publications.

Chapter 11. The Eclipse: The Self HIDEs

1. Allen, J. G., Fonagy, P., & Bateman, A. W. (2008). *Mentalizing in clinical practice*. American Psychiatric Publishing.

2. Bromberg, P. M. (2006). *Awakening the dreamer: Clinical journeys*. Routledge.

3. Damasio, A. R. (1999). *The feeling of what happens: Body and emotion in the making of consciousness*. Harcourt.

4. Dell, P. F., & O'Neil, J. A. (Eds.). (2009). *Dissociation and the dissociative disorders: DSM-V and beyond*. Routledge.

5. Fosha, D. (2000). *The transforming power of affect: A model for accelerated change*. Basic Books.

6. Jung, C. G. (1960). *The structure and dynamics of the psyche* (Collected Works Vol. 8). Princeton University Press.

7. Kalsched, D. (2013). *Trauma and the soul: A psycho-spiritual approach to human development and its interruption*. Routledge.

8. Levine, P. A. (2010). *In an unspoken voice: How the body releases trauma and restores goodness*. North Atlantic Books.

9. Ogden, T., & Ogden, T. H. (1989). *The primitive edge of experience*. Jason Aronson.

10. Porges, S. W. (2011). *The polyvagal theory: Neurophysiological foundations of emotions, attachment, communication, and self-regulation.* W. W. Norton & Company.

11. Schore, A. N. (2003). *Affect dysregulation and disorders of the self.* W. W. Norton & Company.

12. Siegel, D. J. (2012). *The developing mind: How relationships and the brain interact to shape who we are* (2nd ed.). Guilford Press.

13. Stern, D. B. (2010). *Partners in thought: Working with unformulated experience, dissociation, and enactment.* Routledge.

14. van der Kolk, B. A. (2014). *The body keeps the score: Brain, mind, and body in the healing of trauma.* Viking.

15. Winnicott, D. W. (1965). *The maturational processes and the facilitating environment: Studies in the theory of emotional development.* International Universities Press.

Chapter 12. Trauma and the Eclipse

1. Bloom, S. L. (2013). *Creating sanctuary: Toward the evolution of sane societies* (2nd ed.). Routledge.

2. Bromberg, P. M. (2011). *The shadow of the tsunami: And the growth of the relational mind.* Routledge.

3. Cozolino, L. (2017). *The neuroscience of psychotherapy: Healing the social brain* (3rd ed.). W. W. Norton & Company.

4. Fisher, J. (2017). *Healing the fragmented selves of trauma survivors: Overcoming internal self-alienation.* Routledge.

5. Fosha, D. (2000). *The transforming power of affect: A model for accelerated change.* Basic Books.

6. Herman, J. L. (1997). *Trauma and recovery: The aftermath of violence—from domestic abuse to political terror.* Basic Books.

7. Kalsched, D. (1996). *The inner world of trauma: Archetypal defenses of the personal spirit.* Routledge.

8. Levine, P. A. (1997). *Waking the tiger: Healing trauma.* North Atlantic Books.

9. Levine, P. A. (2010). *In an unspoken voice: How the body releases trauma and restores goodness.* North Atlantic Books.

10. Ogden, P., Minton, K., & Pain, C. (2006). *Trauma and the body: A sensorimotor approach to psychotherapy.* W. W. Norton & Company.

11. Porges, S. W. (2011). *The polyvagal theory: Neurophysiological foundations of emotions, attachment, communication, and self-regulation.* W. W. Norton & Company.

12. Schore, A. N. (2003). *Affect dysregulation and the repair of the self.* W. W. Norton & Company.

13. Siegel, D. J. (2012). *The developing mind: How relationships and the brain interact to shape who we are* (2nd ed.). Guilford Press.

14. Stern, D. B. (2010). *Partners in thought: Working with unformulated experience, dissociation, and enactment.* Routledge.

15. van der Kolk, B. A. (2014). *The body keeps the score: Brain, mind, and body in the healing of trauma.* Viking.

Chapter 13. Echoes of the Eclipse

1. Bromberg, P. M. (2006). *Awakening the dreamer: Clinical journeys.* Routledge.

2. Cozolino, L. (2017). *The neuroscience of psychotherapy: Healing the social brain* (3rd ed.). W. W. Norton & Company.

3. Damasio, A. R. (1999). *The feeling of what happens: Body and emotion in the making of consciousness.* Harcourt.

4. Fisher, J. (2017). *Healing the fragmented selves of trauma survivors: Overcoming internal self-alienation.* Routledge.

5. Gendlin, E. T. (1996). *Focusing-oriented psychotherapy: A manual of the experiential method.* Guilford Press.

6. Haley, J. (1991). *Strategic therapy and its relevance to the unconscious*. Zeig, Tucker & Theisen.

7. Jung, C. G. (1959). *Aion: Researches into the phenomenology of the Self* (Collected Works Vol. 9, Part II). Princeton University Press.

8. Kalsched, D. (2013). *Trauma and the soul: A psycho-spiritual approach to human development and its interruption*. Routledge.

9. Levine, P. A. (2010). *In an unspoken voice: How the body releases trauma and restores goodness*. North Atlantic Books.

10. Maté, G. (2022). *The myth of normal: Trauma, illness, and healing in a toxic culture*. Avery.

11. Ogden, P., & Fisher, J. (2015). *Sensorimotor psychotherapy: Interventions for trauma and attachment*. W. W. Norton & Company.

12. Porges, S. W. (2021). *Polyvagal safety: Attachment, communication, self-regulation*. W. W. Norton & Company.

13. Rothschild, B. (2000). *The body remembers: The psychophysiology of trauma and trauma treatment*. W. W. Norton & Company.

14. Stern, D. B. (2015). *Relational freedom: Emergent properties of the interpersonal field*. Routledge.

15. Winnicott, D. W. (1965). *The maturational processes and the facilitating environment: Studies in the theory of emotional development*. International Universities Press.

Chapter 14. Circles of Survival: The Loop of Repetition

1. Bromberg, P. M. (2011). *The shadow of the tsunami: And the growth of the relational mind*. Routledge.

2. Cozolino, L. (2014). *The neuroscience of human relationships: Attachment and the developing social brain* (2nd ed.). W. W. Norton & Company.

3. Fisher, J. (2017). *Healing the fragmented selves of trauma survivors: Overcoming internal self-alienation*. Routledge.

4. Fosha, D. (2000). *The transforming power of affect: A model for accelerated change*. Basic Books.

5. Gergen, K. J. (2009). *Relational being: Beyond self and community*. Oxford University Press.

6. Haley, J. (1976). *Problem-solving therapy*. Jossey-Bass.

7. Herman, J. L. (1997). *Trauma and recovery: The aftermath of violence—from domestic abuse to political terror*. Basic Books.

8. Jung, C. G. (1953). *Two essays on analytical psychology* (Collected Works Vol. 7). Princeton University Press.

9. Kalsched, D. (1996). *The inner world of trauma: Archetypal defenses of the personal spirit*. Routledge.

10. Levine, P. A. (2010). *In an unspoken voice: How the body releases trauma and restores goodness*. North Atlantic Books.

11. Ogden, P., Minton, K., & Pain, C. (2006). *Trauma and the body: A sensorimotor approach to psychotherapy*. W. W. Norton & Company.

12. Porges, S. W. (2021). *Polyvagal safety: Attachment, communication, self-regulation*. W. W. Norton & Company.

13. Schore, A. N. (2003). *Affect dysregulation and disorders of the self*. W. W. Norton & Company.

14. Siegel, D. J. (2020). *The power of showing up: How parental presence shapes who our kids become and how their brains get wired*. Ballantine Books.

15. Winnicott, D. W. (1960). *Ego distortion in terms of true and false self*. In *The maturational processes and the facilitating environment* (1965). International Universities Press.

Chapter 15. Beyond the Label: Reframing Psychiatric Diagnosis

1. American Psychiatric Association. (2013). *Diagnostic and statistical manual of mental disorders* (5th ed.). American Psychiatric Publishing.

2. Andreasen, N. C. (2007). DSM and the death of phenomenology in America: An example of unintended consequences. *Schizophrenia Bulletin, 33*(1), 108–112. https://doi.org/10.1093/schbul/sbl054

3. Breggin, P. R. (1993). *Toxic psychiatry*. St. Martin's Press.

4. Fisher, J. (2017). *Healing the fragmented selves of trauma survivors: Overcoming internal self-alienation*. Routledge.

5. Frances, A. (2013). *Saving normal: An insider's revolt against out-of-control psychiatric diagnosis, DSM-5, big pharma, and the medicalization of ordinary life*. William Morrow.

6. Gergen, K. J. (2009). *Relational being: Beyond self and community*. Oxford University Press.

7. Kinderman, P. (2014). *A prescription for psychiatry: Why we need a whole new approach to mental health and well-being*. Palgrave Macmillan.

8. Kirmayer, L. J., & Gómez-Carrillo, A. (2019). Healing in cultural context: Traditions, discourse and practice. *Transcultural Psychiatry, 56*(4), 720–741. https://doi.org/10.1177/1363461519855860

9. Paris, J. (2015). *The intelligent clinician's guide to the DSM-5®* (2nd ed.). Oxford University Press.

10. Porges, S. W. (2011). *The polyvagal theory: Neurophysiological foundations of emotions, attachment, communication, and self-regulation*. W. W. Norton & Company.

11. Ross, C. A., & Pam, A. (1995). *Pseudoscience in biological psychiatry: Blaming the body*. Wiley.

12. van der Kolk, B. A. (2014). *The body keeps the score: Brain, mind, and body in the healing of trauma*. Viking.

13. Wakefield, J. C. (1992). The concept of mental disorder: On the boundary between biological facts and social values. *American Psychologist, 47*(3), 373–388. https://doi.org/10.1037/0003-066X.47.3.373

14. Watters, E. (2010). *Crazy like us: The globalization of the American psyche*. Free Press.

15. Widiger, T. A., & Samuel, D. B. (2005). Diagnostic categories or dimensions? A question for the Diagnostic and Statistical Manual of Mental Disorders–Fifth Edition. *Journal of Abnormal Psychology, 114*(4), 494–504. https://doi.org/10.1037/0021-843X.114.4.494

Chapter 16. The Role of Physiology in Coherogenesis

1. Ahn, A. C., Tewari, M., Poon, C.-S., & Phillips, R. S. (2006). The clinical applications of a systems biology approach to traditional Chinese medicine: An example using the theory of "Qi". *Journal of Alternative and Complementary Medicine, 12*(9), 851–858. https://doi.org/10.1089/acm.2006.12.851

2. Berntson, G. G., Cacioppo, J. T., & Quigley, K. S. (1993). Autonomic determinism: The modes of autonomic control, the doctrine of autonomic space, and the laws of autonomic constraint. *Psychological Review, 100*(6), 459–491.

3. Cozolino, L. (2017). *The neuroscience of psychotherapy: Healing the social brain* (3rd ed.). W. W. Norton & Company.

4. Damasio, A. R. (1999). *The feeling of what happens: Body and emotion in the making of consciousness*. Harcourt.

5. Germain, A., Buysse, D. J., & Nofzinger, E. A. (2008). Sleep-specific mechanisms underlying posttraumatic stress disorder: Integrative review and neurobiological hypotheses. *Sleep Medicine Reviews, 12*(3), 185–195. https://doi.org/10.1016/j.smrv.2007.09.003

6. Goleman, D., & Davidson, R. J. (2017). *Altered traits: Science reveals how meditation changes your mind, brain, and body.* Avery.

7. Kelley, K. W., Bluthe, R. M., Dantzer, R., Zhou, J. H., Shen, W. H., Johnson, R. W., & Broussard, S. R. (2003). Cytokine-induced sickness behavior. *Brain, Behavior, and Immunity, 17*(S1), S112–S118. https://doi.org/10.1016/S0889-1591(02)00077-6

8. Lipton, B. H. (2005). *The biology of belief: Unleashing the power of consciousness, matter & miracles.* Hay House.

9. McEwen, B. S. (2007). Physiology and neurobiology of stress and adaptation: Central role of the brain. *Physiological Reviews, 87*(3), 873–904. https://doi.org/10.1152/physrev.00041.2006

10. Pert, C. B. (1997). *Molecules of emotion: Why you feel the way you feel.* Scribner.

11. Porges, S. W. (2011). *The polyvagal theory: Neurophysiological foundations of emotions, attachment, communication, and self-regulation.* W. W. Norton & Company.

12. Rossi, E. L. (2002). *The psychobiology of gene expression: Neuroscience and neurogenesis in hypnosis and the healing arts.* W. W. Norton & Company.

13. Scaer, R. C. (2005). *The trauma spectrum: Hidden wounds and human resiliency.* W. W. Norton & Company.

14. Schore, A. N. (2003). *Affect regulation and the repair of the self.* W. W. Norton & Company.

15. van der Kolk, B. A. (2014). *The body keeps the score: Brain, mind, and body in the healing of trauma.* Viking.

Chapter 17. Pathways of Return

1. Bateson, G. (1972). *Steps to an ecology of mind: Collected essays in anthropology, psychiatry, evolution, and epistemology.* University of Chicago Press.

2. Berzoff, J., Flanagan, L. M., & Hertz, P. (Eds.). (2011). *Inside out and outside in: Psychodynamic clinical theory and psychopathology in contemporary multicultural contexts* (3rd ed.). Rowman & Littlefield.

3. Bromberg, P. M. (2011). *The shadow of the tsunami: And the growth of the relational mind.* Routledge.

4. Campbell, J. (2008). *The hero with a thousand faces.* New World Library.

5. Cozolino, L. (2017). *The neuroscience of psychotherapy: Healing the social brain* (3rd ed.). W. W. Norton & Company.

6. Damasio, A. R. (2010). *Self comes to mind: Constructing the conscious brain.* Pantheon.

7. Fischer, J. (2017). *Healing the fragmented selves of trauma survivors: Overcoming internal self-alienation.* Routledge.

8. Fosha, D. (2000). *The transforming power of affect: A model for accelerated change.* Basic Books.

9. Gendlin, E. T. (1996). *Focusing-oriented psychotherapy: A manual of the experiential method.* Guilford Press.

10. Jung, C. G. (1960). *The structure and dynamics of the psyche* (Collected Works Vol. 8). Princeton University Press.

11. Levine, P. A. (2010). *In an unspoken voice: How the body releases trauma and restores goodness.* North Atlantic Books.

12. McGilchrist, I. (2009). *The master and his emissary: The divided brain and the making of the Western world.* Yale University Press.

13. Ogden, P., & Fisher, J. (2015). *Sensorimotor psychotherapy: Interventions for trauma and attachment.* W. W. Norton & Company.

14. Schore, A. N. (2003). *Affect regulation and the repair of the self.* W. W. Norton & Company.

15. Siegel, D. J. (2012). *The developing mind: How relationships and the brain interact to shape who we are* (2nd ed.). Guilford Press.

16. Stern, D. B. (2010). *Partners in thought: Working with unformulated experience, dissociation, and enactment*. Routledge.

17. Turner, V. (1969). *The ritual process: Structure and anti-structure*. Aldine.

18. van Gennep, A. (1960). *The rites of passage*. University of Chicago Press.

19. Varela, F. J., Thompson, E., & Rosch, E. (1991). *The embodied mind: Cognitive science and human experience*. MIT Press.

Chapter 18. Breaking the Cycle

1. Anderson, H. (1997). *Conversation, language, and possibilities: A postmodern approach to therapy*. Basic Books.

2. Berman, B. A. (2013). *Trauma-informed mindfulness: Teaching mindfulness to people with PTSD, addiction, and other mental health challenges*. W. W. Norton & Company.

3. Boszormenyi-Nagy, I., & Spark, G. M. (1973). *Invisible loyalties: Reciprocity in intergenerational family therapy*. Harper & Row.

4. Fosha, D. (2000). *The transforming power of affect: A model for accelerated change*. Basic Books.

5. Gilligan, S. (2017). *The courage to love: Principles and practices of a relationship-based self-worth therapy*. Routledge.

6. Herman, J. L. (1997). *Trauma and recovery: The aftermath of violence—from domestic abuse to political terror*. Basic Books.

7. Linehan, M. M. (1993). *Cognitive-behavioral treatment of borderline personality disorder*. Guilford Press.

8. Maté, G. (2022). *The myth of normal: Trauma, illness, and healing in a toxic culture*. Avery.

9. Ogden, P., Minton, K., & Pain, C. (2006). *Trauma and the body: A sensorimotor approach to psychotherapy*. W. W. Norton & Company.

10. Porges, S. W. (2011). *The polyvagal theory: Neurophysiological foundations of emotions, attachment, communication, and self-regulation*. W. W. Norton & Company.

11. Rosenberg, M. (2003). *Nonviolent communication: A language of life*. PuddleDancer Press.

12. Siegel, D. J. (2010). *The mindful therapist: A clinician's guide to mindsight and neural integration*. W. W. Norton & Company.

13. van der Kolk, B. A. (2014). *The body keeps the score: Brain, mind, and body in the healing of trauma*. Viking.

14. Wilson, S. (2014). *Mindful America: Meditation and the mutual transformation of Buddhism and American culture*. Oxford University Press.

15. Wondolleck, J. M., & Yaffee, S. L. (2000). *Making collaboration work: Lessons from innovation in natural resource management*. Island Press.

Chapter 19. The Pattern as Portal

1. Bateson, G. (1972). *Steps to an ecology of mind: Collected essays in anthropology, psychiatry, evolution, and epistemology*. University of Chicago Press.

2. Berzoff, J., Flanagan, L. M., & Hertz, P. (Eds.). (2011). *Inside out and outside in: Psychodynamic clinical theory and psychopathology in contemporary multicultural contexts* (3rd ed.). Rowman & Littlefield.

3. Cozolino, L. (2014). *The neuroscience of human relationships: Attachment and the developing social brain* (2nd ed.). W. W. Norton & Company.

4. Damasio, A. R. (1999). *The feeling of what happens: Body and emotion in the making of consciousness*. Harcourt.

5. Fisher, J. (2017). *Healing the fragmented selves of trauma survivors: Overcoming internal self-alienation.* Routledge.

6. Hayes, S. C., Strosahl, K. D., & Wilson, K. G. (2012). *Acceptance and commitment therapy: The process and practice of mindful change* (2nd ed.). Guilford Press.

7. Jung, C. G. (1959). *The archetypes and the collective unconscious* (Collected Works Vol. 9, Part I). Princeton University Press.

8. Kalsched, D. (2013). *Trauma and the soul: A psycho-spiritual approach to human development and its interruption.* Routledge.

9. Levine, P. A. (2010). *In an unspoken voice: How the body releases trauma and restores goodness.* North Atlantic Books.

10. May, R. (1983). *The discovery of being: Writings in existential psychology.* W. W. Norton & Company.

11. Porges, S. W. (2021). *Polyvagal safety: Attachment, communication, self-regulation.* W. W. Norton & Company.

12. Riso, D. R., & Hudson, R. (1999). *The wisdom of the Enneagram: The complete guide to psychological and spiritual growth for the nine personality types.* Bantam Books.

13. Schore, A. N. (2003). *Affect dysregulation and disorders of the self.* W. W. Norton & Company.

14. Siegel, D. J. (2012). *The developing mind: How relationships and the brain interact to shape who we are* (2nd ed.). Guilford Press.

15. Winnicott, D. W. (1965). *The maturational processes and the facilitating environment: Studies in the theory of emotional development.* International Universities Press.

Chapter 20. Returning to the Symbolic

1. Bromberg, P. M. (2011). *The shadow of the tsunami: And the growth of the relational mind.* Routledge.

2. Byers, A. (2016). The transformation of meaning in psychological trauma: From dissociation to coherence. *Journal of Trauma &*

Dissociation, 17(4), 393–409.
https://doi.org/10.1080/15299732.2016.1146280

3. Damasio, A. R. (2010). *Self comes to mind: Constructing the conscious brain*. Pantheon.

4. Fosha, D. (2000). *The transforming power of affect: A model for accelerated change*. Basic Books.

5. Gendlin, E. T. (1997). *Experiencing and the creation of meaning: A philosophical and psychological approach to the subjective*. Northwestern University Press.

6. Jung, C. G. (1960). *The structure and dynamics of the psyche* (Collected Works Vol. 8). Princeton University Press.

7. Kalsched, D. (2013). *Trauma and the soul: A psycho-spiritual approach to human development and its interruption*. Routledge.

8. Lakoff, G., & Johnson, M. (2003). *Metaphors we live by* (2nd ed.). University of Chicago Press.

9. Ogden, P., & Fisher, J. (2015). *Sensorimotor psychotherapy: Interventions for trauma and attachment*. W. W. Norton & Company.

10. Porges, S. W. (2021). *Polyvagal safety: Attachment, communication, self-regulation*. W. W. Norton & Company.

11. Rossi, E. L. (2002). *The psychobiology of gene expression: Neuroscience and neurogenesis in hypnosis and the healing arts*. W. W. Norton & Company.

12. Schore, A. N. (2003). *Affect regulation and the repair of the self*. W. W. Norton & Company.

13. Stern, D. B. (2010). *Partners in thought: Working with unformulated experience, dissociation, and enactment*. Routledge.

14. Trevarthen, C. (2001). Intrinsic motives for companionship in understanding: Their origin, development, and significance for infant mental health. *Infant Mental Health Journal, 22*(1–2), 95–

131. https://doi.org/10.1002/1097-0355(200101/04)22:1<95::AID-IMHJ6>3.0.CO;2-1

15. Winnicott, D. W. (1971). *Playing and reality*. Routledge.

Chapter 21. The Sensorial Reawakened

1. Caldwell, C. (2018). *Bodyfulness: Somatic practices for presence, empowerment, and waking up in this life*. Shambhala Publications.

2. Damasio, A. R. (1999). *The feeling of what happens: Body and emotion in the making of consciousness*. Harcourt.

3. Fisher, J. (2017). *Healing the fragmented selves of trauma survivors: Overcoming internal self-alienation*. Routledge.

4. Fogel, A. (2009). *Body sense: The science and practice of embodied self-awareness*. W. W. Norton & Company.

5. Gendlin, E. T. (1996). *Focusing-oriented psychotherapy: A manual of the experiential method*. Guilford Press.

6. Levine, P. A. (2010). *In an unspoken voice: How the body releases trauma and restores goodness*. North Atlantic Books.

7. McGilchrist, I. (2009). *The master and his emissary: The divided brain and the making of the Western world*. Yale University Press.

8. Ogden, P., Minton, K., & Pain, C. (2006). *Trauma and the body: A sensorimotor approach to psychotherapy*. W. W. Norton & Company.

9. Pert, C. B. (1997). *Molecules of emotion: Why you feel the way you feel*. Scribner.

10. Porges, S. W. (2011). *The polyvagal theory: Neurophysiological foundations of emotions, attachment, communication, and self-regulation*. W. W. Norton & Company.

11. Rothschild, B. (2000). *The body remembers: The psychophysiology of trauma and trauma treatment*. W. W. Norton & Company.

12. Scaer, R. C. (2005). *The trauma spectrum: Hidden wounds and human resiliency*. W. W. Norton & Company.

13. Siegel, D. J. (2012). *The developing mind: How relationships and the brain interact to shape who we are* (2nd ed.). Guilford Press.

14. Tronick, E. (2007). *The neurobehavioral and social-emotional development of infants and children*. W. W. Norton & Company.

15. Wallin, D. J. (2007). *Attachment in psychotherapy*. Guilford Press.

Chapter 22. Resting in the Unitive

1. Almaas, A. H. (2004). *The inner journey home: Soul's realization of the unity of reality*. Shambhala Publications.

2. Barbezat, D. P., & Bush, M. (2014). *Contemplative practices in higher education: Powerful methods to transform teaching and learning*. Jossey-Bass.

3. Bohm, D. (1980). *Wholeness and the implicate order*. Routledge.

4. Brown, M. (2007). *The presence process: A journey into present moment awareness* (Rev. ed.). Namaste Publishing.

5. Gendlin, E. T. (1997). *Experiencing and the creation of meaning: A philosophical and psychological approach to the subjective*. Northwestern University Press.

6. Goleman, D., & Davidson, R. J. (2017). *Altered traits: Science reveals how meditation changes your mind, brain, and body*. Avery.

7. James, W. (1902/2004). *The varieties of religious experience: A study in human nature*. Barnes & Noble Classics.

8. Levine, P. A. (2010). *In an unspoken voice: How the body releases trauma and restores goodness*. North Atlantic Books.

9. Maté, G. (2022). *The myth of normal: Trauma, illness, and healing in a toxic culture*. Avery.

10. McGilchrist, I. (2009). *The master and his emissary: The divided brain and the making of the Western world.* Yale University Press.

11. Nhat Hanh, T. (1991). *Peace is every step: The path of mindfulness in everyday life.* Bantam Books.

12. Ruiz, M. (1997). *The four agreements: A practical guide to personal freedom.* Amber-Allen Publishing.

13. Tolle, E. (2005). *A new earth: Awakening to your life's purpose.* Penguin Group.

14. Tolle, E. (2004). *The power of now: A guide to spiritual enlightenment.* New World Library.

15. Wallace, B. A. (2007). *Contemplative science: Where Buddhism and neuroscience converge.* Columbia University Press.

16. Wilber, K. (2000). *Integral psychology: Consciousness, spirit, psychology, therapy.* Shambhala Publications.

17. Winnicott, D. W. (1965). *The maturational processes and the facilitating environment: Studies in the theory of emotional development.* International Universities Press.

Chapter 23. Coherence Through Conscious Awareness

1. Almaas, A. H. (2004). *The inner journey home: Soul's realization of the unity of reality.* Shambhala Publications.

2. Bromberg, P. M. (2011). *The shadow of the tsunami: And the growth of the relational mind.* Routledge.

3. Cozolino, L. (2017). *The neuroscience of psychotherapy: Healing the social brain* (3rd ed.). W. W. Norton & Company.

4. Damasio, A. R. (2010). *Self comes to mind: Constructing the conscious brain.* Pantheon.

5. Fosha, D. (2000). *The transforming power of affect: A model for accelerated change.* Basic Books.

6. Gendlin, E. T. (1996). *Focusing-oriented psychotherapy: A manual of the experiential method*. Guilford Press.

7. Goleman, D., & Davidson, R. J. (2017). *Altered traits: Science reveals how meditation changes your mind, brain, and body*. Avery.

8. James, W. (1902/2004). *The varieties of religious experience: A study in human nature*. Barnes & Noble Classics.

9. Levine, P. A. (2010). *In an unspoken voice: How the body releases trauma and restores goodness*. North Atlantic Books.

10. McGilchrist, I. (2009). *The master and his emissary: The divided brain and the making of the Western world*. Yale University Press.

11. Ogden, P., & Fisher, J. (2015). *Sensorimotor psychotherapy: Interventions for trauma and attachment*. W. W. Norton & Company.

12. Schore, A. N. (2003). *Affect regulation and the repair of the self*. W. W. Norton & Company.

13. Siegel, D. J. (2012). *The developing mind: How relationships and the brain interact to shape who we are* (2nd ed.). Guilford Press.

14. Stern, D. B. (2010). *Partners in thought: Working with unformulated experience, dissociation, and enactment*. Routledge.

15. Tolle, E. (2004). *The power of now: A guide to spiritual enlightenment*. New World Library.

16. Wallace, B. A. (2007). *Contemplative science: Where Buddhism and neuroscience converge*. Columbia University Press.

17. Wilber, K. (2000). *Integral psychology: Consciousness, spirit, psychology, therapy*. Shambhala Publications.

Chapter 24. Consciousness Aware of Itself

1. Almaas, A. H. (2004). *The inner journey home: Soul's realization of the unity of reality*. Shambhala Publications.

2.   Bays, J. (2011). *The illusion of separateness: A practical guide to spiritual awakening*. Sentient Publications.

3.   Bohm, D. (1980). *Wholeness and the implicate order*. Routledge.

4.   Brown, M. (2007). *The presence process: A journey into present moment awareness* (Rev. ed.). Namaste Publishing.

5.   Chittick, W. C. (2000). *The heart of Islamic philosophy: The quest for self-knowledge in the teachings of Afdal al-Din Kashani*. Oxford University Press.

6.   Forman, R. K. C. (1998). *Mysticism, mind, consciousness*. State University of New York Press.

7.   Goleman, D., & Davidson, R. J. (2017). *Altered traits: Science reveals how meditation changes your mind, brain, and body*. Avery.

8.   James, W. (1902/2004). *The varieties of religious experience: A study in human nature*. Barnes & Noble Classics.

9.   McGilchrist, I. (2009). *The master and his emissary: The divided brain and the making of the Western world*. Yale University Press.

10. Nisargadatta Maharaj. (1973). *I am that* (M. Frydman, Trans.). Acorn Press.

11. Tolle, E. (2005). *A new earth: Awakening to your life's purpose*. Penguin Group.

12. Tolle, E. (2004). *The power of now: A guide to spiritual enlightenment*. New World Library.

13. Varela, F. J., Thompson, E., & Rosch, E. (1991). *The embodied mind: Cognitive science and human experience*. MIT Press.

14. Wallace, B. A. (2007). *Contemplative science: Where Buddhism and neuroscience converge*. Columbia University Press.

15. Wilber, K. (2000). *Integral psychology: Consciousness, spirit, psychology, therapy*. Shambhala Publications.

Chapter 25. Living the Rhythm: Daily Life as Coherogenesis

1. Abram, D. (1996). *The spell of the sensuous: Perception and language in a more-than-human world*. Vintage.

2. Buber, M. (1970). *I and Thou*. Charles Scribner's Sons.

3. Damasio, A. R. (1999). *The feeling of what happens: Body and emotion in the making of consciousness*. Harcourt.

4. Eisenstein, C. (2007). *Sacred economics: Money, gifting, and society in the age of transition*. Evolver Editions.

5. Gendlin, E. T. (1996). *Focusing-oriented psychotherapy: A manual of the experiential method*. Guilford Press.

6. Halprin, D. (2003). *The expressive body in life, art, and therapy: Working with movement, metaphor, and meaning*. Jessica Kingsley Publishers.

7. Kelman, D. (2007). *Ecological psychology: Understanding our place in the world*. Havard University Press.

8. McGilchrist, I. (2009). *The master and his emissary: The divided brain and the making of the Western world*. Yale University Press.

9. Pert, C. B. (1997). *Molecules of emotion: Why you feel the way you feel*. Scribner.

10. Porges, S. W. (2011). *The polyvagal theory: Neurophysiological foundations of emotions, attachment, communication, and self-regulation*. W. W. Norton & Company.

11. Rosenberg, M. (2003). *Nonviolent communication: A language of life*. PuddleDancer Press.

12. Suskind, R. (2014). *A hopeful heart: Yoga for recovery, rebalancing, and self-empowerment*. Skylight Paths Publishing.

13. Wheatley, M. J. (2006). *Leadership and the new science: Discovering order in a chaotic world* (3rd ed.). Berrett-Koehler.

14. Wilber, K. (2000). *Integral psychology: Consciousness, spirit, psychology, therapy*. Shambhala Publications.

15. Winnicott, D. W. (1965). *The maturational processes and the facilitating environment: Studies in the theory of emotional development*. International Universities Press.

Chapter 26. The Unfinished Path: Trusting the Mystery

1. Almaas, A. H. (2004). *The inner journey home: Soul's realization of the unity of reality*. Shambhala Publications.

2. Bateson, G. (1972). *Steps to an ecology of mind: Collected essays in anthropology, psychiatry, evolution, and epistemology*. University of Chicago Press.

3. Bromberg, P. M. (2011). *The shadow of the tsunami: And the growth of the relational mind*. Routledge.

4. Cozolino, L. (2017). *The neuroscience of psychotherapy: Healing the social brain* (3rd ed.). W. W. Norton & Company.

5. Damasio, A. R. (1999). *The feeling of what happens: Body and emotion in the making of consciousness*. Harcourt.

6. Fosha, D. (2000). *The transforming power of affect: A model for accelerated change*. Basic Books.

7. Gendlin, E. T. (1996). *Focusing-oriented psychotherapy: A manual of the experiential method*. Guilford Press.

8. Goleman, D., & Davidson, R. J. (2017). *Altered traits: Science reveals how meditation changes your mind, brain, and body*. Avery.

9. Kegan, R. (1982). *The evolving self: Problem and process in human development*. Harvard University Press.

10. Kalsched, D. (2013). *Trauma and the soul: A psycho-spiritual approach to human development and its interruption*. Routledge.

11. McGilchrist, I. (2009). *The master and his emissary: The divided brain and the making of the Western world*. Yale University Press.

12. Siegel, D. J. (2012). *The developing mind: How relationships and the brain interact to shape who we are* (2nd ed.). Guilford Press.

13. Tolle, E. (2005). *A new earth: Awakening to your life's purpose.* Penguin Group.

14. van der Kolk, B. A. (2014). *The body keeps the score: Brain, mind, and body in the healing of trauma.* Viking.

15. Wilber, K. (2006). *Integral spirituality: A startling new role for religion in the modern and postmodern world.* Shambhala Publications.

16. Winnicott, D. W. (1965). *The maturational processes and the facilitating environment: Studies in the theory of emotional development.* International Universities Press.

Chapter 27. The Play of Being and Becoming

1. Bateson, G. (1972). *Steps to an ecology of mind: Collected essays in anthropology, psychiatry, evolution, and epistemology.* University of Chicago Press.

2. Bohm, D. (1980). *Wholeness and the implicate order.* Routledge.

3. Brown, M. (2007). *The presence process: A journey into present moment awareness* (Rev. ed.). Namaste Publishing.

4. Csikszentmihalyi, M. (1990). *Flow: The psychology of optimal experience.* Harper & Row.

5. Fosha, D. (2000). *The transforming power of affect: A model for accelerated change.* Basic Books.

6. Gendlin, E. T. (1996). *Focusing-oriented psychotherapy: A manual of the experiential method.* Guilford Press.

7. Goleman, D., & Davidson, R. J. (2017). *Altered traits: Science reveals how meditation changes your mind, brain, and body.* Avery.

8. Heidegger, M. (1927/1962). *Being and time* (J. Macquarrie & E. Robinson, Trans.). Harper & Row.

9. James, W. (1890/1983). *The principles of psychology*. Harvard University Press.

10. Kegan, R. (1982). *The evolving self: Problem and process in human development*. Harvard University Press.

11. McGilchrist, I. (2009). *The master and his emissary: The divided brain and the making of the Western world*. Yale University Press.

12. Siegel, D. J. (2012). *The developing mind: How relationships and the brain interact to shape who we are* (2nd ed.). Guilford Press.

13. Stern, D. N. (1985). *The interpersonal world of the infant: A view from psychoanalysis and developmental psychology*. Basic Books.

14. Varela, F. J., Thompson, E., & Rosch, E. (1991). *The embodied mind: Cognitive science and human experience*. MIT Press.

15. Wilber, K. (2000). *Integral psychology: Consciousness, spirit, psychology, therapy*. Shambhala Publications.

16. Winnicott, D. W. (1971). *Playing and reality*. Routledge.

More Information

Center for Integrative Psychiatry, LLC

Integrative Psychiatry Education

Offering training on the practice of integrative psychiatry. In over 100 presentations, Dr. Hatcher expands on the implementation of integrative psychiatry principles for a holistic yet personalized approach to care. He has also developed training on a psychotherapeutic procedure that incorporates the principles described in this book. Visit https://www.DrNicholasHatcher.com/ipp/ to learn more.

Catharsis Health, LLC

Private Integrative Psychiatry Practice

Offering virtual trauma-informed integrative (holistic) psychiatry in Washington and Minnesota incorporating a blend of pharmaceuticals, nutraceuticals, laboratory and diagnostic evaluation, lifestyle modification, and psychotherapy personalized to each unique individual's needs and preferences. Visit https://www.Catharsishealth.org/ to learn more.

Connect

Social media and YouTube handles are listed on the copyright page where you can follow and subscribe to Dr. Hatcher's ongoing work.